Contested Terrain

Contested Terrain

A New History of Nature and People
in the Adirondacks

Philip G. Terrie

The Adirondack Museum/Syracuse University Press

First Paperback Edition 1999
99 00 01 02 03 04   6 5 4 3 2 1

Editor: Alice Wolf Gilborn

A note on illustrations: Except where noted otherwise, all reproductions of photographs, maps, lithographs, and paintings in this book are from the collections of the Adirondack Museum. For a photograph, "P" indicates its photograph number (except for those cases where one has not been assigned). For paintings and lithographs, the accession number and collection number are provided. In certain cases, no such number exists.

Permission by the Forest History Society, Inc., to reprint material from the following source is gratefully acknowledged: Philip Terrie, " 'Imperishable Freshness': Culture, Conservation, and the Adirondack Park," *Forest & Conservation History* 37, no. 3 (July 1993): 132–41.

The paper used in this publication meets the minimum requirements of American National Standard for Information Sciences—Permanence of Paper for Printed Library Materials, ANSI Z39.49-1984. ∞™

Library of Congress Cataloging-in-Publication Data
Terrie, Philip G.
　　Contested terrain : a new history of nature and people in the
　　Adirondacks / Philip G. Terrie.—1st ed.
　　　　p.　　　cm.
　　Includes bibliographical references and index.
　　ISBN 0-8156-0445-9 (cloth: alk. paper) 0-8156-0570-6 (pbk.: alk. paper)
　　　　1.　Adirondack Mountains (N.Y.)—History.　　2.　Land use, Rural—New
　　York (State)—Adirondack Mountains—History.　　1.　Title.
　　F127.A2T43　1997
　　974.7'5—dc21　　　97-11058

Manufactured in the United States of America

For Larkin and Ellen

Philip G. Terrie is Professor of English and American Culture Studies at Bowling Green State University. He is former Assistant Curator at the Adirondack Museum and is the author of *Forever Wild: A Cultural History of Wilderness in the Adirondacks, Wildlife and Wilderness: A History of Adirondack Mammals,* and numerous articles on Adirondack history and environmental literature.

Contents

Illustrations

Foreword

The Adirondack Museum is a large regional museum of history and art located in Blue Mountain Lake, New York. The museum explores and presents the history of the Adirondacks, the place and its people. For more than forty years the museum has collected historical and cultural artifacts that document the complex interaction between people and the land over time. Since opening to the public in 1957, the museum has mounted exhibitions, offered programs, and sponsored publications that bring this history to the public. Over the past forty years an explosion in historical scholarship has brought attention to new areas of inquiry including social and labor history and, most recently, environmental history, a rich perspective for understanding the Adirondacks. In recent years, this research has been encouraged and supported by the museum in hopes of enriching the public's understanding of Adirondack history.

One of the insights from the field of environmental history is that our perceptions of nature are shaped and influenced by human activity. Many visitors to the Adirondacks, and to the Adirondack Museum, are surprised to learn that the region is not only a "natural" place, but also has a complex and surprising human history. What appears to many as a wild landscape is actually a special kind of cultural landscape that human activity has shaped and continues to shape to the present day.

The Adirondack Museum seeks to act as a catalyst for scholarship on the Adirondack region and to bring this new research to the broadest possible audience. There are many ways in which museums do this. Through exhibitions, for example, a museum can tell stories, contrast points of view, and present challenging issues. In a similar way, a publication like this book deepens our understanding of the many ways in which people have thought about and valued the Adirondacks. Philip Terrie looks at Adirondack history as the story of a contested territory. He explores how cultural and economic factors have influenced the way people perceive the region and examines the many kinds of stories told about the Adirondacks. The voice of the outsider and the seasonal visitor is heard in these pages, as is the voice of the year-round resident. Only by listening to these many voices and the stories they tell, can we hope to understand what is at stake in the Adirondacks today.

This publication is the result of a collaboration between the museum and historian Philip Terrie. The project reflects our shared belief that what is presented here can help people better understand the special history of the Adirondacks. Our thanks go to author Philip Terrie for his energy and dedication to this project. I also want to thank museum staff, Alice Gilborn and Jim Meehan, and Syracuse University Press, our publishing partner in this and many other enterprises.

Jacqueline F. Day
Director

Acknowledgments

I am grateful to Jackie Day at the Adirondack Museum for responding positively when I first proposed to write this book; the Museum has generously supported the project and provided an ideal place for work. Alice Gilborn assiduously read, meticulously edited, and thoroughly improved my manuscript through numerous drafts. Museum Librarian Jerry Pepper answered frequent calls of distress by mail, telephone, fax, and email, and Jim Meehan labored diligently in the photo collection. Hallie Bond, Warder Cadbury, and Michael Wilson read the manuscript and made excellent suggestions for improving it. At Bowling Green State University, Joan Conrad was helpful in more ways than I can count, a summer research grant from the BGSU Faculty Research Committee pushed along the early writing, and a faculty improvement leave gave me the time to finish the manuscript. To all, I am grateful. Needless to say, errors or misinterpretations that remain are my responsibility. Portions of this book were originally published, in somewhat different form, in the following journals, and are reprinted here with permission: *Adirondack Journal of Environmental Studies*, *Adirondack Life*, *Hudson River Valley Review*, *Journal of Forest and Conservation History*, and *New York History*.

Introduction

The aims of this book are easy to describe. I hope to provide here an introduction to the history of the Adirondacks, a book that will be the first one people will read about this endlessly fascinating and appealing region. I want to show that the history of the Adirondacks is a tale of contested terrain and to connect current conflicts to their historical, social, and cultural roots. Further, I want to look at how the contests over the Adirondacks originate in stories—narratives about the land and its potential. Finally, I want to bring into the dialogue certain groups, mainly the year-round residents, whose voice has been noticeably absent from most previous efforts to write Adirondack history—including my own.

Available histories of this region are valuable, but they fall short of providing the combination of continuity, readability, and coherence that I hope to achieve here. Alfred L. Donaldson's *A History of the Adirondacks* is three quarters of a century old. While it contains much useful information, it is eccentrically organized and occasionally inaccurate. Frank Graham's *The Adirondack Park: A Political History* is an excellent overview of legislative and judicial events, but it dwells too much on non-Adirondack history and does not try to assess the larger social and cultural forces at play in the complex drama of Adirondack history. Jane E. Keller's *Adirondack Wilderness: A Story of Man and Nature* is replete with errors. My own *Forever Wild: A Cultural History of Wilderness in the Adirondacks* is narrow in its focus on wilderness and elitist in its emphasis on the views of bourgeois or wealthy writers and other intellectuals from outside the region. The different nature of my current approach to materials I have discussed in previous books and articles will, I hope, excuse the repetitions in this new book.

It is difficult to describe with precision exactly what I mean by the Adirondacks. The Adirondack Park has changed its boundaries several times since its establishment in 1892. Does that mean that Westport, which was not in the original Park but is now, was not in the Adirondacks in 1892 but is now? The word "Adirondacks" conjures up a variety of often conflicting images and places. The hustling, busy village of Lake Placid is in the Adirondack Park, and so is the remote back country of the West Canada Lakes Wilderness Area. Purveyors of stylish mail-order clothing use a certain image of the Adirondacks as rustic yet genteel to sell expensive shirts to affluent American consumers, and the Adirondack chair has become a symbol of leisure recognized around the United States. At the same time, unemployment rates in Adirondack counties are among the highest in New York state. What and where *is* the place we call the Adirondacks?

In 1854 Farrand N. Benedict, a professor at the University of Vermont and one of the first great Adirondack enthusiasts, grappled with the same questions. Writing in *Putnam's Monthly Magazine,* he proclaimed confidently, "In my observations concerning the wilderness of Northern New York, I shall endeavor to give as clear an idea as I can of, *where it is—what it is*—and *what it is good for.*"[1] My aim in this book is not so much to give my answers to Benedict's questions as to discuss the complex, contentious history of claims about the social and cultural meaning of the Adirondacks. The answer to the most important question, what is this region good for, is elusive and endlessly arguable; the story of the many attempts to insist on the virtues of one answer over others is the history of the Adirondacks.

Like Benedict, I am referring to that part of northern New York enclosed by the current boundary of the Adirondack Park (though that boundary did not yet exist when he wrote, and though he probably meant an area somewhat smaller than the contemporary Park). I shall be emphasizing the central Adirondacks, the lake country of the central plateau, the Fulton Chain, the high peaks, the forests of the northwest, the towns of the inner core. While I shall refer to certain illustrative episodes, personalities, and cultural trends from the history of the Champlain Valley, for the most part I shall dwell on the higher ground to the west, the area most associated in the popular mind with the word *Adirondacks.*

The Adirondack region today is a complex and diverse place, existing both in the geographical reality of the physical landscape and in the imaginations of the millions of people who have lived in, worked in, traveled through, or thought about it. Now larger than each of six states (Connecticut, Delaware, Hawaii, Massachusetts, New Jersey, and Rhode Island) and containing over 2.4 million acres of state-owned Forest Preserve along with nearly 3.6 million acres of land privately owned but governed by a regional zoning plan, the Adirondack Park possesses both placid wilderness ponds and noisy theme parks. It is home to 130,000 year-round residents and to black bears, bald eagles, and the occasional moose. The eerie cry of the loon can be heard on the same lakes roiled by speedboats, seaplanes, and jet skis. The trees of the Forest Preserve, protected in perpetuity by the state constitution, cannot be cut for any reason, but hundreds of thousands of acres of private land are intensively logged. It is largely a land of nature, treasured for the fragile tundra of its alpine summits and for its open spaces of forest and water, yet threatened by acid precipitation, crowding, overdevelopment, and a host of other environmental assaults.

Popular conceptions of the Adirondacks come from a complex set of images and narratives. Purveyed through a seemingly endless array of books, journals, official documents, personal narratives, maps, paintings, etchings—in short, though all the varied media of life, exploration, description, recreation, contemplation, and government—the diverse and often contradictory images of the Adirondacks have imprinted themselves on the popular consciousness. When first penetrated by Europeans in the eighteenth century, the Adirondacks appeared to them to be a barren desert, while later observers saw a sublime wilderness of mountains, rivers, lakes, and forests; to others it has appeared to be a landscape of trees ripe for harvest, a source of great mineral wealth, a land where ordinary people could establish ordinary American lives, an arena for genteel hunting and fishing, or a retreat for wealthy capitalists from the pressures of business. One of the most enduring images of the region is of an ancient land untouched—or at least not inordinately corrupted—by the gritty realities of urban, industrial civilization. To many people the appeal of the Adirondacks has rested on the persistent notion that the region remains strikingly *different* from the largely human-shaped modern world.

The recorded history of the Adirondacks begins with a story of contested terrain. In 1609, Samuel de Champlain, the first white man
known to have set foot in what is now the Adirondack Park, along with
a party of Algonquin Indians from the St. Lawrence, defeated a gathering of Mohawks in a brief though deadly battle near Crown Point. This
battle set the tone for what has been nearly four centuries of conflict, as
the Adirondack landscape has been fought over with bows, harque-
buses, fleets of warships, and, more recently, legislation and lawsuits.

As a cultural historian, I find it useful that our conception of the
Adirondacks as contested terrain begins in narrative, in the almost
mythic tradition that the Adirondacks served as the frontier between
the Iroquois and the Algonquins. According to this narrative, the battle
between Mohawks (one of the Iroquois Five Nations) and Algonquins
of 1609 was but one skirmish in a lengthy contest for control of northern New York. The story that different Indian cultures fought one another over the Adirondacks reflected both European assumptions
about Native American politics and warfare and the European need to
perceive the North American landscape as a prize to be struggled for
by colonizing powers from abroad. In other words, the story that
Champlain told about the events of July 30, 1609, in the details he emphasized and in those he left out, reflected and reinforced European
cultural, political, and economic needs. It is a shame that we do not
have the Mohawk and Algonquin stories of that battle.[2]

The chief organizing device of this book is the notion that our contests over land—conducted through warfare or lawsuits, among other
devices—simultaneously derive from, retell, reinforce, and develop
certain stories. People tell stories about the land that reflect their needs.
They project their needs onto the land in the stories they tell about it.
They define—in a sense, create—the land in their stories. These stories
either achieve currency in the popular imagination or they fail to do so.
When a story becomes widely accepted, it helps to promote certain attitudes toward the land and thus eventually contributes to the forma-
tion of public policy. By "story" I do not mean fiction; I mean widely
shared understandings about the land's meaning deriving from accounts of actual encounters with the land and from generalizations
concerning the land's status and future. A surveyor's notes, a hunter's
tale of bagging a white-tailed deer, a diarist's account of a stormy winter, a legislative debate over a conservation law, an oil painting or an

engraving—each of these and many other expressive, descriptive, or prescriptive media constitute the narrative threads that add up to stories about what the land is and what it is good for.[3] The answer to the question, what are the Adirondacks, is ultimately found in the stories people have told about the region.

For example, one story about the Adirondacks that was widely circulated in the nineteenth century described the region as an ideal hunting and fishing ground for urban sportsmen. This story in turn helped to promote a popular image of the region. It had its roots in the indisputable realities of the landscape and experience, and it emerged at just the time when middle and upper class American men were searching for recreation and an opportunity to get closer to nature. It thus easily entered the collection of shared stories about the American landscape.

But it was only one of several concurrent realities. Another story might have been of a landscape inhabited by farm families struggling to make a living, of poor Americans stitching together a life from farming, guiding, and logging and engaged in such ordinary American pursuits as raising children, establishing schools and churches, and starting small businesses. This, too, was a reality of the nineteenth-century Adirondacks, but it did not find its voice in the narratives of the land that reached the popular imagination outside the Adirondacks. The powerful existence of the one narrative and the virtual absence of the other had significant consequences at the end of the nineteenth century when the state of New York was deciding, through statutes and the state constitution, what it wanted to do with the Adirondacks. One of the major aims of this book is to examine the power of stories in determining our understanding of and decisions about place.

Historians also tell stories. Most historians, argues J. Donald Hughes, especially those writing the lengthy tomes used in survey classes in both World or American history, employ "development" as the fundamental organizing principle of their narratives.[4] Titles such as *The Development of Civilization,* the name of a popular textbook, illustrate the tendency of historians, and no doubt most others, to understand the human story in terms of a putative rise from one level of economic and social organization to another. That this "rise," which is nearly always tied to an emphasis on "growth," is an altogether good thing is seldom if ever questioned. Among other things, Hughes asks whether the last several millennia of human history have been good for the land, air, water, and living things of the earth. Is this notion of growth-equals-good the only lens through which we should perceive history? Should it continue to function as the primary organizing device for the stories through which we understand our relationship with the non-human world?

The whole world needs to learn to live with stability, with predictability, with a life that we hope can get better but not necessarily bigger, faster, slicker, or newer. It might as well start here in the Adirondack Park; in many respects it already has. Can we learn to think of development and progress not in terms of growth but in terms of better health care, better education, better access to cultural amenities, better relations between parents and children or between people and nature? Bill McKibben, with his characteristic eloquence, puts it this way: "The whole world is going to have to learn to live differently. The whole warming, depleting, unraveling planet will no longer be able to grow its way out of problems. [W]e in the Adirondacks [must] learn to find joy in our situation—to see ourselves made rich and not poor by loon and beaver and pine and bog and trackless snow."[5]

In the Adirondacks, the way we think about development and limits inevitably brings us to the political and cultural conflicts of the last twenty-five years, to what we think of the Adirondack Park Agency and the Private Land Use and Development Plan (discussed below in Chapter Eight), and to what role local people have had in constructing the Adirondack story of conservation and planning. I should say here at the outset that I believe that over the last century and a half the local voice has been consistently ignored as New York state has tried to decide what to do with the Adirondacks. One of the aims of this book is to reintroduce that voice to the Adirondack historical narrative. At the same time, I resolutely believe in and support the conservationist agenda for the Adirondacks, including region-wide zoning. These are not mutually exclusive understandings, as I hope this book demonstrates.

If there is agreement that limits are necessary, then there is hope for reconciliation and for the future in the Adirondacks; how those limits are described and implemented can be worked out by people of good will. I hope that people concerned with the future of this region can accept it as a cultural landscape, a place of people, their artifacts, and nature. The Adirondack Park has both a natural and a human history. If we can look for new strategies for telling the region's stories, moving from narratives that polarize and exclude to one of harmonious relations between people and nature, then the Adirondacks can indeed provide the first chapter in a new story for the whole world.

Contested Terrain

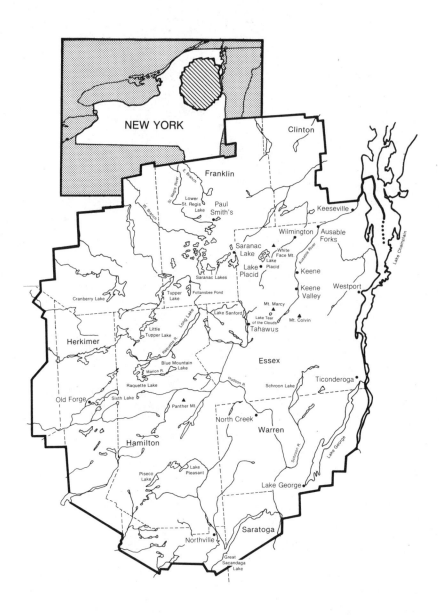

NEW YORK

Clinton

Franklin

E. Branch

St. Regis River

Lower
St. Regis
Lake

Paul
Smith's

W. Branch

Keeseville

Lake Champlain

Wilmington

Ausable
Forks

Ausable River

Saranac
Lake

White
Face Mt.

Lake
Placid

Lake
Placid

Saranac Lakes

Keene

Cranberry Lake

Tupper
Lake

Follansbee Pond

Keene
Valley

Westport

Lake Sanford

Mt. Marcy

Long Lake

Lake Tear
of the Clouds

Mt. Colvin

Herkimer

Little
Tupper Lake

Raquette R.

Tahawus

Blue Mountain
Lake

Marion R.

Essex

Raquette Lake

Hudson R.

Schroon Lake

Ticonderoga

Old Forge

Sixth Lake

Panther Mt.

North Creek

Warren

Schroon R.

Lake George

Hamilton

Piseco
Lake

Lake
Pleasant

Lake George

Northville

Saratoga

Great
Sacandaga
Lake

1

"A Broken Unpracticable Tract"

The earliest stories about the Adirondack landscape were undoubtedly told by Native Americans—hunters, warriors, or traders who traveled through the region's forests or navigated the rivers and lakes. But what the Adirondacks as a place meant to these people has not survived. In any case, these narratives were, largely, tales told by transients, for while parts of the Adirondacks appear to have served as hunting grounds for various Native American cultures living in the nearby river valleys, no serious evidence suggests that Indians lived permanently in the central Adirondacks. Wildlife would have been more plentiful and agriculture more productive in the surrounding lowlands of Lake Champlain and the Mohawk, St. Lawrence, and Black rivers, where better soils, longer growing seasons, and a warmer climate offered a more secure life than did the cold and steep Adirondacks. Archaeological finds indicate that Indians routinely passed through the Adirondacks, but year-round settlements were apparently rare.[1]

The place that would later be called the Adirondacks entered the European-American consciousness relatively late. The same characteristics of climate and terrain that discouraged Native Americans also delayed the arrival of Europeans. And when the Adirondacks began to appear on or in the first European-American narratives—early maps and exploration accounts—the dominant story involved not so much what the Adirondack country *was* but what it was *not*. Both cartographers and explorers were looking for land that appeared suitable for agriculture. Eighteenth-century Americans were mostly an expanding population of farmers, and as the coastal plains became cleared and

settled, a constant pressure for new arable lands developed. Throughout the British colonies, land subject to cultivation was valued, while
land that resisted cultivation was often dismissed as worthless.[2] Hence
the first encounters of Europeans with the Adirondack region emphasized the inaccessibility and ruggedness of a mountainous, swampy
country.

In 1755, Lewis Evans, one of the first great English cartographers in
North America, released his *General Map of the Middle British Colonies
in America*. This was the most detailed map of its day, yet in the com-
mentary accompanying it Evans was able to say more about the Ohio
Valley, where the lay of the land appeared promising for agriculture,
than about the Adirondacks. Of the country lying between the Mohawk and St. Lawrence rivers Evans wrote, "[It] is entirely impassable
by Reason of Ridges and Hills, not being yet broken, to drain the vast
drowned Land and Swamps."[3]

Sir William Johnson advanced a similar impression in the 1770s,
writing that the southern Adirondack country was "so verry [sic]

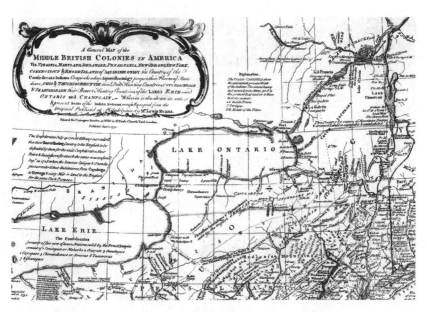

*This detail from a 1771 edition of Lewis Evans's map shows the minimal
knowledge of northern New York acquired by Europeans by the mid-
eighteenth century. Adirondack Museum Library.*

mountainous & barren that it is worth nothing. The Snow was 5 feet deep on these Mountains the 30th of March."[4] And in 1784 Thomas Pownall composed a lengthy *Topographical Description* to be published with a reissue of Evans's map. Pownall noted that he possessed more "Ignorance" than "Information" about the region we know today as the Adirondacks, reporting only that it was

> called by the Indians Couxsachrage, which signifies the Dismal Wilderness or Habitation of Winter, [and] is a triangular, high mountainous Tract, very little known to the Europeans; and although a hunting Ground of the Indians, yet either not much known to them, or, if known, very wisely by them kept from the Knowledge of the Europeans. It is said to be a broken unpracticable Tract; I own I could never learn any Thing about it.[5]

Thus the very first story told about the Adirondacks by Europeans emphasized the region's mystery, wildness, and unsuitability for agriculture. At the beginning of European-American efforts to construct a narrative about the Adirondacks, the key elements in the story were established by people—Evans, Johnson, Pownall, among others—who did not live or work there and who saw the land exclusively in terms of those natural characteristics that resonated, or failed to resonate, with their needs, in this case the eighteenth-century inclination to see land in terms of its agricultural potential. The first Adirondack story was of a land of mountains, swamps, and bad weather.

At about this time, scattered trappers and hunters were pursuing mostly solitary lives in the northern wilderness. Probably the first whites to see the central Adirondacks were trappers, who may have been sources of information for cartographers and geographers like Evans and Pownall. Among the best known of these early trappers were Nicholas Stoner and Nat Foster, both of whom began trapping in the southern and southwestern Adirondacks after the American Revolution. They trapped beaver, otter, and muskrat, selling pelts at settlements to the south.[6]

Shortly after Pownall's lament about the scarcity of accurate information, at least one Native American family was taking up permanent residence in the central Adirondacks. Sabael Benedict, a Penobscot Indian from Maine, who had fought for the British at the battle of Quebec in 1759, became the first known permanent settler in what is now

Sabael Benedict, first known settler in
Hamilton County, portrait by unknown
artist. P. 218.

Hamilton County. At about the time of the American Revolution, he settled on the shore of Indian Lake (which subsequently received its name from Benedict's presence there) with his wife, three daughters, and a son. There they lived, hunting and trapping.[7]

The son, Lewis Elijah Benedict, played a prominent role in the gradual process by which downstate New Yorkers slowly learned about this vast, largely unmapped region in the northern part of their state. In 1840, geologist Ebenezer Emmons hired Benedict to guide him through the central Adirondacks. Emmons, a professor at both Williams College and the Albany Medical College, was working for the New York Natural History Survey. Beginning field work in 1836, the Natural History Survey examined the state's geology, botany, zoology, mineralogy, and agriculture. This was part of a nation-wide effort to identify and exploit natural resources.[8] Emmons led the first recorded ascent of Mount Marcy, reaching the summit on a chilly August morning in 1837. And it was Emmons who proposed the name "Adirondacks" for the entire mountainous region and "Marcy" for the premier summit.[9]

Geologist and explorer Ebenezer Emmons led the first recorded ascent of Mount Marcy and proposed the name Adirondacks *for the region of the high peaks. Reproduced from Harold K. Hochschild's* Township 34.

Emmons's annual reports to the legislature—submitted from 1837 to 1841—along with his monumental final report, *Geology of New-York, Part II: Comprising the Second Geological District* (1842–44), advanced important new elements in the nascent story of the Adirondacks. All the reports were published, and while they hardly became best sellers, they were perused by the educated and inquisitive of the day. Henry David Thoreau, for example, ruminating over them in Concord, Massachusetts, was astonished to learn that Emmons was unable to find his way through the tangled Adirondack wilderness without an Indian guide, and he remarked admiringly on the persistence of so much wild land in so civilized and developed a state as New York: "New-York has her wilderness within her own borders; and though the sailors of Europe are familiar with the soundings of her Hudson, and Fulton long since invented the steamboat on its waters, an Indian is still necessary to guide her scientific men to its head-waters in the Adirondac [sic] country."[10] What struck Thoreau and many others of the time was the fact that so large a piece of New York state, as late as the 1830s and '40s, remained in a frontier or even less settled condition. The Adirondacks, in other words, were fundamentally different from the rest of New York.

Emmons was writing at a time when a variety of cultural factors were coalescing that would encourage an image of the Adirondacks as a place defined almost exclusively by natural, as opposed to social or cultural, characteristics. The romantic temperament, with its faith in the redemptive powers of nature, exercised enormous power among the American middle and upper classes and thus influenced profoundly the way that Emmons and people like him responded to and constructed narratives about the Adirondacks. Developing in Europe during the last decades of the eighteenth century and responding to the wrenching cultural, social, and environmental changes effected by industrialization, romanticism found modern (especially urban) life to be inherently stressful, corrupting, debilitating, and spiritually enervating. The antidote to these widely perceived evils of modernity was a retreat to nature. Where the modern city seemed a pit of iniquity and woe, nature was a fount of divine virtue and regenerative power. The romantic movement encouraged Americans to appreciate the beauties of their country in ways that their seventeenth- and eighteenth-century ancestors had often ignored.[11] As a literate, culturally alert man of his day, Emmons was sensitive to the changes in American life that would inevitably accompany the shift from a rural, agricultural society to one that was largely urban and industrial. Emmons understood that America would follow western Europe down the path of industrialization, and he knew that the beauty and opportunities for spiritual renewal offered by the Adirondacks would be an invaluable treasure in a state where mills and smokestacks were even then beginning rapidly to replace forests and farms.

Emmons found the entire Adirondack region to be a land "unrivaled for its magic and enchantment," declaring,

> It is not, however, by description that the scenery of this region can be made to pass before the eye of the imagination: it must be witnessed; the solitary summits in the distance, the cedars and firs which clothe the rock and shore, must be seen; the solitude must be felt; or, if it is broken by the scream of the panther, the shrill cry of the northern diver [loon], or the

shout of the hunter, the echo from the thousand hills must be heard before all the truth in the scene can be realized.[12]

Emmons's account of the natural beauty of the Adirondacks reflected
an American aesthetic of nature that was focusing intensely and increasingly on wild scenery. The same landscape that had seemed
rugged and difficult to Evans or Pownall now appealed to Emmons because it reminded him of the romantic canvases of painters that were
becoming popular even as he wrote and would later be recognized as
the Hudson River School.

Indeed, Charles C. Ingham, a New York city artist (whose career had
mostly been dedicated to painting portraits of the socially prominent),
accompanied Emmons on the expedition of 1837 that completed the
first ascent of Marcy. Ingham's painting of Indian Pass, "The Great
Adirondack Pass—Painted on the Spot" (first exhibited in 1839 and one
of the earliest oil paintings depicting an Adirondack scene) illustrated

This sketch of the high peaks by Ebenezer Emmons was among the earliest picto-
rial evidence of the grand scenery of the northern mountains. Lithograph by
John H. Bufford for Emmons's report to the legislature for 1837. 58.321.2 (168).

Charles Cromwell Ingham's The Great Adirondack Pass *(1837) typified the romantic fascination with sublime scenery. 66.114.01 (138).*

well an important feature of the romantic fascination with the American landscape, its inclination to search out striking scenery.[13] Wild American nature, it was widely believed, would become the subject of a great national art, an art that would erase the nagging sense of cultural backwardness that many Americans felt when they compared their country with Europe.[14] The towering cliffs and summits of the Adirondack high peaks and the magnificent lakes of the central plateau appeared providentially consonant with this hope.

The fact that Ingham was part of the 1837 expedition was but one important way that Emmons promoted and refined the first great narrative attempting to define the Adirondacks—a narrative that has exercised enormous power ever since. In this view the Adirondack country is "nature," a place of wildness, a place defined by non-human attributes. In its emphasis on an unpeopled landscape, it is descended from the picture of the Adirondacks advanced by Evans and Pownall, though it finds positive characteristics where they found negative. The most important version of this story combined the love of the merely pictorial features of wild scenery with a personal search for recreation and rejuvenation amidst the very mountains and lakes that furnished the scenery.

In June of 1840, Emmons met zoologist James DeKay, also employed by the Natural History Survey, at Lake Pleasant, where they began a lengthy and mostly water-borne tour of the Adirondacks. They trekked by foot to Lewey Lake near Indian Lake, where they rendezvoused with Lewis Elijah Benedict. From Emmons's account of their subsequent adventures, it is hard to tell whether Benedict's skills as woodsman or his trusty canoe were more vital to the success of their mission, which eventually carried them all the way to the Saranac lakes, with a side trip to Old Forge. Emmons was immensely impressed with Benedict's

> birch canoe [which] gave us a safe transport through the wilderness for at least one hundred miles, together with our camp equipment, as tents, pork, bread, fish, guns, traps, hammers, and various objects caught by the way, making, in the whole, a tolerable load for so frail a bark, considering that it must necessarily pass over stones and sandbars and against rocks and logs, and overcome the various obstructions incident to a wild and unfrequented country.[15]

At Raquette Lake Emmons visited the rough compound established by that lake's first settlers, a pair of rugged men named, amazingly, Beach and Wood. After admiring their vegetable garden, Emmons went on to display more precisely his prescient vision of the region's future. He described Raquette Lake in detail:

> The waters are clear but generally ruffled with the breeze. It is well supplied with lake trout which often weigh twenty pounds. The neighboring forests abound also in deer and other game. Hence it is finely suited for the temporary residence of those who are troubled with *ennui,* or who

wish to escape for a time during the months of July and August from the
cares of business or the heat and bustle of the city. To enable the traveller
or invalid to make the most of the situation, a supply of light boats are
[sic] always on hand for fishing or hunting, or for exploring the inlets
and neighboring lakes which are connected with the Racket [sic].[16]

Emmons and DeKay did not know it, but they were helping to establish what would become the major elaboration of the story of the
Adirondacks as a romantic landscape. They were outsiders who came
to the Adirondacks to see the wilderness, and they needed both the
woodcraft and the small boat of a local man to get them from place to
place and to keep them fed and healthy. The men (and a few women)
who followed Emmons to the wilderness were usually not scientists.
They came just to fish, hunt, and restore body and soul amid the scenic
and recreational glories of the Adirondacks, but Emmons and DeKay
set the pattern for these increasingly popular camping trips. The
Adirondacks became that nature to which middle- and upper-class
gentlemen from outside the region repaired to recapture the vigor of
body and soul weakened by the stresses of modern life. These visitors,
as Emmons foresaw, would be "temporary," and the success of their
visit would depend on the resources of the year-round residents,
whose existence in Emmons's picture of the future was elided into the
equipment ("supply of light boats") they furnished the tourists.

Obviously, in antebellum America, the people most in need of an escape from the miseries of overwork, the wage slaves of the North and
the actual slaves of the South, were denied access to the sort of bourgeois vacation that Emmons envisioned on Raquette Lake. Likewise,
those Americans who lived and worked in the countryside—farmers
and loggers, for example—were unlikely to be reading Ralph Waldo
Emerson's "Nature" and meditating on the salutary influences of a life
in the wilderness.[17] But to the growing managerial and professional
class, that is, to those Americans profiting from the new economy and
culture developing around the nation's rapidly expanding cities, a retreat to the seacoast or the mountains became increasingly appealing
and available. The loci of these vacations ranged from the opulent and
cosmopolitan, as at Newport or Saratoga Springs, to the rustic and isolated, as at Maine's Moosehead Lake or the central Adirondacks.[18]

Emmons thus predicted what would become a prominent feature of
the Adirondack story. As he so eloquently announced, here was a re-

gion whose recreational opportunities appeared limitless. The tourist seeking an escape from the drudgeries and distractions of modern life would find solace and rest amidst the scenic lakes of the central Adirondacks. All the tourist needed was a boat and a guide, preferably one as "safe and intelligent" as Lewis Elijah Benedict.[19]

That Benedict was an Indian undoubtedly also appealed to Emmons's romanticism. Intellectuals of that era, especially in the East, projected a host of associations onto the very idea of Native Americans, and in Emmons's case this led to an especially lasting vestige of his imprint on the Adirondacks, the name that he proposed for the high peaks and that subsequently came to identify the entire region. In the annual report to the legislature in which he discussed the field work for 1837, Emmons suggested a name for the mountainous country he was exploring:

> The cluster of mountains in the neighborhood of the Upper Hudson and Ausable rivers, I propose to call the Adirondack Group, a name by which a well-known tribe of Indians who once hunted here may be commemorated.

He went on to assert that the "Adirondacks or Algonquins in early times held all the land north of the Mohawk," admitting, significantly, that "whether this is literally true or not" was not known.[20]

By the time Emmons named the Adirondacks, Native Americans were seldom seen in the eastern United States, except on reservations. No longer an obstacle to American "progress" (of which the Natural History Survey was manifestly a vehicle), they could be romanticized in, by, and for the popular imagination. That these Indians were thought to have "once" hunted in the Adirondacks was a telling detail of Emmons's rationale for choosing the name he did. It was part of the popular American inclination to sentimentalize Indians. The best known example of the eastern American romanticization of Indian culture in the antebellum era was Henry Wadsworth Longfellow's *The Song of Hiawatha* (1855), itself based on a collection of Ojibwa tales compiled by Henry Rowe Schoolcraft and published in 1839, just a couple of years after Emmons named the Adirondacks.[21] Emmons was not the last white man to project the romantic symbolism of Indian associations onto the Adirondack landscape, but his was certainly the most important regional example of this widespread cultural project.

Emmons's impulse to create Indian associations for the Adirondacks appears in this engraving of "View of the Indian Pass from Lake Henderson." Lithograph by John H. Bufford for Emmons's report to the legislature for 1837. 58.321.2 (171).

Nowhere is Emmons's romantic conception of the Adirondacks more clear than in the name he bestowed upon the high peaks that he was among the very first to explore and climb.

So pervasive was this need to establish Indian associations that Emmons was in fact criticized for naming mountains (e.g., Marcy and Seward) after European Americans. People of his era wanted to believe that features of the Adirondack landscape had once possessed authentic Indian names, even though there was absolutely no evidence that this was the case. The popular outdoor writer Charles Lanman blasted Emmons for his "folly . . . in attempting to name the prominent peaks of the Adirondac [sic] region after a brotherhood of living men. . . . A pretty idea, indeed, to scatter to the winds the ancient poetry of the poor Indian, and perpetuate in its place the names of living politicians!"[22]

Alongside Emmons's romanticism—sometimes contradicting it, sometimes complementing it—was a keen awareness of the potential for economic development. To Emmons, the Adirondacks seemed capable of providing both beautiful scenery for the tourist and wealth for the businessman; that these two expectations might eventually generate conflict did not occur to him. Nor should we be surprised that it did not; the Adirondack region was an enormous, largely unexplored wilderness. That nature should be protected from exploitation would have been unimaginable to most Americans in the early nineteenth century.

The romantic temperament emerged in America during, and largely coexisted with, an era of feverish expansion and development. While the politicians of Emmons's day often disagreed with one another over the role of the federal government in promoting such aids to economic development as turnpikes and canals or assistance to industry through tariffs, there was widespread consensus that nature was a source of wealth, that the natural resources of the still relatively young nation were a divinely provided opportunity for rapid exploitation. The natural wealth of North America also offered, so went the prevailing wisdom of the age, a way for the United States to avoid the evils of the social system that condemned people to lives of class-bound poverty in Europe. In a society that was continually expanding economically and geographically, ambitious and entrepreneurial individuals would always have the opportunity to change their status.[23] The fundamental American ideology of individually achieved success was from the very beginning tied to widely shared convictions about the inexhaustibility of American nature.

All these impulses to settle the continent, extend American institutions from sea to sea, and exploit natural resources added up to what generations of historians have discussed as the doctrine of the "manifest destiny" of the American people.[24] Though the dominant focus of this notion was on the West, it operated in the Adirondacks just as powerfully as it did in the rest of the country. The only thing that distinguished the Adirondacks from western frontier regions was that exploitation of local riches—real or imaginary—did not involve the removal or slaughter of indigenous peoples.

Otherwise, the idea that nature was an apparently endless resource to be exploited (which obviously contradicted the earlier image of the

Adirondacks as cold, forbidding, and resistant to human use) became an increasingly important element in the growing body of narratives defining the Adirondack landscape. Ebenezer Emmons, who promoted the romantic ideal of retreat to the land as antidote to the evils of modernity, simultaneously advanced the banner of economic exploitation. Thus, for Emmons and the many Americans who shared his views, the word "nature" and the physical landscape it described belonged to two quite distinct narratives: nature was a place of scenery, recreation, and rejuvenation, and it was also and at the same time a locus for utilitarian exploitation. As Emmons's fellow explorer, Farrand Benedict, wrote, "There is much in this region to draw hitherward the pleasure-loving, many inducements for the money-loving."[25] The contest between these two narratives has been fiercely engaged in the Adirondacks (and in innumerable other places) ever since Emmons's day.

The first utilitarian contribution that Emmons foresaw for the Adirondacks involved mining. Iron mining and smelting began in the Lake Champlain foothills of the Adirondacks in 1801 and was a prominent feature of the local economy for the rest of the century. By the time of the Civil War iron from the eastern Adirondacks was considered to be among the best in the world. While most of the Adirondack mines and forges were close to Lake Champlain, an important exception to this was the McIntyre development near Newcomb. There a company controlled by a group of downstate investors, the chief of whom was Archibald McIntyre of New York City and Albany, mined ore discovered in 1825 by Lewis Elijah Benedict.[26]

When Emmons set off for the summit of Marcy in 1837, his base camp was a small village at the McIntyre iron works on the upper Hudson. Emmons explored this area carefully and concluded that it held iron deposits of national significance: "The most extensive beds of this kind of ore in the district, and perhaps in the world, are found at Newcomb, in the vicinity of Lake Sandford [sic]." Emmons waxed eloquent about the ostensible potential of the iron deposits on the upper Hudson and predicted a rosy future of huge profits for the mine's owners.[27]

Like many Americans of his day, moreover, Emmons believed that agriculture was the best possible use of land and maintained high hopes that the Adirondacks would someday support a population of thrifty yeomen and their families. The wilderness that otherwise he

ADIRONDACK VILLAGE.

Sketch of one of the two villages near the McIntyre iron development, from Benson J. Lossing's The Hudson, from the Wilderness to the Sea *(1866).*

found to be the source of "truth" would be replaced by fields and gardens:

> The axe has been laid at the foot of the tree, and ere long where naught now greets the eye but a dense, and to appearance impenetrable forest, will be seen the golden grain waving with the gentle breeze, the sleek cattle browsing on the rich pastures, and the farmer with well-stored granaries enjoying the domestic hearth.[28]

This vision of georgic prosperity derived from the same traditions that had led Evans and Pownall to disparage the Adirondacks as cold and useless; in either case, the land is understood only in terms of agricultural productivity. And the prevailing wisdom of Emmons's day had an answer to the old claims about the uncooperative Adirondack climate. It was widely believed, with some empirical evidence, that once the forests were cleared from a previously forested landscape, the climate would get warmer. This was the beginning of awareness of the potential for human activities to effect climate change.[29] Emmons himself asserted, "When the country is settled extensively, and the timber

and wood removed, there will be an amelioration of climate; it will become drier and less frosty, and the summer warmer and better suited
to the raising of corn."[30]

In describing what he was certain was the Adirondack future, even
when engaging in what seems like an almost supernatural faith, Emmons invoked a vocabulary—"golden grain," "rich pastures,"
"domestic hearth"—that would have been familiar and of mythic significance to most Americans. Like Thomas Jefferson and many other
eighteenth-century thinkers who helped establish this view in the national set of cultural values, most Americans believed the farmer to be
the true exponent of democracy and the farmed landscape to be the
best protector of republican virtue and Christian values. When Emmons constructed his narrative of rural wholesomeness, he was describing a future for both the American people and the American
landscape that was unconsciously and nearly universally understood.[31]

As it turned out, Emmons underestimated both the severity of
Adirondack winters and the relative thinness of the soil, and the dream
of prosperous agricultural communities was never realized, though
many a poor family had to learn the hard way that their labors in clearing the forest from a parcel of Adirondack land would never be ade-
quately rewarded. Likewise, difficulties of transportation and
impurities in the ore prevented Archibald McIntyre's iron company
from achieving the financial success predicted by Emmons. But the importance of Emmons's picture of an intensely peopled and cultivated
landscape is critical to what has been ever since a contest between competing narratives about the Adirondacks, both of which appear in
the various pronouncements of Ebenezer Emmons about the region's
future.

In one story the Adirondacks exist as a natural landscape, one to be
defined and appreciated as the embodiment of all the goodness and
virtue of nature, a nature that is defined as fundamentally outside the
social world of commerce and industry. Here the Adirondack country
is inhabited by fish and animals, the hillsides are forested, and people
are either visitors or scattered residents who live close to nature in order to serve the needs of the visitors. In the competing story, the
Adirondack country is just another American place where people go
about the daily business of working, raising children, and engaging the

For explorers and early settlers and tourists, the first Adirondack roads were little more than primitive tracks through the forest. Log Road in Hamilton County *(1844) by Regis Francois Gignoux. 64.005.01 (92).*

national economy. There were at least two important and inherently conflicting variations of this latter story. In the first the dominant theme is the notion of sustainable frontier communities based on agriculture; in the other the critical theme is the extraction of natural resources capitalized by outside corporations. Emmons failed to distinguish between these, just as he failed to distinguish between the stories of the Adirondacks as nature or as locus for economic activity. In his ambivalence, we find the source of the confusion that has vexed New Yorkers ever since. Is the Adirondack region a landscape of wild nature treasured for its beauty, recreational potential, and immanent divinity? Is it a place where people live? Is it a place to make money? Can it be all of these?

2

"Long Lake Was a Hard Place to Live"

Even as Ebenezer Emmons and his colleagues on the Natural History Survey were exploring the wilderness of northern New York, families were struggling to carve out an existence there. The same landscape that appealed to Emmons either as a recreational retreat for jaded professionals from the city or as a source of natural resources awaiting exploitation by downstate capital was simply a new home to settlers looking for cheap land and a fresh start on life. Beginning on the Adirondack margins and gradually penetrating to the central core, families cleared plots for crops, built log cabins, started small businesses like saw- or gristmills, and eked out a living in a beautiful but harsh land. Their story is similar to that of many other nineteenth-century American frontier regions. It is the story of mostly poor people looking for a chance for a better life for themselves and their children.

In other parts of the United States, especially the trans-Mississippi West, the story of poor migrants' establishing new communities on the frontier has achieved mythical status, with certain inevitable elements—the arrival of sturdy pioneers, their struggles with hardship and deprivation, their perseverance and industry, and their eventual triumph. Beginning with the Pilgrims in Massachusetts and running through ranchers, farmers, and missionaries throughout the West, the story of frontier settlement has become part of the national narrative. Oddly, a similar story has not become a key element of the larger Adirondack narrative. Yet the same ingredients are here.

Before there were settlers in the Adirondacks, there was ownership of the land, usually by downstate speculators. In the late eighteenth century, most of what would eventually become the Adirondack Park was purchased by wealthy men who never laid eyes on their northern lands. Huge chunks of northern New York were bought for speculation and carved into smaller tracts for resale. The three most important of these were the Totten and Crossfield Purchase, Macomb's Purchase, and the Old Military Tract. These huge tracts were in addition to many smaller tracts around the margins of the Adirondacks.

The Totten and Crossfield Purchase involved a series of complex transactions among a consortium of wealthy speculators, chiefs of Mohawk Valley Indian tribes, and the British crown. By the onset of the American Revolution, the investors, for whom the New York City shipwrights Totten and Crossfield were apparently little more than front men, owned over a million acres of northern wilderness, stretching from Long Lake to Lake Pleasant, from northern Herkimer County to the high peaks. The owners sided with the British during the Revolution, after which this huge tract reverted to the ownership of the new state of New York, though the diagonal survey lines, running southwest-northeast and southeast-northwest, subdividing it into townships, became a permanent feature of Adirondack maps and property titles.[1]

Alexander Macomb, son of an Irish immigrant who settled in Albany, made a fortune in the fur trade at Detroit, returned to New York a rich man, and decided to put some of his great wealth to work speculating in the northern wilderness. Between 1792 and 1798, patents for nearly four million acres of lands in northern New York were issued to Macomb. None of these lands stayed in his hands for long, however, but like Totten and Crossfield, the name Macomb remains part of Adirondack maps and titles as a reminder of the earliest efforts to realize a profit in Adirondack real estate.[2]

The other major apportionment of Adirondack land was the Old Military Tract consisting of about 665,000 acres in Clinton, Franklin, and Essex counties and containing Keene Valley, Lake Placid, and the Chateaugay lakes. Its name derives from the fact that these lands were set aside by the state in 1781 to pay troops raised to protect the northern frontier from Indian raids. Practically none of the lands it contained were so distributed; most were subsequently sold by the state as "wild lands."[3]

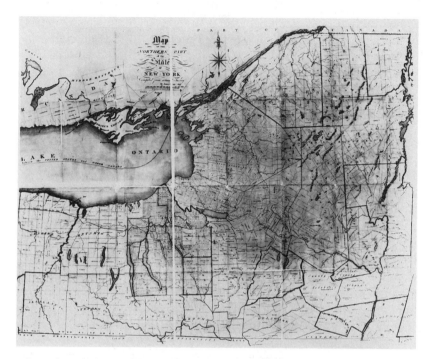

By early in the nineteenth century, as this 1812 map by Amos Lay illustrates, the Adirondack country was divided into counties, towns, and numerous large lots, many never visited by their absentee owners. Adirondack Museum Library.

Beginning in the late eighteenth century, families from other parts of New York or from New England began moving onto scattered parcels of these and lesser Adirondack tracts. Settlement in the Lake Champlain and Lake George valleys was well established by 1790. From there and from the Mohawk Valley slim fingers of settlement inched up Adirondack rivers or skipped ahead to lowlands around the central lakes, where land was cleared, houses built, and crops planted.[4]

These settlers came mostly from New York state or New England. Hard evidence on precisely where all of the early nineteenth-century immigrants to the Adirondacks came from is elusive, but U. S. and state census schedules as well as the few surviving diaries and other bits of personal reminiscence suggest that the families who moved into the region during this period were predominately Anglo-Saxon and had been born in the United States. (As was the case throughout the country, the non-Anglo-Saxon often encountered ethnic prejudice. In the 1840s in the town of Long Lake, young Robert Shaw was told by the mother of a young lady that he could not take her daughter to a Christmas ball because he was "an uncouth, no-mannered Irishman, and . . . not educated, besides being profane and rough."[5])

The *History of Hamilton County* notes that the early settlers in that county were all from other New York counties or from New England.[6] A look at census schedules for Hamilton County confirms this. Beginning in 1850 enumerators indicated the place of birth for everyone counted in the federal census. For that year the birthplaces for residents of Hamilton County, including children, were overwhelmingly in New York, with a handful from Vermont, New Hampshire, Canada, England, Ireland, and Scotland.[7] A number of Adirondack place names derive from the New England origins of early settlers: Brandon in Franklin County, for example, is named after Brandon, Vermont.[8]

In any case, migration to the Adirondacks was sparse. Population densities throughout what is now the Adirondack Park were far below those of the rest of New York. By 1850, New York was a settled state— except for the Adirondack plateau, which retained its frontier character with only a few communities boasting populations of more than a hundred residents. The state census of 1855, moreover, showed that what population there was in the Adirondacks remained native born, to an extent significantly greater than the rest of the state: for the most part, immigrants from abroad steered clear of the central Adirondacks.[9]

The main source of immigrants to the Adirondacks was previously settled parts of New York and New England, where, by 1800, agriculture was entering a period of eclipse. The shift from subsistence to market agriculture, promoted by the rise of urban centers and increasing connections between the United States and far-off population centers, led to overcultivation and overproduction. In the following decades, as fertility declined and opportunities for clearing new land diminished, northeastern agriculture began to collapse, though the worst was not reached until after the Civil War. Farmers and their families looked west for a chance to improve their fortunes. Most took advantage of new transportation arteries like the Erie Canal (which was completed in 1825) and headed for the rich lands of Ohio and Indiana. New England and New York (that part of the state east of the Appalachian height of land) were the major sources of migration to the Old Northwest.[10]

But a few people heeded the rumors of cheap and abundant land in a little-known, barely explored northern corner of New York. These hardy souls became the first white settlers in the Adirondacks. Poor to begin with (otherwise, most would never have made the desperate stab at establishing a new life in such a remote, harsh environment), they arrived with little but enthusiasm and a willingness to work hard. William Reed, who moved to the northern Adirondacks as a small boy in 1823, recorded his memories of a difficult time and wrote of his family and their neighbors, most of whom had trekked from New England: "They were generally poor, hardworking laborers with no capital and could barely pay the expense of migration on the most economical scale. A few brought teams and a little household furniture, but very rarely one brought money enough to pay for land."[11] Or, as Henry Conklin, author of another memoir of early nineteenth-century local life, put it, "we had been so poor that we had only one suit of clothes to our backs, and when mother wanted to wash them she had to do it while we were abed at night or undressed and go to bed in the day time while she washed and dried our clothes."[12]

Some of the early settlers had in fact set out for better lands to the west but had been forced by circumstance or bad luck into the Adirondacks. The Shaw family, for example, which left Ireland in 1834 hoping to make it to Ohio by way of Quebec, found themselves waylaid by typhus shortly after reaching North America; after nine years of suffering and poverty, they landed in the frontier village of Long Lake, New York, trying to achieve there, far from the fertile lands of Ohio, the immigrants' dream of success and prosperity in the new world.[13]

The purchase of land was difficult for many, especially since ownership was often uncertain and township and other lines of subdivision had been hastily run. More important, immigrants generally lacked the cash or credit to buy from downstate speculators the few pieces of land even remotely suitable for agriculture. One observer of the difficulties facing Adirondack settlers trying to buy land noted that high prices were a major obstacle to "poor men," the only people who "can be induced to go in at first and endure the hardships of pioneer life."[14] This was but the first of many subsequent instances of uneasy relations between people living in the Adirondacks and those, generally possessed of greater wealth and hence greater power, living elsewhere. Here, as later, the issue was who should control the land—those living on it or someone else? As Reed acidly observed, "The land was owned in immense tracts by individuals, who had either stolen or purchased them."[15] Some settlers, no doubt, simply moved onto unoccupied land and ignored the technicalities of ownership.[16]

Occasionally, families moved into houses or cabins abandoned by others who had given up their hopes for a new life. The family of four-year-old Livonia Stanton (who, as a married adult, Livonia Stanton Emerson, composed a lengthy and invaluable reminiscence about her early years in the central Adirondacks) moved into a vacant log cabin on the west side of Long Lake in 1849. They arrived in the winter, and her father had to shovel several feet of snow out of the house and break the ice on the floor with his ax before he could start a fire.[17] The Shaw family, as well, arrived in winter, finding a cabin full of snow and lacking a working chimney.[18] Conklin's family moved from hovel to hovel in Herkimer County, until his father was able to make a down payment on a hundred-acre plot. There the family built a

Log Cabin in the Adirondacks Near North Woods Club *(ca. 1857) by Eliphalet Terry. 69.051.01 (209).*

small log cabin in a few months and moved in—a total of fourteen people—before winter.[19]

In the spirit of community that was common throughout the American frontier, houses were often erected by an entire neighborhood for a poor family. When Henry Conklin's brother and his family were "in the meshes of poverty and so poor they were not decently clothed and the children in rags, . . . [t]he neighborhood got together one day and went to work cutting and hauling logs and put him up a log house. Some brought nails, some lumber, and some shingles and before night we had it nearly completed." With donated furniture and the father working at odd jobs for friends and relatives, the family "lived from hand to mouth."[20]

Settlers occupied houses that were cramped, drafty, small, and cluttered. Conklin described one log cabin with a first floor of eighteen by twenty feet. This was divided into a small bedroom, where his parents slept in one bed and his seven sisters in another, and a center room that was combination kitchen and parlor. The six boys all slept in one bed in a narrow, low-ceilinged loft, reached by a ladder. Any guests stayed in the loft with the boys.[21]

Even with minimal housing secured, life for these families in the Adirondack wilderness offered all the deprivations, hardships, and disasters that have become familiar elements of the American frontier story. Many families—beset with miserable weather, short growing seasons, and scant opportunities to accumulate capital—found life in the north country more than they could handle and moved away, looking for better opportunities in the West: as Livonia Stanton Emerson recalled, "When we had lived in this wilderness about 8 or 10 years, the town seemed to be at stand still, there were as many people got discouraged and moved away as there were families that moved in to town." A sad but common activity in Adirondack towns was saying good-bye, almost certainly forever, to neighbors or relatives heading west.[22]

But others persevered and achieved at least part of the American dream. "You may ask why a man would move into such a place with a family?" wrote Livonia Stanton Emerson:

> The only reason I know was this:—land was cheap, wood was plenty, all it cost was to cut it, fish, venison and fur were plenty. That was quite an

inducement to a poor man, when he has to pay rent, and buy his wood, it took quite a little of his hard earnings. Long Lake was a hard place to live and yet it had many comforts. We had six months of winter, that was a dreary time, the summer came, it was so pleasant we forgot all about the long winter, until it was here again.[23]

For those who endured, wrote William Reed, came the rewards of industry and dedication: "They encountered all the hardships and self-denial of a new settlement with cheerfulness and worked on for years with a persistence and energy worthy of commendation."[24] Success for some was more than merely modest. Robert Shaw arrived in Long Lake at the age of fourteen. Nearly illiterate and abysmally poor, he educated himself, cleared land for his father's farm, worked as a lumberjack and a dozen other trades, and ended his life as the respected proprietor of a prosperous general store.[25] For Reed's family, for Robert Shaw, and for many others like them, the Adirondack story of the nineteenth century was a story of hard-working Americans making a new life in a new land.

For them all, hopes were high, encouraged by the optimistic boosterism endemic throughout America in the age of Andrew Jackson. Whereas Ebenezer Emmons emphasized exploitable natural resources, others, applying the same doctrine of manifest destiny but in a variation that focused on communities rather than capital-intensive extractive industry, predicted a rapidly growing population of successful husbandmen. The most fulsome of these predictions for the central Adirondacks came from a summer tourist from Massachusetts, Congregational minister John Todd, who visited Long Lake for several summers in the 1840s. Todd was certain that the energy, industry, and dedication of the settlers he met there would be the foundation of a thriving society: "When the day shall arrive in which these forests shall be cut down, and along the lakes and valleys and around the base of these glorious mountains there shall be a virtuous, industrious and Christian population, I have no doubt it will easily support a million of people."[26] Todd's vision of a cleared and settled Adirondacks was the ultimate distillation of one version of the Adirondack story. Todd took the story of the Adirondacks as a place for American families to realize the American dream and reduced it to its mythic essence.

In pursuit of this dream, nearly all Adirondack families tried to make farming their primary occupation, though most had to combine this with various other jobs. When Reed's family moved to the north country in 1823—into a log cabin, where a blanket hung over the only opening—they worked a farm of seventy-two acres, of which seven acres were cleared for wheat, a half acre for corn, and a small patch for potatoes.[27] For all these early settlers, clearing the forest was a never-ending task, involving cutting and burning away tree after tree. Henry Conklin wrote, "It was all woods, a great dense forest." But the woods gave way; Conklin noted later, "As soon as spring opened we all went to work chopping and clearing. What a crashing there was in the old dead girdled trees as they came crashing to the ground under the mighty strokes of the axe."[28] And Livonia Stanton Emerson remembered the first spring at Long Lake, with all the family, including herself, aged four, helping to get enough land ready for cultivation. Among charred stumps, they planted turnips, potatoes, oats, rye, and flax.[29]

The Martin Byrne family, who settled near Minerva in 1837, tried a wide variety of crops, looking to diversify their yield, identify which crops could best withstand the harsh climate, and protect themselves when blight or other failures inevitably destroyed one of the crops. In 1855, for example, Martin Byrne planted rye, oats, peas, corn, beans, potatoes, buckwheat, and onions. Peas were considered a good crop on newly cleared land still infested with weeds and brush and were often fed to hogs. The rye was threshed by hand and mixed with wheat and oats as feed for horses, while the corn was taken to the mill. One bushel of planted corn yielded a crop of 193 bushels, which, when ground, supplied the family with mush and cornbread for a whole year.[30]

An additional crop that nearly all Adirondack families harvested was maple sugar. In the days before glass or metal containers were cheap and plentiful, the sap was boiled all the way down to sugar; making and keeping maple syrup came later. Maple sugar was a welcome treat and even part of courting rituals; one April in Long Lake Robert Shaw, perhaps still striving to overcome prejudice against the Irish, celebrated his twenty-first birthday by "treating the neighbors' girls to warm maple sugar."[31]

Sugaring occurred during March and April, and the fires it required demanded yet further labor chopping away at the Adirondack forest— beyond the seemingly endless labor of laying up wood for heating the

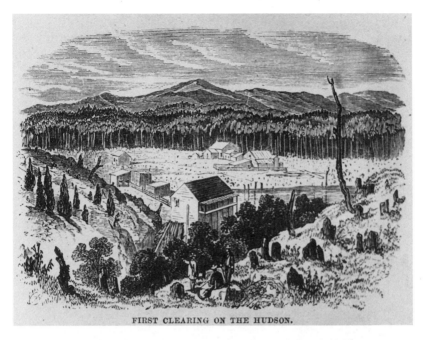

FIRST CLEARING ON THE HUDSON.

The Newcomb farm, first cleared in 1816, from Benson J. Lossing's The Hudson *(1866).*

house and cooking. "There was always wood to be cut for boiling sap, to keep the house warm during the winter, and to cook with the year round." And "there was always another wood lot to be cleared and added to the farming land."[32] During the nineteenth century, barely a day passed for an Adirondack family when someone wasn't chopping wood. It should come as no surprise that the forest constituted a part of the Adirondack experience that was quite different from what it meant to romantics like Emmons and the tourists who followed him. To Adirondackers the forest was both a resource and an obstacle to their own prosperity.

Around the house, most important tasks were performed by women, without whose contributions to the family economy life would have been even harder. Soap making, spinning and weaving cloth, sewing and mending clothes, gardening, food preparation, and all the other labor of keeping a family together and healthy occupied women throughout the year.[33]

Inside and out, Adirondack families endured a difficult life. Besides a forest that must have often seemed ominous, there were the unavoidable realities of the Adirondack climate and growing season combined with such horrors as fire, illness, and the psychological trauma resulting from isolation and day-to-day drudgery. It was a hardy lot that survived these travails and made a go of it in the Adirondacks. The family of Henry Conklin moved repeatedly and suffered a series of hardships, yet he noted after one of their moves in Herkimer County (a move made especially chaotic by the presence of no fewer than twelve children, including a new-born baby),

> We were all well and healthy, thanks to plain food, plenty of outdoor exercise and a father and mother with iron constitutions and no hereditary disease lurking in their bodies. What a tough lot of children we were. Al-

An idealized rendition of the early spring ritual of boiling down maple sap for sugar. Currier and Ives lithograph, "American Forest Scene. Maple Sugaring," after a painting by Arthur Fitzwilliam Tait. 72.137.1 (221).

though poor and at times pinched with hunger we were comparatively happy going to our new home in the wilderness.[34]

Not everyone was so lucky. Martin Byrne's wife died of typhoid fever when she was forty-five, and her daughter, aged seventeen, died of the same disease about a week later. Even in the Adirondacks, polluted water was a threat to health and life; after the Byrnes dug a new, stone-lined well, they had no further trouble with this scourge.[35]

When accidents occurred, Adirondackers were left to their own resources. After an employee mangled his leg horribly in an accident involving a huge circular saw blade at Robert Shaw's sawmill, no reliable doctor was available. Shaw himself gathered some assistants to hold down the bleeding man. He cleaned sawdust out of the deep wound, steeled his nerve, and sewed up the leg. The victim survived.[36] The unavailability or uselessness of professional doctors also meant the persistence of folk remedies. When Henry Conklin's father appeared to be dying of "an inflamation [sic] in his bowels" and the doctors had abandoned hope, a local woman saved his life with a poultice made from freshly dug earthworms.[37]

The isolation of north-country life led some to drink—or at least led some observers to insist that drinking was a problem. The Reverend John Todd arrived in the fledgling community at Long Lake when it was barely a decade old and found intemperance to be a threat to social stability: "before they had a road, before they could get flour or comfortable food, they used to get in whiskey by the barrel."[38] And William Reed perceived a similar problem in Franklin County:

> there was drunkenness in all its horror, poverty, filth, ferocity and foulness. Liquor selling was unrestrained; the pious deacons, Luther and Clark, retailed it without scruple; the variety store keeper never failed to have a supply on hand, and topers could indulge in a glass, gill, pint or quart and have a jolly young revel at almost any store. Whisky sold at twenty-five cents a gallon retail, and there were sixteen distilleries for making it from corn and rye, within the limits of Franklin County about 1830 to 35.[39]

As it was throughout rural America, one response to the ostensible evils of liquor was the revival meeting, led by an itinerant preacher.

The vacationing John Todd led services in Long Lake, and other Protestant ministers did the same at communities throughout the Adirondacks. Because Adirondack settlements were often so remote, revivals did not occur frequently enough for some residents. Henry Conklin treasured the memory of a revival held in a Herkimer County schoolhouse, after which he was baptized in the waters of West Canada Creek: "We had been deprived of having meetings or going to church so long that we had almost become like the heathen and needed a good shaking by something."[40]

Other problems were less social and more material. The Shaw family of Long Lake, after working hard for five years, watched helplessly as their harvest—a "meager crop"—went up in flames in a barn fire of suspicious origins. With no rye to take to the mill, no hay for their cows, and winter approaching, the Shaws were ready to quit, abandon the slim opportunities for living independently in the Adirondacks, and return to working for low wages in Vermont. But their son Robert took a job chopping wood for the forge at the McIntyre iron mine. He worked hard, aiming to cut two cords a day and take home twelve dollars a month.[41]

It became an unavoidable feature of Adirondack life that no one could expect to make a living with only one skill. Even though conditions in the central Adirondacks remained those of the frontier, the days of the purely subsistence economy were fading. Adirondackers needed ways to generate cash to buy essentials like stoves, clothing, and the paraphernalia of hunting, fishing, and trapping. The census schedules for 1850 showed that the overwhelming majority of the heads of families in Hamilton County identified agriculture as their occupation (510 in agriculture, seventy-two in manufactures and trades, and two in commerce), but the accounts of actual life show that nearly everyone pursued other occupations as well. Among the non-farming trades listed in the census were laborer, carpenter, blacksmith, merchant, logger, and joiner.[42] In his memoirs, Long Lake's Robert Shaw claimed to have worked at no less than thirteen trades: at one time or another this self-identified "self-made backwoods genius" was a carpenter, wheelwright, blacksmith, sleigh maker, stone mason, cobbler, plasterer, millwright, farmer, logger, doctor, lawyer, and preacher.[43]

Martin Byrne "hired out" to other farmers, especially during haying season. As his sons grew older and better able to manage the home farm, Martin could spend more time working for others and bringing needed cash into the household economy.[44] Likewise, Livonia Stanton Emerson's father earned a little cash by doing "day work" for slightly more prosperous neighbors. This involved much travel and long hours, but "that was the way men had to work in those days." Later, he worked on a logging crew, forced to leave home just as he was trying to finish building a new house. The work was twenty miles from Long Lake and required him to stay there from late fall until spring. His labors were productive, though; when he returned, he brought with him nine sheep.[45]

The Byrnes, who lived relatively close to a commercial center, Glens Falls, opted to open a small general store to bring in cash. This was operated in the house, for some years right in the kitchen. Martin Byrne traveled to Glens Falls once a week to pick up supplies and to sell what surplus he could gather from his farm.[46] Another common way to pick up extra cash was trapping. Henry Conklin, shortly after marrying, noted, "My money for the fur helped me along quite considerable through poverty's vale." A few years later, still relying on trapping for needed cash, he sold his furs and used the money to buy clothes: "Fur was then bringing a good price and mink pelts were bringing from two and a half to three dollars. I made more out of fur while I was at it than I did get elsewhere."[47]

Adirondack families looked for a supply of cash wherever they could, and cottage industries, whereby a family would manufacture some item in the home for sale either locally or to buyers from beyond the neighborhood, were another source of cash. Near their cabin the Conklins built a log shanty, where the boys cut spruce shingles during the winter months. These were hauled by their father to Utica and Herkimer and were for many years the only way the family could acquire cash. The return for labor was scant; spruce shingles brought between two and two and a half dollars per thousand. Years later Henry Conklin observed, "I tell you we had to work or starve."[48] The contributions of women were critical to earning cash; they sewed and knitted garments for sale, hired out to work as housekeepers, and oversaw the care and feeding of lodgers.[49]

In the Champlain valley an economy significantly different from that of the central Adirondacks developed. There, beginning roughly at the time of the Natural History Survey, the iron industry—boosted by new discoveries of ore, protective tariffs, and growing demand for iron from northeastern manufacturers—became a major factor in the local economic picture. This in turn stimulated agriculture; miners and mill workers and their families needed agricultural products on a rapidly expanding scale. At the same time, farmers in search of a source of cash found it through working part-time at the forges. Towns in Essex and Clinton counties—Ausable Forks, Mineville, Clintonville, and Moriah, for example—typified the culture and economy that grew up around the eastern Adirondack iron industry before the Civil War.[50]

The one central Adirondack town that developed along these lines was Newcomb, where the McIntyre concern was mining and smelting what it believed was high-quality ore. By mid-century the company's two villages, Tahawus and Adirondac, had stable populations, numerous dwelling houses, a post office, a company bank, a school, churches, and stores—all supported by sawmills, gristmills, charcoal kilns, and two substantial farms. All this changed when continuing difficulties associated with transporting ore from the remote site near Newcomb to ports on Lake Champlain, combined with the death of founder Archibald McIntyre, floods on the upper Hudson that washed out dams, and the financial panic of 1857 led to a sudden and complete halt in operations. The villages' residents abandoned their homes, and the area became known as a picturesque vestige of failure and faded glory.[51]

But in the Lake Champlain region, the iron industry thrived, utterly dominating both the landscape and the economy. By the eve of the Civil War agriculture supplying a population connected with iron mines and forges was firmly established, and many areas that a few decades before had been largely an untouched forest had been cleared for cultivation or pasture. Villages, industrial sites, and transportation corridors served the needs of iron interests.[52]

The other important extractive industry was logging. Settlers had been cutting down trees since they first came to the Adirondacks, and they immediately found a variety of uses for most of the trees they felled. Some went into their own cabins, in the form of log walls and shingles, while settlers burned countless cords of firewood for heating and cooking. Around the iron forges hardwoods were cut by the hundreds of acres for charcoal. All around the Adirondack margins hemlocks, a common Adirondack species, were harvested for their bark,

Long after the McIntyre mine closed, its imprint on the landscape remained.
Photograph by Seneca Ray Stoddard, 1888. P. 1713.

which was used in tanning hides for leather. And softwoods, chiefly
white pine and red spruce, were cut for lumber wherever they were
accessible.

The story of logging in the Adirondacks is a long and complex one.
It has been a major industry throughout the region's recorded history.
It reached its peak in the decades around the beginning of the twentieth century, but its roots go back well before the Civil War. It has
been—and remains—a major producer of income for Adirondackers,
as well as a source of raw materials and profits for corporations mostly
headquartered outside the Adirondacks. It is omnipresent and controversial and has been seen both as an essential, ultimately benign feature of regional culture and as a brutal assault on the landscape.
Logging is a part of nearly every Adirondack story, whether as picturesque, dangerous, and highly skilled labor or as just another human
rape of nature in the name of profits.

Cutting hemlock bark for tanneries was one of the earliest extractive industries in the Adirondacks.

Cutting hemlocks for their bark was beginning in the southern and southeastern Adirondacks by the time of the Natural History Survey, though the peak of its role as a significant element of the Adirondack economy occurred between 1860 and 1880. Tanneries appeared near towns and transportation corridors, but these remained limited to local operations with little impact until after the Civil War. In Warren County a small tannery was using hemlock bark at Warrensburg as early as 1810, and a large-scale tannery began there in 1831. In southern Hamilton County a tannery was operating in Wells early in the nineteenth century; by 1855 three Hamilton County tanneries—at Wells, Hope, and Morehouseville—were employing over sixty men.[53]

At these and similar sites scattered around the eastern and southern Adirondack margins, local residents could work for cash on a seasonal basis. Conklin and several of his brothers worked many years supplying bark to tanneries. At one point, he wrote, "We were making a good living and did not lack the necessities of life." They felled hemlock trees and peeled off the bark, which was carted by the cord to tanneries. There, as part of a complicated process involving profligate levels of waste and pollution, tannin from the hemlock bark was used to cure cow hides.[54]

At the same time, logging for lumber was developing as a major occupation. Adirondack logging began as a locally centered industry, as each new Adirondack community needed a sawmill to produce lumber. Running on water power, these quickly became important elements in the local culture, and sawmill owners were key players in the establishment and maintenance of the regional economy. The mills began as individually or family-owned businesses, where the proprietors bought logs from or processed them for their neighbors. In the town of Wells in southern Hamilton County, for example, Nicholas Bratt and William Wells were operating both saw- and gristmills by the first decade of the nineteenth century. Both had immigrated from outside the area (Wells from Long Island, Bratt from Saratoga County) looking for business opportunities. Other mills soon appeared in the vicinity, and by the 1830s there were at least three additional sawmills in Wells. By 1855 twenty-three sawmills were operating in Hamilton County, all in the southern part of the county, where a growing population could both use finished lumber and supply a labor force.[55]

The mill owners were beginning to change their businesses from operations serving strictly local needs to larger enterprises processing Adirondack lumber for a modernizing economy. As the sawmills enlarged their operations, they were able to channel limited amounts of outside cash into the hands of Adirondack families, for whom logging—including cutting trees, skidding logs to loading stations, building roads and camp buildings, and a host of related jobs—and working at the mills supplemented the always meager return from farming. For some, the cash earned as a logger was a ticket away from the Adirondacks; Henry Conklin's brother worked all one summer "pulling a cross cut saw in the Hinkley lumber woods," saving money to get himself to the California gold fields.[56]

The export of logs to mills outside the Adirondacks began in this period. Though the peak of Adirondack logging would not be reached until the early twentieth century, the era before the Civil War saw the emergence of what eventually became a major industry wherein local labor and resources served the interests of outside capital. In 1813, Norman and Alanson Fox floated logs down the Schroon and Hudson rivers from the Brant Lake tract in Essex County to Glens Falls. Before then logs had been hauled to mills relatively close to the standing timber.[57] Once the Fox brothers had identified this efficient and inexpensive method for transporting raw materials to mills, where they could be cut into finished lumber for sale on a national market, the story of Adirondack logging slowly evolved from small local affairs harvesting timber for more or less local needs to heavily capitalized and labor-intensive operations closely tied to the national economy.[58]

Expanded logging also began to exercise a noticeable impact on the landscape. Henry Conklin recalled both remunerative employment and environmental change in the year of his seventeenth birthday. A new mill was "buying spruce and hemlock logs and the boys and men in the neighborhood were engaged in working for them or cutting logs and banking them for the new firm. This together with peeling hemlock bark made business quite lively along through our place. . . . The wilderness began to be stripped of the hemlock and spruce and good shingle timber was scarce near the creek."[59] As the Adirondacks became more implicated in the national economy, Adirondackers watched (and helped) their landscape enter a period of profound change.

Eventually, yet another cluster of trades developed—trades that would increasingly come to define life and work for people who lived in the Adirondacks. The summer sportsmen, whose arrival Emmons had so accurately predicted, needed hotels, guides, and a variety of services. The scenery and field sports drew visitors, but the whole camping-out routine involved a "fatigue which few can be willing to endure." The solution, wrote John Todd (as Emmons had noted), was to hire "an experienced hunter for a guide and aid."[60] Guiding sportsmen during the summer became another source of cash for local men, who worked at other trades at other times of the year. John Cheney, for example, who led Ebenezer Emmons and his survey team to the summit of Marcy and who subsequently became celebrated as one of the region's most famous and reliable guides, was originally hired by the McIntyre mine company to supply venison for its workers.[61]

Of greater long-range significance was the appearance of hotels and inns; many tourists interested in hunting, fishing, and enjoying the scenery had no wish to camp out. Having braved the often horrible roads of the mid-nineteenth century, they arrived at central Adirondack villages in need of a dry bed and a hot dinner. Livonia Stanton Emerson's family seized this opportunity and offered lodging and board to "some of the sporting people that came from the cities to spend the summer months here."[62]

Local entrepreneurs began building hotels throughout the Adirondacks. In 1860, the Hamilton County supervisors saw clearly that the future of their region depended on cash brought in by "residents of the cities, who, with their families, would come among us, expending their money" at local hostelries.[63] Though providing room and board to tourists did not become a major local industry until after the Civil War, its roots, too, are in the antebellum years. Martin's Hotel on Lower Saranac Lake, for example, was begun in 1849. It was one of the first

A LODGE IN THE WILDERNESS.

The first Adirondack hostels were constructed from rough local materials. Benson J. Lossing's The Hudson *(1866).*

Adirondack enterprises undertaken to meet the opportunities offered
by the nascent tourist industry.[64]

The arrival of tourists was a pivotal moment both in the history of
the Adirondacks and in the lives of the local residents. While the
tourist-based economy became absolutely essential to the livelihoods
of Adirondackers, it necessitated a fundamental change in the way local people related to the Adirondack landscape. From the beginning,
some Adirondack residents appear to have appreciated the special
quality of the landscape they were calling home. While the visitors they
lodged and guided came from the cities in search of the nature that the
romantic temperament told them would heal their bodies and souls,
the year-round residents knew the Adirondacks as the nature that sus-
tained and always surrounded them—in all its obstinacy and harsh-
ness. This is not to say that one of these sets of perceptions was
somehow superior to or more genuine than the other. The point is that
the development of a culture of tourism added a complex new narrative thread to the story of people and nature in the Adirondacks.

One obvious connection between Adirondackers and their environment was through hunting and fishing. There is a significant difference
between the sport hunting conducted by the romantic tourists who followed Emmons to the Adirondacks and the hunting of people trying to
feed themselves and their children. Livonia Stanton Emerson remembered that her father hunted deer whenever he needed to: "In those
days any one had a right to kill deer any time. No law preventing it."[65]
Likewise, Henry Conklin recalled how the forest supplied his family's
table:

> That summer we had plenty of trout. The boys used to go fishing after
> supper and would sometimes get enough for three meals a plenty to last
> all the next day. Some times they would catch a big pan full in an hour
> or two, and such great nice beauties. During the summer season for ten
> or twelve years our table was well supplied with fish, and they helped
> us along wonderfully. Some times we had venison during the summer
> and fall. There was no law against killing deer anytime of year. Or if
> there was it was never put in force. . . . Everybody got them and sup-
> posed they were as free as water. There was never any wasted, for they
> were not killed expressly for their saddles to supply the market. . . . No,
> they were killed because we were poor and had to have meat and none
> was wasted.[66]

In fact, New York statutes governed legal seasons for hunting white-tailed deer, and at the time that Livonia Stanton Emerson's father and the Conklins were shooting deer in the summer it was technically illegal. Conklin was correct in guessing that the law was not enforced. It was only after the Adirondacks became a popular recreational retreat for bourgeois sportsmen from eastern cities that state authorities took an interest in Adirondack fish and game.[67]

For Adirondackers, hunting in the deep forests around them could be more than food gathering, and it could lead to an awareness of the possibility that tourists brought more to their region than money. In 1852 Conklin went on a winter hunting trip to Jock's Lake (now called Honnedaga Lake and owned by the Adirondack League Club). There he and his friends enjoyed a grand time in the wilderness. Years later Conklin recalled the delights of the experience and contrasted the site as he first encountered it with its condition after it was discovered and used by summer sportsmen: "The ruthless hand of the tourist, hunter, fisherman, guide and hotel and cottage builder had . . . left their devastating, cruel and haggling mark around its evergreen points and bays." Even the road deteriorated with overuse; on his first visit to this remote pond, "it was not worn into deep channels and down among the rocks and mud as the road is now."[68] The arrival of tourists was more than just a welcome source of outside cash; to some Adirondackers it meant the end of an era marked by self-sufficiency and personal intimacy with the wild country all around them. As the tourists made their mark on the wilderness, the Adirondacks that the local residents had known began to disappear. This was a development both welcomed and questioned.

Ties between the Adirondack landscape and local people also developed via avenues other than hunting. Henry Conklin's mother was weary and weak by the time her family had made its last move. She had borne fifteen children and had worked heroically to keep her family fed, clothed, and sane. "After all her hardships and hard work she was happy here in the wilderness. She declared she never wanted to move again and wanted to stay here until she died. . . . Here with [her baby] in her arms she . . . used to gather the wild flowers that grew there. She said she never wanted to move anywhere, only to this sacred spot."[69] The inevitability that some Adirondackers would come to love the land around them and consider it their spiritual home was largely

ignored by downstate writers and policy makers who eventually determined the fate of the region.

Conklin expressed his own strong sense of place in his recollection
of the pain of leaving his Adirondack home after enlisting in the Union
Army in 1861. After tearfully hugging his wife and children for what
might have been the last time, he hurried out of the cabin and into the
snow: "I halted a moment to take one more glance at the dear old place
and my 'log cabin in the lane' where so many loved ones had clustered
around me. As I glanced at the creek as its gurgling waters were running under the ice, whose music had often lulled me to sleep, I looked
back at the cabin and the light was still burning, and I fancied I heard
their cries of anguish."[70] Such scenes doubtless occurred all across the
country, North and South—no less so in the Adirondacks, where families were subject to the same joys, pains, and love of place experienced
by Americans throughout the land.

The relationship between Adirondackers and the landscape around
them was based on personal history and intimacy with a demanding
land, and it was often fundamentally different from a relationship
based on recreational, seasonal access to the same land. But it was not
without its ambiguities and contradictions. Conklin's family and many
others like it responded to the notion that the Adirondack landscape
was a "wilderness" with considerable ambivalence. The wilderness
was where they hunted and fished, and it was a feature of a landscape
they came to love. In this respect it was associated with home, family,
and shared experiences, including both the trials endured while establishing new communities and the individual pleasures of exploring
and getting to know the forests and lakes.

But the wilderness condition of the Adirondacks was also a source
of hardship, and every family's goal was to secure a good living by
eliminating at least that part of the wilderness around their home and
farm. Henry Conklin recalled the sense of progress achieved when
the vicinity of his home yielded to civilization, "Our little neighborhood was now quite prosperous and we thought we were getting out
of the wilderness. We had a new bridge and a new schoolhouse."[71]
The Adirondack forests and their wilderness condition often seemed
endless and a constant and real impediment to personal comfort, material success, and cultural advancement. When children attended
school or families worshipped in churches where the wilderness had

once prevailed, this was, in the minds of Adirondackers, genuine progress.

Nowhere was this antipathy to wilderness more pronounced than in the unexamined disposition of virtually every Adirondack community to kill off wolves and mountain lions. These predators represented everything that was untamed and threatening about the wilderness and consequently were universally hated. Livonia Stanton Emerson, who "could often hear the screams of the panther and howls of hungry wolves," used the presence of these much mythologized beasts to symbolize her sense of the terror of life on the Adirondack frontier.[72] The campaign to eradicate predators began early; in the part of Montgomery County that would become Hamilton County, bounties were paid for wolves as early as 1823. In 1837, the first official town meeting held in Long Lake voted to spend town money on only two items: building roads and paying bounties for the corpses of wolves and mountain lions.[73] So it went throughout the Adirondacks, as every town and county passed ordinances aimed at eradicating predators, the most powerful symbol of the persisting wilderness.[74]

In terms of everything from the animals hunted to the forest itself, the Adirondacks constituted a nature in the minds of the people who lived there that was both similar to and in important ways distinct from the nature recommended by Ebenezer Emmons to affluent romantic tourists. In either case, a story about the land and what it was good for developed out of experience and cultural needs. The feeling of Adirondackers for the land was as deep as it was ambivalent. The paradoxes of this relationship would be simultaneously intensified and buried as downstate interests became increasingly concerned with constructing their own stories about the north country.

3

"The Freedom of
the Wilderness"

After the Natural History Survey had announced the existence of, and had given a name to, the largely unknown Adirondacks, New Yorkers and other Americans seized upon this land of peaks, lakes, and forests as the ideal locale for communing with nature. There they hunted and fished and sought to restore bodies and souls weary from the demands of modern life. The journey to the Adirondacks became part of an American travel craze, which swept the nation in the years between the opening of the Erie Canal in 1825 and the onset of the Civil War.[1] The canal, along with a growing network of railroads, allowed those Americans who could afford it to inspect personally their country's landscape; such travel had been largely impossible for earlier generations.

Tourists traveled to Niagara Falls, the White Mountains, the springs of Virginia, the Hudson Highlands, and a host of other spots to admire the scenic glories of the United States. For those unable to make such journeys in person, urban exhibitions of the lavish canvasses of Hudson River School artists like Thomas Cole and Asher B. Durand made the American wilderness come alive in all its natural splendor.[2] By the 1840s, ministers, doctors, businessmen, and other professionals from urban centers throughout the northeastern United States were beginning to take a few weeks away from work during the summer and head for the Adirondacks, among other places, where they admired the scenery, hunted, fished, and generally lounged about, while their guides did most of the work.[3]

The first tourist to arrive in the central Adirondacks did so hard on the heels of the Emmons expedition's first recorded ascent of Mount

Marcy. Within two weeks of the published account of the Marcy climb, which Emmons's colleague William C. Redfield had described in a series of letters to a New York newspaper, Charles Fenno Hoffman—journalist, poet, novelist, intimate of the New York City literary scene—had arrived at the McIntyre iron works.[4] There he hired John Cheney and hiked, despite the encumbrance of a wooden leg, to Indian Pass, which Emmons and Redfield had also visited and which Redfield had also glowingly described. A few days later Hoffman was bitterly disappointed when he found himself unable to follow Cheney up the rugged Opalescent River to the summit of Marcy.[5]

On his return to the city, Hoffman published a series of letters in the *New York Mirror;* these became the earliest examples of what became a sub-genre of American letters, as subsequent genteel camping trips in the Adirondacks quickly generated their own distinctive literature.[6] Hoffman's example inspired scores of other writers, one of the first of whom was the Reverend Joel T. Headley, a Protestant minister in search of mental and physical health after suffering what was apparently a nervous breakdown. Headley, who climbed Marcy and traveled by boat through the central lake region in the 1840s, typified the bourgeois, romantic travelers who began appearing in the central Adirondacks during the decades before the Civil War.

Headley's 1849 book, *The Adirondack; or, Life in the Woods*—republished, plagiarized, and expanded in numerous editions over the next thirty years—is an excellent example of the genre of wilderness travel narratives about northern New York. Like Hoffman, Headley based his book on letters written to a New York newspaper and elaborated all the familiar romantic tenets about the virtues of closeness to nature, the wilder the better. In particular, Headley found everything in the Adirondacks to be the opposite of what he knew elsewhere; like many American romantics, Headley found nature to be virtuous and benevolent while the city was potentially, if not literally, evil:

> I love nature and all things as God has made them. I love the freedom of the wilderness and the absence of conventional forms there. I love the long stretch through the forest on foot, and the thrilling, glorious prospect from some hoary mountain top. I love it, and I know it is better for me than the thronged city, aye, better for soul and body both. . . . I believe that every man degenerates without frequent communion with

Joel Tyler Headley, author of The Adirondack; or, Life in the Woods *(1849),
the first great Adirondack sporting and
camping narrative. P. 6947.*

nature. It is one of the open books of God, and even more replete with in-
structions than anything ever penned by man. A single tree standing
alone, and waving all day long its green crown in the summer wind, is
to me fuller of meaning and instruction than the crowded mart or gor-
geously built town.[7]

Such convictions—especially the pantheism asserted in the conviction
that nature is "one of the open books of God"—have sent wave after
wave of tourists, sportsmen, and invalids to the Adirondacks. While
the florid style of Headley's account may seem a bit antique to the
modern reader, such expressions of the divinity immanent in nature
have been repeated with equal effectiveness and sincerity ever since.
People who love camping in the Adirondacks today can easily identify
with Headley's enthusiasm for getting back to nature.

Headley was but one of many writers to describe the classic Adirondack camping trip. Sportsmen made their own way to a town or hotel
on the edge of the central wilderness—for example, Martin's Hotel on

Lower Saranac Lake, owned and operated by a remarkable family of guides, woodsmen, and raconteurs.[8] Other popular hotels could be found at Old Forge, along Lake Champlain, and at all the well-frequented gateways to the wilderness, mostly on the southern and eastern margins. Once arrived at these points, the sportsman would hire a guide; groups of sportsmen traveling together usually hired a guide apiece. In addition to furnishing camping gear and dogs for hunting deer, the guide provided the single most important item for an Adirondack sporting expedition—the guideboat, a light, sturdy boat invented by local craftsmen to serve the needs of guides and their clients.[9]

With the sportsmen in the stern, the guide rowing from the bow, and blankets, overcoats, guns, fishing poles, pots and pans, supplies of salt pork and flour, and perhaps a deer hound stowed amidships, these guideboats would set out from Martin's or a similar establishment to tour the central Adirondacks. In 1858, no less a literary figure than Ralph Waldo Emerson himself embarked on an Adirondack camping trip. In "The Adirondacs," a poem he wrote to celebrate his only extended excursion into the American wilderness, he described the trip's beginning:

> At Martin's beach
> We chose our boats; each man a boat and guide—
> Ten men, ten guides, our company all told.[10]

Such parties headed for prime camping spots on Adirondack rivers and lakes. Some sportsmen were content with setting up camp a few miles from the nearest village, while others opted for the remote and isolated. Emerson's party, for example, camped on Follensby Pond, reached from Martin's by a circuitous route of rowing and carrying guideboats. Albany journalist S. H. Hammond was camping near the head of the Bog River in the 1850s, as remote a spot as one could find anywhere in the Adirondacks and one of the most remote in the eastern United States.[11] In any case, the vast majority of these antebellum camping trips stayed close to the interlocking network of rivers and lakes. Campers setting off from Old Forge might be content with a couple of weeks on Raquette Lake or wind their way to Saranac Lake; parties starting from Martin's might head for Long Lake, Tupper Lake, Raquette Lake, or perhaps Blue Mountain Lake. Though a few romantic tourists were interested in climbing the peaks accessible from Keene

For romantic tourists, the experience of roughing it in the wilderness was a mix of the primitive and civilized. A Good Time Coming *(1862) by Arthur Fitzwilliam Tait. 63.037.1 (76).*

Valley or the Ausable lakes, most never strayed far from the rivers and lakes.

After reaching a likely campsite, the guides erected a rough shelter, consisting of a lean-to of hemlock or spruce bark held up by green poles. Inside, blankets and clothing were presumably kept dry. A classic painting by Arthur Fitzwilliam Tait, *A Good Time Coming* (1862), realistically depicts the quintessential Adirondack campsite scene. As soon as the camp was established, the sportsmen occupied themselves hunting and fishing and enjoying the wild scenery. As Emerson described his party's daily regimen,

> All day we swept the lake, searched every cove,
> North from Camp Maple, south to Osprey Bay,
> Watching when the loud dogs should drive in deer,
> Or, whipping its rough surface for a trout;
> Or, bathers, diving from the rock at noon;
> Challenging Echo by our guns and cries;

Or listening to the laughter of the loon;
Or, in the evening twilight's latest red,
Beholding the procession of the pines;
Or, later yet, beneath a lighted jack,
In the boat's bows, a silent night hunter
Stealing with a paddle to the feeding grounds
Of the red deer.[12]

The search for suitable scenery was often a formulaic affair, as travelers responded to certain kinds of landscape according to whether they matched the aesthetic conventions of the day. Antebellum criteria for judging scenery commonly followed dicta articulated (though not invented) by the Irish statesman and writer Edmund Burke in his influential *A Philosophical Enquiry into the Origin of Our Ideas of the Sublime and Beautiful*, first published in 1757. In the Burkean scheme, scenery, at least that scenery in which properly educated people should show an interest, could be divided into two main categories, the sublime and the beautiful. Sublime scenery was understood to be characterized by rugged cliffs, towering precipices, gloomy gorges, and sharp, angular lines, while the beautiful landscape was gentle, curving, and calm. The viewer of sublime scenery was powerfully impressed with his or her insignificance compared to the grandeur of God's creation. Enjoying the beautiful, on the other hand, put one at peace with God's benevolence as shown in the more soothing features of nature.[13]

With these distinctions well absorbed, tourists found the visually magnificent Adirondacks replete with splendid examples of both the sublime and the beautiful. Journalist Thomas Bangs Thorpe, after a hunting and fishing trip on the Fulton Chain in the early 1850s, wrote, "I question if there is in the wide world a place where the natural scenery so strongly combines every possible variety of expression to gratify the eye and call forth admiration."[14] And John Todd was equally impressed by the loveliness of the lakes on the central plateau: "The scenery of these lakes is grand and beautiful beyond any thing of which I ever conceived."[15] The Adirondack landscape offered grandeur and beauty aplenty. With majestic peaks, stunningly lovely lakes and rivers, and vast expanses of untouched forest, the Adirondacks greeted tourists with scenery spectacularly different from the urban or rural places most Americans knew.

The artist Thomas Cole, on a trip to Schroon Lake in 1837, wrote appreciatively in his journal of the "wild sort of beauty" he encountered there and went on to record his keenly felt personal response to the "quietness—solitude—the untamed—the unchanged aspect of nature." To the north he spotted the high peaks: "retiring in the purple haze of distance, a company of mountains lift their heads, some dark with ancient forests, others broken, brown, and bare; the whole surmounted by a majestic form, whose serrated summit, at sunset, lifts among the clouds."[16] Throughout the literary and artistic communities of America's eastern cities, the Adirondacks quickly became known as one of the most alluring and lovely examples of what remained of the American wilderness.

The cliffs on Wallface Mountain at Indian Pass satisfied everyone's sense of the sublime. Charles Ingham's painting of this spot emphasized its overpowering sublimity, depicting awesome cliffs towering over two minuscule human figures. When Hoffman encountered Indian Pass a few weeks after Ingham's initial visit, he employed the standard rhetoric of the sublime, trying to capture the sensational view, which he judged "one of the most savage and stupendous among the many wild and imposing scenes at the sources of the Hudson."[17] Writing about the same spot a few years later, New York State Librarian Alfred Billings Street stretched the vocabulary of the sublime to its utmost. To Street, Indian Pass was truly "a sublime and terrible sight." On reaching Summit Rock, Street grew dizzy and disoriented; then "after a few moments of bracing my system and recovering from the first sickening shock, I again looked. What a sight! horrible and yet sublimely beautiful—no, not beautiful; scarce an element of beauty there— all grandeur and terror."[18]

In contrast to the craggy sublimity associated with the high peaks, the more serene landscape of the lakes, rivers, and forests of the central Adirondacks appealed to the contemporary taste for the beautiful. Both artists and writers found a divine and peaceful immanence in the lake country. In painter Sanford Gifford's *A Twilight in the Adirondacks* (1864), for example, we see a typical lakeside scene, imbued with the radiant grace of a benevolent God.[19] Joel Headley expressed the same sentiment in words in his response to a lovely sunset viewed across the placid waters of Forked Lake:

All was wild but beautiful. The sun was stooping to the western mountains, whose sea of summits were calmly sleeping against the golden heavens: . . . green islands, beautiful as Elysian fields, rose out of the water; . . . I was never more struck by a scene in my life: . . . the evening—the sunset—the deep purple of the mountains—the silence and solitude of the shores, and the cry of birds in the distance, combined to render it one of enchantment to me.[20]

The cult of sublime and beautiful scenery provided a ready-made vocabulary for tourists trying to convey their heartfelt response to the natural splendors of the Adirondacks. The pervasiveness of the rhetoric of the sublime and beautiful in virtually every nineteenth-century account of camping or touring in the Adirondacks testifies to its authority in bourgeois American culture. It allowed tourists to articulate one feature of the appeal of Adirondack nature—its correspondence to the conventions of a popular genre of paintings.

When not admiring the magnificent Adirondack scenery, romantic tourists were busy fishing or hunting. Casting for the native brook

George Henry Smillie's Ausable Lake, Adirondack Mts. *(1868), combining lakeside beauty and distant mountain sublimity, captures the romantic conception of the grandeur of Adirondack scenery. 74.292.02 (377).*

trout, tourists typically implied an important distinction between their sport and the fishing for sustenance conducted by Adirondack residents. Where local people commonly fished with live bait for whatever fish were available, the sportsmen, who considered this mere fishing, styled themselves anglers and invoked the rituals and forms of fly fishing. In the minds of the sportsmen, fishing with bait was vulgar; fishing with flies, especially for brook trout, was genteel. Fly fishing, invented in England in the Middle Ages, was coming into fashion among affluent Americans at just the time that they were discovering the Adirondacks.[21]

Hunters were after white-tailed deer, which were bagged by one of two popular methods. In jacklighting, a sportsman and his guide would set out quietly by boat onto a lake or river after dark. In the bow, where the sportsman sat, with shotgun loaded and ready, was a torch or lantern, to catch the attention of any deer feeding along shore. When a deer spots a bright light, it will become almost hypnotized by it; if not startled by some sudden noise or movement, the deer will remain still. The trick for the guide was to row or paddle the sportsmen to within shooting range without scaring the deer.

The other popular technique for hunting deer was hounding. The guide released hounds, which invariably belonged to him, trained to scent deer in the woods and drive them to water. While the hounds were locating and driving the deer, the sports and their guides would station themselves in boats. If the deer took to water, a well-rowed boat could almost always catch it. Once within range, the sport could begin blasting away as the guide tried to get him closer and closer. If the sport happened to be a particularly bad shot, as many apparently were, the guide might "tail" the deer, which meant grabbing its tail and holding on while the frantic deer lunged desperately and the hunter continued reloading and shooting.[22]

Essential to all the activities of these sportsmen was the Adirondack guide, a figure who, in some accounts, assumed nearly mythic stature. The guide set up and managed the camp, took the sportsman to prime fishing spots, found the deer, furnished guideboat and hounds for hunting, regaled the sportsman with tales of hunting adventures, and generally made sure his client survived the trip. As one tourist praised the guides' many skills,

The guides perform all the necessary camp services; accompany you in fishing and hunting; transport you in their boats over lakes and rivers, carrying the boats on their shoulders around rapids and across portages; . . . entertain you with amusing and exciting incidents of their hunting grounds; and communicate so much valuable information respecting the country.[23]

But the ambiguous depictions of guides in the travel literature of this period tell us much about how the tourists were constructing an image of the Adirondacks and how they related to the year-round residents. While romantic writers extolled the guides as possessors of a natural wisdom and virtue, they often condescended to them for their illiteracy and rough ways. They patronized the guides' frontier accents at the same time that they obviously admired and envied the guides' woodcraft and self-sufficiency.

To romantic tourists, the Adirondack guide was an anachronism in an intellectually and scientifically progressive age. The guide was like the Indian—interesting, but as a picturesque object of historical study or as the subject of a novel or epic poem. When A. B. Street's guide, Harvey Moody, encountered an Indian near Tupper Lake, Street meditated on how they were

representatives of a class unknown to cultured life; the old, bronzed hunter and trapper; and the wild red man, united by their habits and modes of life, and both so perfectly in keeping with the scenes where I saw them—the natural meadow—the primeval woods—the lonely lake—the log hut—the wolf dogs—all so different from the objects to which I had become accustomed.[24]

Other writers were less condescending but also dwelt on an ostensible difference between the guides and themselves, seeing the guides as possessors of self-reliance and virtue quite distinct from that formed by an urban, academic education. According to S. H. Hammond, the guides

were all jolly, good-natured and pleasant people, with a vast deal of practical sense and valuable experience in woodcraft, albeit they were rough and unpolished. Their hearts were in the right place, and they com-

manded our respect always for their kindness and attention to our
wants, while they maintained at all times that sturdy independence
which enters so largely into the character of the border men of our
country.[25]

Both Street's association of Indian and guide with the "scenes" around
them and Hammond's sense of the guide as naturally noble suggest
how the tourist's construction of a story about the Adirondacks depended on a specific understanding of both the locale and its inhabitants as parts of a nature greatly valued by the outside world, and thus
eventually worthy of protection, but considered fundamentally different "from the objects to which I had become accustomed."

Through accounts of both their guides and the entire camping experience, romantic tourists—seeking wild scenery, white-tailed deer,
brook trout, and a respite from modern life—helped to construct a
multi-faceted image of the Adirondacks that has largely determined
popular attitudes ever since. Eastern, urban writers established the
conventions of what has been one of the dominant, if not *the* dominant,
story about the Adirondacks. In the voluminous travel and camping literature composed about the Adirondacks after the Natural History
Survey, as well as in oil paintings and engravings, the Adirondack
landscape became synonymous in much of the popular mind with
"wilderness."

The idea of wilderness in American culture is complex, and it has
generated a substantial scholarly literature.[26] The first English settlers
in Massachusetts found what they considered a "hideous and desolate
wilderness" to be the chief obstacle to the establishment of God's king-
dom in the New World. The absence of a familiar landscape of farms
and villages was alienating and frightening, and the English set out to
eliminate both the wilderness and its native inhabitants.[27] But by the
time of the Natural History Survey and the arrival of tourists in the
central Adirondacks, many Americans, at least along the Atlantic coast,
where the landscape was either cultivated or urban, had nearly completely turned around the Puritan hostility toward wilderness and
adopted the wilderness as the symbol of American virtues and vigor.
In both cases, the understanding of what "wilderness" meant depended on projections of deeply felt cultural anxieties onto the natural
landscape. Where the Puritans saw the wilderness as threatening and

dangerous, as the literal dwelling place of Satan, romantics, under-standably anxious about the spiritual and moral direction of an in-creasingly urban, industrialized society, saw the wilderness as the place where they could re-establish contact with both nature and their country's history.

The writers and artists who came to the Adirondacks had mostly grown up in places where opportunities to encounter the wild had be-come rare, where children had little sense of natural history. They had experienced childhoods much like that of Henry Adams, who, having passed his boyhood in the suburbs of Boston in the 1840s, later lamented how separate from the natural world his life had been:

> As a rule boys could skate and swim and were sent to dancing school; they played a rudimentary game of baseball, football, and hockey; a few could sail a boat; still fewer had been out with a gun to shoot yellowlegs or a stray wild duck; one or two may have learned something of natural history if they came from the neighborhood of Concord; none could ride across country, or knew what shooting with dogs meant.[28]

For people like this, the discovery of the Adirondack wilderness seemed a godsend, a much-appreciated antidote to a life increasingly alienated from nature.

The existence in the Empire State itself of a wilderness wilder and larger than anyone had previously dreamed, therefore, fit perfectly with the spirit of the age. Writers and artists were inspired by their own specific cultural circumstances to emphasize the obvious and indis-putable wildness of much of the Adirondacks—the magnificent scenery, the unexplored forests, the crystalline lakes and rivers. But these features of the Adirondacks often impressed themselves in the minds of tourists and artists at the expense of another, different story—the story of a frontier, of a peopled landscape of families, farms, and towns.

Despite the villages where they stopped for the night, despite the guides who rowed them from lake to lake, despite the meager fields where Adirondack farmers struggled to raise their crops, romantic writers and artists constructed a story about the Adirondacks that de-fined the entire region as wilderness, with no significant human pres-ence. This was a story that suited their genuine longing for a landscape

characterized by the redemptive qualities of nature, sublime and beautiful scenery, and opportunities for the genteel pursuit of hunting and
fishing. It was both a story reflecting the power of the obvious marvels
of the Adirondack landscape and a selective response to Adirondack
reality.

But the establishment of the wilderness motif as the dominant
Adirondack story was not instantly accomplished. The equally powerful disposition of romantic tourists toward appreciation of the agricultural landscape had to be overcome before the wilderness story
prevailed. In the 1840s, John Todd's prediction of a prosperous agricultural future for the central Adirondacks led to an argument, conducted
in New York City newspapers, between Todd and Joel T. Headley,
whose vision of Adirondack reality both promoted and derived from
the notion of the Adirondacks as wilderness retreat for tourists.

Having read of Todd's hopes for a landscape supporting a thriving
population, Headley, who had visited the Adirondacks, including
Long Lake, where Todd had helped to start a church, wrote to the *New
York Observer* in 1844 to offer his view of the Adirondack future. With
the village of Long Lake in mind, Headley noted the "slow growth of
the colony" and concluded, "that this should ever be a good farming
country is impossible." He went on to insist that the only value of the
Adirondacks was as wilderness retreat for professional men, repeating
the familiar romantic convictions about the utility to modern, urban
culture of a vacation spent hunting and camping in the woods: after
time in the wilderness, the tired, jaded urbanite "will come back to his
toils and studies with a firmer frame and freer heart. Nature in her
grand and solitary places remoulds a man before he is aware of it, and
a new existence is born within him."[29] To Headley, the only logical role
for the Adirondacks in American life was to serve as the locus of vacations for people from outside the region.

Todd, who understood the Adirondacks primarily as a frontier
evolving toward the pastoral, read Headley's account and bristled at
being disputed. He wrote to the same *New York Observer* to insist that
Headley's knowledge of Adirondack geography was hopelessly limited and that the central Adirondack valleys were full of locales
promising prosperity and security to both farmers and miners. Among
other things, he repeated Emmons's hope that once the trees were cut

down, the climate would improve to the point where agriculture would become profitable: "When the sun shall be let in to warm the earth, . . . is it not reasonable to suppose the climate will be softened and milder?" Todd concluded this response to Headley with a rapturous description of a growing, pious community on Long Lake.[30] Nor was Todd the only writer promulgating this pastoral fantasy: S. H. Hammond foresaw the same future for the Adirondacks, which would be a land of "beautiful and productive farms. Where meadows and green fields would stretch away from the river toward the hills. and where fine farm-houses and barns would be seen, and flocks and herds would be grazing in rich pastures."[31]

In 1847 Headley published further letters in the *Observer*, asserting that the Long Lake farmers were abandoning their homesteads, that the church Todd had helped to found had but one member, and that Long Lake instead of "being a centre from which shall radiate an intense population, covering the whole of this wild region . . . will drag on a miserable existence, composed, two thirds of it, by those who had rather hunt than work."[32] The realities of climate and terrain proved too much for the pastoral narratives of Todd and others who shared his hopes. The story of the Adirondacks as what Thomas Pownall had called "a broken unpracticable Tract" resurfaced in the years before the Civil War, and the prediction that the central Adirondacks would ever be significantly devoted to agriculture largely disappeared. As a traveling journalist remarked in 1860, "The broken surface of the country, the nature of the soil, the distance from markets, and the superior inducements afforded by more fertile sections, must continue to divert an agricultural population from these barren, uninviting regions."[33]

The disagreement between Headley and Todd crystallizes the major, continuing conflict in Adirondack history—what is the Adirondack country good for and who decides what will happen to it? Headley believed that the ideal future for the Adirondacks would be for the entire region to remain as wilderness, a vacation land, and he promoted a story about the Adirondacks that suited this conviction; Todd saw a different future and advanced his set of stories. Ever since their day, and particularly in the last quarter century, similar debates have raged, as exponents of contesting stories about the Adirondacks have maneuvered to achieve dominance in the public mind. The eventual disappearance of the agricultural dream did not mean that Headley won the argument. It meant that the terms of the debate over what the Adirondack landscape was and what it was good for shifted to new ground as new players in the Adirondack narrative, notably commercial loggers, arrived on the scene.

Samuel H. Hammond dismissed the pastoral vision, took the wilderness story to a logical extreme, and called in 1857 for the permanent preservation of the Adirondacks. Justifiably worried that the ruthless commercial impulses of American life would completely eliminate opportunities for spiritual redemption in nature, Hammond wondered,

> When that time shall have arrived, where shall we go to find the woods, the wild things, the old forests, and hear the sounds which belong to nature in its primeval state? Whither shall we flee from civilization, to take off the harness and ties of society, and rest for a season,

Frederic Rondel's A Hunting Party in the Woods. / In the Adirondac [sic], N. Y. State, 1856. *65.051.01 (104).*

from the restraints, the conventionalities of society, and rest from the cares and toils, the strifes and competitions of life? Had I my way, I would mark out a circle of a hundred miles in diameter, and throw around it the protecting aegis of the constitution. I would make it a forest forever.[34]

Noticeably absent from Hammond's view of the perfect disposition of the Adirondacks are the towns and villages even then punctuating the wilderness. Hammond was fantasizing about a region without human inhabitants, raising the romantic preoccupation with wilderness to one of its conclusions.

But Hammond's adoption of the wilderness story and his concern with preserving nature developed in a context suddenly different from the debate between Todd and Headley. Where these two ministers argued about whether farming was viable and disagreed about the sustainability of villages like Long Lake, neither's narrative accounted for what might happen to the Adirondacks once significant exploitation of natural resources financed by outside capital began. When Hammond expressed his hope that the Adirondacks might be protected as a "forest forever," it was not plows operated by Todd's thrifty yeomen or pastures supporting a local family's cow he feared; it was commerce—"worldliness, greed for progress, thirst for gain," the mentality that believed "everything in the heavens, or on the earth, or in the waters, were [sic] to be measured by the dollar and cent standard."[35]

The new figure in the always changing Adirondack narrative was the commercial logger. The earliest logging had been locally conducted for local needs, and lumberjacks had at first appeared to romantic tourists as a picturesque and appropriate presence on the land. Headley, especially impressed with the skill with which loggers felled trees and then ran the logs down river, described with rapt enthusiasm a logging operation he encountered near Indian Lake.[36] But by the decade before the Civil War, loggers' shanties had appeared far from the settlements on remote streams like the Cold and Bog rivers.[37]

At this time loggers cut only white pine or spruce and only those trees immediately adjacent to the rivers down which the logs were run to mills. To most antebellum tourists the logger did not appear to threaten the wilderness (nor did the iron mines in the Champlain Valley). But a few, like Hammond or William James Stillman, who organized the camping trip that brought Emerson to the Adirondacks, perceived that commercial logging might compromise irrevocably the integrity of the landscape. Along the Saranac River, Stillman observed sadly that the big white pines had all been cut; finding traces of logging on the Raquette, he regretted that "the river [had] lost much of its solemnity."[38] T. Addison Richards similarly predicted and lamented that the Raquette would eventually serve as a major conduit whereby the Adirondack logs would reach the St. Lawrence, "to whose markets it will, by and by, bear the immense freights of timber which this wilderness is destined to yield."[39]

The regrets of tourists like Richards and Stillman and the agenda for conservation first articulated by Hammond constituted a significant elaboration of the story of the Adirondacks as redemptive nature. It was in direct conflict with the story, given its first important expression by Ebenezer Emmons, of the Adirondacks as repository of natural resources ripe for exploitation. The contest between these stories would define Adirondack history for the following century and a half and continues to frame how we both understand Adirondack realities and plan for the future.

4

"The Genius of Change Has Possession of the Land"

After the Civil War the image of the Adirondacks as a recreational paradise was given one of its most forceful expressions in an 1869 best seller, *Adventures in the Wilderness; or, Camp-Life in the Adirondacks.* William H. H. Murray, minister at the Park Street Congregational Church in Boston, repeated, in an especially eloquent and appealing style, all the claims advanced by Headley and his generation.[1] Murray particularly emphasized recreation in his book. Like his predecessors, he subscribed to the romantic faith in nature as a holy and redemptive place, but this appeared less important to him than the opportunities for wholesome sport and exercise. *Adventures in the Wilderness* recounts story after story of exciting exploits with the rod and gun and bracing, sometimes perilous, boat trips on the network of Adirondack rivers and lakes. So many eager campers and sportsmen were lured to the Adirondacks by Murray's tales of idylls in the woods and arrived there so utterly unequipped, psychologically or materially, for the realities of insects, damp bedding, and uncooperative weather that the popular press began calling them "Murray's Fools." For the rest of his life Murray himself was known as "Adirondack Murray."[2]

Murray's image of the Adirondacks continued and built on that first constructed by romantic writers of the previous generation. Like Headley, Street, Hammond, and others, Murray understood the Adirondacks as a beautiful domain of nature to be treasured for its lakes, rivers, and forests, its spectacular scenery, its white-tailed deer and brook trout, and, mostly, its difference from urban America. Although he had been born and raised in the country, by the time he

wrote *Adventures in the Wilderness*, Murray was a man of the city, drawn
to the urban world for its cultural and professional opportunities but
full of reservations about the manifest urban threats to physical and
spiritual health.[3] Murray's Adirondacks, like Headley's, were the opposite of the city. He gratefully found there a nature that was everything the city was not. But in his narrative of the Adirondacks as the
antidote to the urban, Murray, like both his predecessors and his disciples, generally ignored the existence of another Adirondacks,
where people—including his guides—lived throughout the year and
where they struggled to feed their children and pay their bills.

In its emphasis on sport and recreation, *Adventures in the Wilderness*
represents a significant development in the evolving image of the
Adirondacks. Before the Civil War the Adirondack camping trip was
largely, though not at all exclusively, an experience of the soul. Panthe-
istic romantic travelers looked for, and found, divinity in the landscape, and they worshipped the wilderness for the immanence of God.
They hunted and fished, of course, and they traveled by boat and occasionally by foot through the northern wilderness, but these activities
were, to a large extent, part of the ceremonies of the religion of nature.
To Murray and scores of subsequent writers working in the same
genre, the importance of the Adirondacks was as an arena for manly
recreation.

The opening of the Adirondacks promoted by Murray and a host of
other writers after the Civil War, moreover, suited perfectly an explosion in American interest in field sports. Middle-class men (and a few
women) from Eastern cities repaired in droves to American seashores,
forests, and fields to hunt and fish. They angled for trout in the
Catskills, hunted white-tailed deer in Pennsylvania and moose in the
Maine woods, shot ducks and geese along the Chesapeake Bay, and
rode after foxes in the rolling hills of the Virginia hunt country. The
more affluent headed west, where they chased elk and big horn sheep.
The truly adventurous might shoot lions or elephants in Africa or po-
lar bears in the Arctic.[4] This was both a continuation of patterns established before the Civil War and evidence of the existence of a new
moneyed class created by the industrial and commercial growth of the
mid-nineteenth century. The Adirondacks, within a day's travel of several major metropolitan areas, provided a perfect and relatively acces-

sible locus for the pursuit of field sports. Adirondack deer and trout were caught and killed with abandon throughout the summer and early fall.

All this was part of a growing cult of recreation, exercise, and health.[5] The Adirondacks—and similar wilderness retreats throughout the United States—moved from being the home of God to being the place where, the dominant culture declared, men from the elite and middle classes developed the muscles, self-reliance, and independence needed for success in the competitive world of industry and commerce. In this sense, Murray and his disciples anticipated the obsession with rugged exercise and the promotion of manly attributes that characterized Theodore Roosevelt (some of whose earliest camping experiences occurred in the Adirondacks) and his generation.[6]

This concern with what were commonly considered masculine attributes became even more important when social commentators perceived a decline in American masculinity itself. Throughout the final decades of the nineteenth century, various theorists on American culture routinely observed that American manhood was in a state of precipitous decline, that the masculine ruggedness displayed so heroically at Valley Forge, the Alamo, and Gettysburg had somehow been eroded by the combined forces of urbanization, over-civilization, and an extremely vaguely articulated notion that women had achieved a questionable hegemony in white, bourgeois culture. Americans feared that their young men were becoming effete, refined, and delicate.[7]

The answer to this threat to national security, wrote many cultural critics, was to have America's youth return to the wilderness, where healthy sports and vigorous exercise would restore the national will. The prominent New Yorkers charged by the legislature in 1872 to investigate the possibility of establishing an Adirondack Park, for example, believed that wilderness recreation could address the alarming decline in masculinity, fatuously declaring,

> The field sports of the wilderness are remarkably exhilarating, and strengthen and revive the human frame. The boating, tramping, hunting and fishing expeditions afford that physical training which modern Americans . . . stand sadly in need of, and which we must hope will, with the fashionable young men of the period, yet replace the vicious, enervating, debasing pleasures of the cities. It is to their eager pursuit of

field sports that metropolitan Englishmen owe their superiority in physical power, with that skillful use of fire-arms, independence, fearlessness,
cool presence of mind, and ability which they possess to bear the fatigues
of war and exigencies of military service.[8]

American girls, though to a lesser extent, were also subject to this fear
of declining vitality. Just as the boys who were supposed to furnish the
nation its military and business leaders were accused of a loss of vigor,
so too young women, whose destiny was to be healthy wives and productive mothers, were said to be but fragile shadows of their sturdy
grandmothers. Neurasthenia, the stylish malady of the nervous system
that afflicted upper- and middle-class women of the end of the nineteenth century, was evidence of the crisis of health.[9] For both boys and
girls, the answer was the hardy life of the wilderness.

Prosperous Easterners found a new reason for an Adirondack vacation; where the father's hunting and fishing had been an initial rationale, now the whole family could improve body and soul by paddling,
sailing, or swimming across an Adirondack lake. As one observer of
the Adirondack scene put it, "To the wealthy dwellers of cities, debili-
tated by a tainted atmosphere, the breezes and the mountain springs
bring life, while the free, joyous exercises of their children in these summer homes, lay for them the foundations of continued health."[10]

The Adirondacks promoted the health of more than just the relatively fit in need of a little exercise. Partly because of a tale recounted
in Murray's *Adventures in the Wilderness*, the Adirondacks became
famous for their capacity to cure tuberculosis, or consumption, as this
scourge was generally known in the nineteenth century. Murray insisted that "the mingled perfume of cedar, of balsam and the water
lily" had cured a young man whom the "best skill that money could
buy" had given up as doomed. Taken to the Adirondacks, lain in a
"boat half filled with cedar, pine, and balsam boughs," he was rowed
into the wilderness, his friends assuming that he would die there.
After five months of camping, he emerged from the forest, "bronzed
as an Indian, and as hearty." He had gained sixty-five pounds and
bore the boat on his own shoulders at all the carries. "The wilderness
received him almost a corpse. It returned him to his home and the
world as happy and healthy a man as ever bivouacked under its
pines."[11]

Stories like this, true or not, promoted an image of the Adirondacks as a miraculous landscape, a place of mystical powers. They derived both from the obvious benefits of time spent away from the filthy air of industrial cities and from a growing faith in the divine goodness inherent in the American wilderness. Murray was able to pass on such a tale because it fit so well with American hopes that the powers of nature could help people resist the diseases and corruptions of modern life.

A decade or so after the publication of *Adventures in the Wilderness*, a cluster of tuberculosis sanitaria began to emerge in the vicinity of Saranac Lake. The key figure in this development was Dr. Edward Livingston Trudeau, who suffered from consumption himself and came to the hotel at Paul Smith's in 1873, searching for relief. Relief he found, and he dedicated the rest of his life to working with victims of TB. By the time of his death in 1915, the Adirondack Cottage Sanitorium, which he established on a slope of Mount Pisgah near Saranac Lake, was a world renowned center for tuberculosis research and patient care. Among Dr. Trudeau's clients were the British writer Robert Louis Stevenson and a New York banker, Alfred L. Donaldson, who made Saranac Lake his permanent home and wrote a two-volume history of the Adirondacks.[12]

The larger context of this faith in the wilderness to revive the nation's vitality and cure its diseases was a renewed and widespread American compulsion to get back to nature. Murray was thus an early exponent of what a decade or two later became a national cultural phenomenon. Intellectually, this movement was a logical extension and descendent of the romanticism that had pervaded American culture since antebellum days; by the end of the nineteenth century, it had acquired a remarkably recharged authority. Middle-class Americans sent their children to summer camps, spent Sunday afternoons promenading in their cities' recently redesigned public parks, traveled on family vacations to newly established national Parks like Yellowstone and Mount Rainier, and read assiduously in the works of nature writers like John Burroughs and John Muir.[13] As before, opportunities to experience the restorative powers of nature were limited to the relatively well-to-do; the millions of inhabitants of the nation's slums, either unemployed or working for starvation wages in horribly unsafe and unsanitary factories and sweat shops, had woefully little access to the rural or wild corners of their country.

To middle-class Americans, the existence of just this teeming prole-
tariat seemed but one more reason to abandon, at least for a few weeks,
the filthy and slum-ridden cities. For the managerial and professional
classes, moreover, despite their relative affluence, work was often te-
dious and alienating. And conventional religion, which in an earlier
age might have provided a relief to a life that sometimes seemed ster-
ile, was circumscribed by science and appeared to be surrendering to
secularization. For those who could afford it, a retreat to nature supplied the antidote to, or at least an escape from, the travails of a society
struggling toward the twentieth century. Adirondack lakes and rivers
especially appealed to back-to-nature sentiments and became a popular destination for Americans searching for healthy recreation far from
the pressures of everyday routine.

A further development, which both resulted from and promoted this
growing interest in the Adirondacks, was improved transportation,
making it easier for the denizens of eastern cities to reach the North
Woods. A railroad line constructed under the leadership of Dr. Thomas
Clark Durant, who had been a key player in the construction of the first
transcontinental railroad, reached from Saratoga to North Creek by
1871. This company, a successor to the Saratoga and Sacket's Harbor
Railroad first planned before the Civil War, hoped to extend service all
the way to Lake Ontario, but for the next seventy years no track was
laid past North Creek.

Though this line never paid dividends to its investors, it played a
significant role in opening up the central Adirondacks to tourists. Travelers journeyed to North Creek by rail; from there stagecoach connections provided access to the beautiful country around Raquette Lake
and Blue Mountain Lake.[14] Meanwhile, travelers connecting through
Albany from New York City, Philadelphia, or Boston used other lines
along the Lake Champlain Valley to reach the Adirondack interior.
From railroad termini in towns like Ausable Forks, travelers would
switch to stagecoaches. On the southwest corner of the Adirondacks,
the Utica and Black River Railroad reached Boonville, from which a
rough road meandered through the forest to the Fulton Chain.[15]

These coaches were heading for a rapidly growing collection of hotels. From the Chateaugay lakes to the Moose River, hotels and board-
ing houses popped up along Adirondack waters. Some were humble
affairs with straw-tick beds and indifferent food; others were opulent,

Blue Mountain stagecoach meeting tourists at the North Creek train station, ca. 1888. Photograph by Seneca Ray Stoddard. P. 9534.

modern hostels, like the Prospect House (the first hotel in the world to provide electric lights in every guest room) at Blue Mountain Lake, which opened its doors in 1882.[16] The hotel begun on Lower St. Regis Lake by entrepreneur Paul Smith in 1861 quickly moved past its modest origins and by 1874 was described by guidebook author Seneca Ray Stoddard (who went on to a distinguished career as one of the country's first great landscape photographers) as "a very popular resort, and patronized extensively by a wealthy class of visitors, who prefer to rough it in a voluptuous sort of way." Commenting on the variety of lodging establishments in the Adirondacks, Stoddard observed, "Scattered all over this wild tract are places of entertainment, ranging all the way from elegantly furnished hotels on the border to the rude log-house of the interior, but all 'hotels,' and willing to take strangers in at from $2.50 per day to $7.00 per week. 'Martin's' is the largest; 'Paul Smith's' the most fashionable." Paul Smith's hotel was known throughout the Northeast as the "St. James of the Wilderness."[17]

The life at these hotels evolved into a social scene quite different from that of the rugged camping trips of antebellum days. One of the chief criticisms leveled at Murray was that his book had attracted a new kind of tourist to the Adirondacks, that the hotels, far from enabling their patrons to get back to nature, had become centers of

The stylish opulence of the Prospect House, Blue Mountain Lake, 1880s.
Photograph by Edward Bierstadt. P. 6790.

refinement and pretense. One writer in the *New York Times* insisted
hyperbolically, "The desert has blossomed with parasols, and the waste
places are filled with picnic parties, reveling in lemonade and sardines.
The piano has banished the deer from the entire region, and seldom is
any one of the countless multitude of sportsmen fortunate enough to
meet even the track of a deer."[18] It was all part of an era of rapid, startling change. No one saw this more clearly than surveyor Verplanck
Colvin, who wrote in 1879, "The woods are thronged; bark and log
huts prove insufficient; hotels spring up as though by magic; and the
air resounds with laughter, song and jollity. The wild trails, once
jammed with logs, are cut clear by the axes of the guides, and ladies
clamber to the summits of those once untrodden peaks. The genius of
change has possession of the land."[19]

But not all tourists were interested in the social rituals of the stylish
hotels. The allure of camping out grew stronger than ever, and drew
countless men and women to the lakes and rivers of the central Adirondacks. The most popular trip was a circle route starting on Upper
Saranac Lake. From there the Raquette River was reached via a three-

mile carry. Once on the Raquette, boats could head downstream to Tupper Lake, from which a series of lakes, ponds, and carries led eventually to Forked Lake. From Forked Lake, parties might visit Raquette Lake before heading for Long Lake, the Raquette River, and the return to Upper Saranac. Given time and inclination, parties might drop in on Blue Mountain Lake or any of a variety of lakes and ponds stretching from the St. Regis Lakes to Old Forge.[20]

The continuing interest in getting back to some form of nature combined with the new railroads and hotels led to a proliferation of travel guides, many published by the railroad companies themselves. Stoddard worked for several railroad companies, and his popular series of guidebooks reflected their efforts to advertise the scenic and recreational appeal of the country their lines served.[21] A variation of this genre was the sportsman's guide, offering tips on hunting and fishing. All these books, which were often distributed free, helped to add new features to the ever-evolving Adirondack story. Mostly they purveyed an image of the Adirondacks as a sporting and vacation retreat. But whereas in the days of Headley or Todd, the Adirondacks remained known to a relatively small portion of the population and actually experienced by still fewer people, by the 1870s, and in rapidly increasing numbers thereafter, the Adirondacks were truly discovered. The annoying presence of crowds in the woods—particularly of crowds of people who were said somehow not to belong there—became a major subject of Adirondack literature.

It seems unlikely that Adirondack Murray was single-handedly responsible for the rush to the wilderness that followed the publication of *Adventures in the Wilderness*, but a rush there was. The popularity of Murray's book and the throngs of "Murray's Fools" that changed forever the character of the Adirondacks in the 1870s were indices of a changing country. America was developing a prosperous middle class, many of whom wanted to go on summer vacations to the Adirondacks or to similar more or less wild spots across the continent, and the railroads, by encouraging travelers to visit scenic or other natural attractions along their routes, partially defined what there was for tourists to see and do.

In every traveler's pocket was a book with a title like *The Tourist's Guide through the Empire State, Embracing All the Cities, Towns and Watering Places*, by Mrs. S. S. Colt of Albany, or Charles Hallock's popular

The Sportsman's Gazetteer and General Guide. Such guides provided detailed information on routes to the woods, hotels, how to hire a guide and how much to pay him, what kind of sport to expect, and what clothes to wear and gear to pack. More important, they glowingly described the many opportunities for sport and rest amid the beauties of the Adirondacks. Mrs. Colt praised the Adirondacks as offering the perfect combination "of good fishing, clear, fresh air, and delightful scenery, and honest sport."[22]

In 1873, Charles Hallock, one of the best known and most read writers on field sports of his day, published *The Fishing Tourist: Angler's Guide and Reference Book.* This work typified the voluminous literature of hunting and fishing generated for genteel sportsmen in the Victorian era. In twenty chapters devoted to wild country across North America, from the Canadian Maritimes to the Great Lakes and the Pacific, Hallock wrote glowingly of the joys of fly fishing. The chapter on the Adirondacks is longer than any other in the book, except for those on Nova Scotia and the Saguenay.

Yet the thrust of Hallock's description of field sports in the Adirondacks is to lament a paradise lost. Where Murray and others told of a wilderness where sportsmen worked hard to bag a deer or land a brook trout, Hallock delivered a patronizing account of "ribbons fluttering on the piazzas; silks rustling in dress promenade; ladies in short mountain suits, fresh from an afternoon picnic; embryo sportsmen in velveteen and corduroys of approved cut, descanting learnedly of backwoods experience."[23] Hallock's condescension derives from the same tradition that feared a growing effeminacy in American culture. His barely covert misogyny suggested that women in general and effeminate men in particular had no proper place in the wilderness and that the Adirondacks needed protection from their ilk.

In any case, what Hallock and others alluded to, negatively or not, was becoming an important element in the Adirondack story. The Adirondacks had become a vacation retreat quite different from what Emmons or Headley had foreseen, although plenty of hunters and anglers continued to camp out in the backwoods even while stylish hotels were organizing croquet matches and picnics. The idea of nature remained fundamental to the nation's image of the Adirondacks. But the nature sought by the clients of these hotels was yet another layer for a story of nature that already possessed many strata.

All of these factors—the back-to-nature movement, the search for the strenuous life, and increased facility of access and availability of lodging—combined to make the Adirondacks one of the nation's "sacred places."[24] The travel experience that before the Civil War had been limited to the few was extended by cheap railroad fares across social lines to people of middling means. For increasing numbers of Americans, the Adirondack region, despite, or perhaps because of, the civilized amenities of the hotels, was a retreat from much that appeared negative about modern American life. By the end of the nineteenth century, northern New York was known throughout the nation as a vacation mecca for both the middle class and the wealthy.

It was inevitable that the features of the Adirondacks that continued to appeal to vacationing city people would inspire some of the more affluent to want to own their own piece of the wilderness. The same era that saw the rapid development of a hotel industry also witnessed the phenomenon that has come to be known as the Adirondack Great Camps. These were pseudo-rustic but stately palaces built deep in the woods on privately owned lakes or ponds for millionaires. Wealthy Americans, lured by scenery and sport, eager to experience the social rituals of the stylish hotels but also wishing to avoid the crowds, built exclusive second homes (for some these were third or fourth homes) on private preserves. There, plutocrats of the Gilded Age—people with names like Vanderbilt, Morgan, Whitney, and Rockefeller—repaired for a month or two of sport, recreation, and rustic yet comfortable living.

The prime mover in establishing the tradition of the great camps was William West Durant, son of Thomas Clark Durant. The younger Durant inherited from his father extensive Adirondack lands and an interest in developing the region. Summoned home from Europe by his father in 1874, William West Durant began an Adirondack career that lasted for some three decades, during which he designed and built a series of wilderness mansions, oversaw a family empire that included logging, railroads, a telegraph company, and extensive speculation in real estate, and endured bitter litigation instigated by his sister. By 1904 he had lost all his Adirondack holdings, but the legacy of the camps he designed for and sold to millionaire friends in the vicinity of Raquette Lake became yet another element in the Adirondack story.[25]

Durant's first Great Camp was Pine Knot, which he began in 1876 on Raquette Lake's Long Point. After a series of additions and elabora-

tions, Pine Knot, a synthesis of Swiss chalet elements with local timber
and stone work, was praised by S. R. Stoddard in 1881 as "unquestion-
ably the most picturesque and *recherché* affair of its kind in the wilderness." By 1895, when Durant sold what was by then a compound of
many elegantly appointed buildings set on 200 acres of studiously
landscaped grounds, Pine Knot had become a small village, maintained by an army of maids, servants, and gardeners.[26] Durant's triumph at Pine Knot set the tone for camps on ponds around Raquette
Lake and as far away as Newcomb. Other builders followed his example, though not necessarily his architectural style, and lavish camps offering a sense of closeness to nature but always with the sorts of
amenities and grandeur available only to the rich appeared throughout
the central Adirondacks. Other centers of great camp construction were
Upper Saranac Lake and the St. Regis Lakes.[27]

The combination of the social life at the expensive hotels and stories
about the extravagance of the Great Camps led to a widely shared image of the Adirondacks as a rich man's playground—to the extent that

Camp Fair View on Raquette Lake, built by William West Durant in 1879.
Photograph, ca. 1888, by Seneca Ray Stoddard. P. 8105.

writers of American fiction could use the image of the retreat to the Adirondacks as a symbol of the indifference of American plutocrats to the realities of American poverty. In Hamlin Garland's *Main Traveled Roads*, for example, first published in 1891, a man who has risen from poor midwestern roots to a position of wealth and security is accused by his relatives of ignoring their suffering and refusing to help his mother and brother. Forced to face this, he confronts his sense of guilt: "He had neglected them; he had said, 'I guess they're getting along all right.' He had put them behind him when the invitation to spend the summer on the Mediterranean or in the Adirondacks came."[28]

But the reality was much more complex than this; at the same time, relatively cheap railroad access and more moderately priced hotels had effected a democratization of the Adirondack vacation. While Vanderbilts were ensconcing themselves at a palatial Great Camp near Raquette Lake, a few miles away a middle-class family from Albany might be enjoying a stay at Holland's Blue Mountain Lake Hotel. Alfred Donaldson described this popular establishment, which greeted

Holland's Blue Mountain Lake House, 1876. Photograph by Seneca Ray Stoddard. P. 7164.

its first guests in 1875, the year before Durant began Pine Knot, as "a primitive log structure, but it was clean and comfortable, and well run." Accessible by stage from the North Creek terminus of Durant's railroad, Holland's typified the many hotels, characterized by an 1882 guidebook as "comfortable although generally unpretentious," appearing throughout the region and appealing to middle-class families.[29] By the end of the century, a Delaware and Hudson Railroad brochure on the Adirondacks was titled, simply, *A Summer Paradise.*[30]

But there was more than one season in the Adirondack year, and the throngs of vacationers, rich or otherwise, made up only one thread in the increasingly complex Adirondack story. The specific emphasis in the Delaware and Hudson brochure on summer, the season when virtually all tourists of that day encountered the Adirondacks, suggests the extent to which this image of the Adirondacks as vacation playground was constructed by people from outside the region. Another part of the regional story, that of the lives, fortunes, and hardships of Adirondack residents, continued to be mostly ignored. While William West Durant was serving champagne to the likes of industrialist and railroad magnate Collis P. Huntington at Pine Knot and while popular journals promulgated an image of the Adirondacks that emphasized recreation for urban vacationers, north-country life for ordinary people was slowly moving beyond frontier conditions.

In the parts of the Adirondacks nearest to Lake Champlain, the driving force behind growth and change was a newly revitalized iron industry. In the 1860s and continuing through the 1870s and early 1880s, mining towns—for example, near the large iron fields on Lyon Mountain and elsewhere in the Chateaugay region, to the south, at Moriah and Ausable Forks, and in the Schroon Valley—bustled with activity. New railroads took out the ore and brought in travelers and consumer goods. Populations grew dramatically, requiring further clearing of forested land for agriculture. But after 1885, technological innovations in the iron industry, largely in the western United States, led to the obsolescence of the Adirondack fields, which, except for the mines at Lyon Mountain and Standish, were closed by 1900. This led, in turn, to widespread abandonment of farms in the Champlain region.[31]

A few diaries, memoirs, and other documents provide tantalizing glimpses of the quotidian life of late nineteenth-century Adirondackers, for whom, in many ways, life remained similar to that described by Livonia Stanton Emerson and other diarists of the era before the Civil War. For one thing, households depended on a variety of sources of cash. In the 1880s, for example, Minnie Patterson Stanyon moved with her parents and siblings to the southern Hamilton County village of Newton's Corners (later renamed Speculator), where her uncle had started a small spruce gum gathering business. On a good day a man could collect three pounds of spruce gum and sell it to a chewing gum manufacturer in Vermont for 60 cents per pound. Her father raised potatoes and strawberries in the summer; he made barrels, snowshoes, and pack baskets in the winter; and in the spring he tapped maple trees.[32]

Men often had to work away from home. This inevitably increased the sense of isolation and loneliness felt by those—mostly women—left at home. Juliet Kellogg left a diary describing her rough life on a remote farm near Minerva in the 1860s. A young married woman without children, she complained to her diary about the long periods when

Adirondack farm in the 1880s. Photograph by Allen & Rowen.

her husband was forced to leave her at home. Many of her diary entries record working inside day after day during spells of bad weather. While her husband Wesley was working far away and unable to return home—presumably on a logging crew—she spent cold winter days mending, washing, ironing, baking, and shearing sheep. One chilly February day, she wrote, with biting precision, "I am very lonely." Two months later, she noted, "Wolves killed two more sheep today."[33]

Nowhere is the picture of day-to-day life in the Adirondacks more poignant, more revealing, or more realistic in its efforts to comprehend both hardships and joys than in the poetry and prose of Jeanne Robert Foster. This was the pen name of Julia Elizabeth Oliver, born into a poor family near the Warren County village of Johnsburg in 1879. Foster's mother was well educated, and she passed on to her daughter an abiding interest in literature and culture. Foster herself was teaching school by the time she was fifteen, and two years later she married a Rochester insurance agent whom she had met through neighbors in Chestertown.

Marriage got her out of the mountains and took her to the bustle of the modern world. By the time of her death in 1970 she had been an actress, model, journalist, poet, and social worker. Along the way she knew and worked with the likes of Pablo Picasso, T. S. Eliot, and Ezra Pound. Throughout a life that led her to Europe and back and introduced her to the innermost circles of European art and culture, she retained a fierce affection for the Adirondacks and intense memories of her early years. One product of her Adirondack memories was a series of lovely verses and essays describing both hardship and a distinct love of the land.[34]

Foster knew well the loneliness and isolation of north-country life:

> There was a certain strangeness about folks
> Who lived on solitary farms up north long ago.
> Sometimes they didn't seem to have much reason
> For living at all, life was so bleak.[35]

Foster was especially sensitive to the hardships endured by women. In "Mis' Cole" she describes the momentous day when an unappreciated woman simply walks away from the farm where she has been neglected and considered by George, her husband, to be

> only hands and feet for George,
> Someone to put food on the table,
> Someone to have more children for him,
> And mend and hand-sew their dresses on them
> Until they wear out in rags.[36]

Life was not without its pleasures. Juliet Kellogg recorded pleasant afternoons spent fishing with Wesley: one day in May she finished oiling a harness, then in the afternoon, "went to Loon Pond a fishing. Wesley and I caught 20 pounds."[37] Minnie Stanyon recalled the joys of picnics; when she and her friends planned a picnic, their day was rather different from that of the clients of Adirondack hotels. Where vacationers from the cities were rowed by a guide to a pleasant spot on a lake or pond, she endured a lengthy journey by ox cart. Though her reminiscences were undoubtedly colored by the nostalgia for a simpler age that pervades so much of modern American culture, she thought of her youth in Hamilton County as "unhurried and unperturbed, with enjoyment for the present and without fear for the future."[38]

Foster describes ties to the land that are reminiscent of those suggested by Henry Conklin before the Civil War. They reflect a love of place based on experience beyond that acquired on a camping trip or vacation. Foster's sense of the meaning of place and of how human beings maintain connections with a personally significant place emphasizes not picturesque sunsets or sublime cliffs but the ordinary and everyday. To Adirondack families, the Adirondack landscape, a mix of nature and culture, was where they lived and worked and pursued ordinary activities. And it was the very familiarity of the contact that created a sense of connectedness:

> There are so many ties
> With soil and mountain roads and country stores
> And with folks who lie sleeping that my heart
> Thrills even to the names: Crane Mountain, Gore
> And "No. 11"; they became a part
> Of all I was and all I hoped to be:
> The woolen factory once at Johnsburg
> Where later on they made fine calico.
> The lead mine on the mountain, the paint bed,
> The garnet outcrops, hemlocks—row on row.

In verses invested with the level of intensity and attention to everyday detail with which Robert Frost described his affection for New England, Foster found meaning in "old shanty days, old settlers, old log barns, and houses [that] have vanished out of mind."[39]

Foster's memories embraced a cluster of villages and farming communities in Warren and Essex counties—Minerva, Olmstedville, Johnsburg, and Chestertown. This was a region through which most vacationers passed as quickly as possible on their way to the central Adirondack lakes, and it seldom appeared in the popular sporting or travel narratives. But it nonetheless was part of the Adirondacks, especially for the people living there year round. If the tourists passing through had stopped to look around, they would have discovered vestiges of frontier life. In "The Old Log House," Foster describes the house where she lived with her family as a little girl—a house without running water, where, in winter, "we hung comforters against the logs to keep out draughts and chill." Community ties in this region remained strong; the house had been built as a project for a neighborhood "bee."[40]

For Adirondack families, trying to make a living from agriculture continued to demand a multiplicity of skills and usually a source of cash from some other work. Foster's father worked as a lumberjack, while her brother Francey ran the farm from the time he was twelve. One of Francey's routine chores was driving cattle, by foot and by himself, the thirty-one miles to market in Glens Falls.[41] In the spring, Foster's father tried to be the first in the neighborhood to tap his maples and sell his sugar and syrup, which he put into "fruit jars and the few tin cans that were obtainable." He sold the first and middle "runs," keeping the last, less sweet, for home use.[42]

Foster was well aware that the tourist economy would come to dominate both the Adirondacks and the people who lived there. About this inevitable development, she harbored profound reservations:

> And the way things are going there won't be woods
> Very long, or wilderness; it'll be
> Imitation ranches, and ski runs, and places
> Called by names that the folks who lived there
> Years and years ago never heard of.[43]

Working in the woods during the winter was a much-needed source of cash for Adirondack families. "Lumbering in Winter" (1871) by Winslow Homer appeared in Every Saturday, *a popular magazine. 66.112.2 (439).*

Tourism meant outside cash; it also meant a disruption of old ties between people and place. But the establishment of the Forest Preserve in 1885 meant that tourist amenities did not capture all the land. Remembering her old log cabin, Foster notes, "The house has been taken down, and but for the fact that the side of the mountain is all state land, the summer camp and the motel would now have invaded the old sugar camp."[44]

Other changes were coming, symbolized by the move of Foster's family fifteen miles from an isolated farm to the relatively bustling village of Chestertown in 1886. When Foster was a young woman, she composed a brief essay recalling the day she arrived in Chestertown with her father, riding atop a wagon load of furniture, stoves, kitchenware, and a heap of other household paraphernalia. To an inexperienced country girl, the "illumination from half a dozen oil street lamps" combined with the light cast by a handful of buildings "appeared to be a vast amphitheatre of light." What was even more impressive and more evocative of the transition from frontier to modernity were the telegraph wires "crossing and recrossing against the stars." To both Foster and her father these wires were "mysterious things that . . . girdled the earth, everywhere carrying power and dominion."[45] The move from farm to town and the Fosters' response to the telegraph wires with all they represented of the modern world of commerce and communication are telling symbols of changes in the lives of Adirondack families.

The date is significant in that it occurred just one year after the establishment of the Adirondack Forest Preserve (to be discussed in the next chapter) and the beginning of an era of state involvement in conservation. The American conservation movement itself, of which developments in the Adirondacks were an important feature, was a major addition to the Adirondack narrative, and Adirondack people would be powerfully affected. The move from farm to town symbolized at least the beginning of the end of serious efforts to live by agriculture in the Adirondacks: in the twentieth century, nearly all Adirondackers live in towns. The telegraph wires suggest the end of a period of relative isolation for the Adirondacks. Increasingly, the Adirondacks would be a part of a larger political, commercial, and social culture.

In the villages, life proceeded along lines typical of small-town life across the country. People went to church, played in the village band, and cheered for the local baseball team. Visits from a one-ring circus or the annual tour of a company presenting *Uncle Tom's Cabin* were eagerly anticipated and thoroughly enjoyed. A more frequent event but one that also occasioned a departure from the usual calm was the arrival of the mail. At Newton's Corners it came by stage from Northville every other day: "Mail time was a exciting time, when people gathered at the post office in the Toles Satterlee General Store."[46]

School house near Johnsburg, ca. 1885. Photograph by Grotus Reising. P. 24259.

Local politics were intense but little disturbed by "the distant reverberations of federal politics. . . . No one had heard of Karl Marx."[47] It was a life centering on church, family, and business. In Chestertown, as Foster later recalled, families enjoyed a social life in which the churches provided the predominate focus (with various Protestant sects freely intermingling and viewing Roman Catholics with usually tacit suspicion). And there was "the trade life, a pleasant stir of bustle in the streets, a trade life that held the community of the locality for a radius of ten miles 'round the village. There was bartering of wood and hides, hemlock bark and grain, potatoes, corn, butter, eggs, honey, and what not; or in winter, skins of foxes and mink."[48]

The Adirondack experience for year-round residents continued to be one profoundly different from that of vacationers from the outside. The Adirondack landscape remained an important shaper of day-to-day realities, but it was a nature not so much of scenery and sport as of a place where people lived and worked among exploitable resources.

One crucial index of what nature meant to Adirondackers is the way they wrote in their journals about the weather. Where vacationers visited the Adirondacks almost exclusively in the summer and where their accounts dwell on pleasant days, only occasionally interrupted by rain, the year-round residents knew the realities of cold days, long nights, and what seemed like endless spells of miserable weather. Mrs. H. M. Clark lived at Cranberry Lake at the end of the nineteenth century; her diary for March 1897, for example—a time of year of which tourists and guidebook writers knew nothing and hence completely left out of their contributions to the regional narrative—consists of one entry after another noting wretched weather: "20—thunder storms at noon," "21—Rained all day," "25—stormed all day," and, finally, "28—pleasant but rather cold."[49] It was a nature that local people, at least some of them, knew well.

5

"One Grand, Unbroken Domain"

On May 20, 1892, New York governor Roswell P. Flower signed legislation creating the Adirondack Park. Ever since, the Adirondack Park has been a feature on New York maps—nearly always indicated with a blue line. The creation of the Park was part of a flurry of legislative activity in the 1880s and '90s. This era of activism exercised a profound impact on the landscape and the various groups of people who enjoyed its recreational and spiritual attributes or who made a living based on its resources. Yet the record of this era of conservation suggests uncertainty over precisely what was being protected and why. Recent controversies over what the Park is and should be, moreover, show that New Yorkers as a group remain ambivalent about what the Park means to them and what should be done with it.

The key authors of the Adirondack conservation story were journalists, wealthy businessmen, cut-and-run loggers, government officials, aristocratic hunters and anglers trying to protect their sport, and transportation interests worried about water levels in the Hudson River. In other words, the voices that prevailed during this explicit discussion of the future status of the Adirondacks were almost exclusively from outside the region. Just about all these interests—except the more ruthless of the loggers—wanted to protect their idea of what constituted the North Country, and good intentions were everywhere. But the outcome was less than what many people had hoped for. Much of the recent uncertainty in the Adirondacks derives from ambiguities and shortcomings in the original legislation. In order to see where these ambiguities crept into the story, it is important to take a close look at the development of the legislative and bureaucratic narrative.

The Park created in 1892 was a domain vast and contiguous but made up of a checkerboard mix of public and private land.[1] The blue line on the official map indicated the region in which the state should concentrate its efforts to acquire additions to the Forest Preserve. At the time, the state contemplated adding nearly all of the private land to the Park, but the economic impossibility of this soon became apparent. In any case, the Park law declared that all the lands in the Park—both the public lands in the Forest Preserve and the privately owned lands surrounding them—were special lands; they were an important piece of New York geography, one in which all the state's citizens had a special interest.

The steps toward conservation of Adirondack forests occurred in a complex cultural context, one feature of which was the increasing recreational use of the Adirondacks by tourists and sportsmen in the 1870s and '80s. Encouraged by Adirondack Murray and his disciples and accommodated by a rapidly expanding network of railroads and hotels, tourists had put the Adirondacks on the nation's map. But tourists were not the only people aware of and eager to benefit from the treasures of the Adirondacks. At the same time that Murray's Fools were scattered through the woods—shooting white-tailed deer, angling for trout, relaxing on pristine lakesides, and slapping at the ubiquitous mosquitoes and flies—another, equally important movement was afoot.

One feature of a dramatic economic expansion throughout much of the United States, beginning roughly at mid-century, was an apparently insatiable appetite for lumber and other wood products. The explosion of railroad building, for example, demanded incredible quantities of wood crossties; forest historians estimate that in 1870 alone the nation's railroad-construction frenzy consumed thirty-nine million crossties, requiring the harvest of around 195,000 acres of forest. And this was just one year's consumption. Construction of new buildings and fences, the use of prodigious quantities of hemlock bark in tanning, the continued use of charcoal in iron smelting, and the reliance of the American merchant marine on wooden-hulled ships—all these were further powerful factors in the surge in American wood consumption in the years between 1850 and the turn of the century.[2]

Loggers using a cross-cut saw for the Santa Clara Lumber Company, ca. 1900. P. 26009.

Logging in the Adirondacks played an important part in the massive American exploitation of forest resources. Although Adirondack logging had begun with the earliest human contact, before the Civil War it amounted to relatively small, innocuous operations. By the 1860s, logging companies were working throughout the southern and eastern Adirondacks.[3] A crucial distinction between earlier logging operations and those of this era is the export of large quantities of Adirondack wood to mills and other consumers outside the region. The small, local mills continued to produce lumber for local use, of course, but the key addition to the Adirondack logging story after the Civil War is the appearance of large, heavily capitalized companies using gangs of loggers and other salaried employees to fell trees and run logs down Adirondack rivers to mill towns like Glens Falls.

The growth of Glens Falls as a milling center indicates the importance of Adirondack logging in New York commerce. Beginning in 1851, the Big Boom, a cable across the Hudson just above Glens Falls, captured floating logs. That year 130,000 logs stopped at the Big Boom. The following year the amount more than doubled. By 1872, the Big Boom caught over a million logs. Meanwhile, mills in the Glens Falls region were processing huge quantities of finished lumber to be sold downstate, including a rapidly growing market in New York City.[4] A similar, though somewhat smaller and less concentrated industry was developing in the western Adirondacks; in 1879, for example, lumber baron Gordias H. P. Gould drove spruce logs yielding fourteen million board feet of lumber to his mill at Lyons Falls.[5]

The effect of this logging on the landscape is not clearly understood. Tourists like S. H. Hammond and W. J. Stillman argued that it was, or soon would be, unarguably catastrophic. Taking only high-quality logs of virgin white pine and spruce, loggers often left piles of brush and bark on the ground. In time, given dry weather, this debris turned into tinder waiting for a careless spark. One result of the combination of logging and fires was denuded mountainsides, and this in turn threatened the watershed. Where a healthy forest covered a slope, rain and snow melt, held in a sponge-like mass of topsoil, moss, and decaying leaves, were gradually released to streams and rivers. Where the forest cover was removed, the runoff occurred rapidly, leading to alternating flood and drought.

The understanding of the capacity of mountain forests to control run-off derived, almost certainly, from George Perkins Marsh's influential *Man and Nature* (1864). After several years spent in the Mediterranean basin, where he studied the local history and geography, Marsh concluded that profligate abuse of primeval forests had caused dramatic climate change and had destroyed agricultural productivity. Marsh argued that if modern societies did not change their ways, the earth would be reduced "to such a condition of impoverished productiveness, of shattered surface, of climatic excess, as to threaten the deprivation, barbarism, and perhaps even extinction of the [human] species."[6]

Since loggers were working primarily in the southern Adirondacks and since this was the area feeding the Hudson River and the Erie Canal, New York transportation interests feared just such a disruption of the water supply needed to keep these arteries viable. The politicians were not far behind. It should be remembered, however, that before the 1890s (when the chemical processes by which wood pulp could be used for the manufacture of paper were introduced), loggers cut only selected species—white pine and spruce for lumber and hemlock for tanning. In the Adirondacks, these species are almost always mixed with hardwoods—beech, maples, and birches. In other words, there was no reason, at that time, for loggers to practice what is known today as clear cutting. It is doubtful that logging operations before the turn of the century actually led to wide-spread denuding of Adirondack slopes during this period. The exception to this, as Barbara McMartin has shown, was in parts of the eastern Adirondacks, where the demands of the iron industry for charcoal led to ruinous clear cutting of hardwood forests. Since this was a region though which many travelers passed on the way to popular hotels like Bartlett's, Martin's, and Paul Smith's, the threat of clear cutting was much on the minds of these tourists. Many observers believed either that a disaster had begun to happen or that it easily might.[7]

From the very beginning of popular appreciation of the Adirondacks as a scenic and natural treasure, downstate writers urged some sort of conservation. Tourist-journalists like Hammond and Stillman

Cutting for charcoal led to clear cutting near the Chateaugay Railroad. Photograph by Seneca Ray Stoddard, ca. 1876. P. 27891.

warned that ruthless exploitation of Adirondack resources could lead
to the destruction of the region's greatest asset—all the recreational and
natural attractions that made it so different from the more settled parts
of New York. Their arguments were picked up by the popular press,
and ever since the mid-nineteenth century, one of the most important
features of the Adirondack story has been the conviction that the welfare of the entire state of New York depends in a variety of ways on the
environmental integrity of the Adirondacks. Nineteenth-century writers, of course, did not use an expression like "environmental integrity,"
but whether they were defending watershed or promoting the need to
protect the Adirondacks as a recreational retreat, a belief that the state
of New York had an interest in preserving the Adirondacks as a place
where nature was less violated than in the remainder of the state became a critical element in the Adirondack narrative.

One of the first newspaper articles to take up the Adirondack cause
was an anonymously penned 1864 editorial in the *New York Times*, the
author of which historian Frank Graham, Jr., has identified as Charles
Loring Brace.[8] The occasion was the news that Dr. Durant's railroad
was pushing north from Saratoga and would soon be available to carry
passengers into the Adirondacks. Brace declared that the Adirondacks
could be "a Central Park for the World." This earliest known example
of the use of the word *park* in connection with the Adirondacks, coupled with Brace's eloquent praise of the "pure air and giant scenery"
and the "ceaseless music of mountain streams," argued the case that
the Adirondacks offered nature, in need of protection, a place to be set
aside, a place where, for once, the elimination of nature in the name of
progress might be slowed.

But Brace, like so many both before and after, was ambivalent. In addition to being a recreational paradise, the Adirondacks could be a
place to make money, and Brace, himself a wealthy man, knew it. There
were mines rivaling "the famous iron mountains of Missouri" and
great "resources of timber and lumber." Aware that unchecked exploitation of these resources might destroy both them and the region's
beauty but unwilling to advocate a hands-off policy, Brace called upon
rich New Yorkers to buy up the "choicest of the Adirondack mountains, before they are despoiled of their forests" and "make of them
grand parks" to be used judiciously and visited whenever the owners

found themselves in need of "health or pleasure." The elitism of Brace's prescription—the suggestion that the Adirondacks would be appropriately protected if owned and exclusively enjoyed by the wealthy—has been a periodically alarming presence in the Adirondack story ever since.

The reason that Brace saw private purchase as the solution to potential problems was that up until his time, the state's policy with respect to Adirondack lands was that it did not want any: it sold its holdings whenever it could. When Adirondack lands were acquired by loggers, the owner usually cut the marketable pine and spruce. Then, when taxes to the local towns came due, the owner simply declined to pay them, and the lands were put up for sale at a public auction. Often, since the valued timber was gone, no one wanted to buy, and the land passed by default into state ownership, even though the state saw no point to maintaining an Adirondack domain.[9]

One Adirondack writer who insisted that more active state involvement was the appropriate response to what he was sure was a disaster of biblical dimensions was an energetic young man from Albany, Verplanck Colvin. The son of a prominent attorney, Colvin developed an obsession for the Adirondacks as a teenager, eventually managed to have himself employed by the state as a surveyor, and spent most of his life exploring, writing about, and pleading for some sort of protection for the Adirondacks. Arguably the most important and certainly the most interesting of nineteenth-century Adirondack writers and activists, Colvin presented his earliest useful meditation on the need for conservation and an Adirondack Park in his account (published in 1872) of an 1870 ascent of Mount Seward, a remote peak east of Long Lake, which he and Raquette Lake guide and hunter Alvah Dunning were probably the first to climb.

Colvin closed his description of his Seward ascent with a ringing call for conservation. The chief argument for protecting the forests, in Colvin's view, was the need to preserve watershed. The steadily diminishing flow of water in "principal rivers and . . . canals," he maintained, threatened commerce. The explanation for this potential catastrophe was the "chopping and burning off of vast tracts of forest in the wilderness, which have hitherto sheltered from the sun's heat and evaporation the deep and lingering snows, the brooks and rivulets,

Surveyor and conservationist Verplanck Colvin. P. 22777.

and the thick, soaking, sphagnous moss which, at times knee-deep, half water and half plant, forms hanging lakes upon the mountain sides."[10]

Colvin saw evidence that the forests were disappearing and that "the winter snows that accumulate on the mountains, unprotected from the sun, melt suddenly and rush down laden with disaster." It was just the sort of disaster predicted by G. P. Marsh. At the same time, valuable resources were being wasted, and New York, once a net exporter of lumber, would soon have to turn to other states or Canada for this important raw material. Colvin proposed "the creation of an ADIRONDACK PARK or *timber preserve.*"[11] Colvin's vision of what such a park should do and be is telling. He suggested that the integrity of Adirondack forests was a pressing state concern, that lumbering should be permitted, and that the utilitarian protection of watershed and promotion of scientific forestry could easily coexist with the recreational pursuits of "sportsmen, artists, and tourists."

Colvin's oft-quoted proposal is worth noting for one further reason: it completely failed to acknowledge the existence and needs of the

communities which even then dotted the region. On the way to Seward, Colvin and Dunning passed through the village of Long Lake,
where they profited greatly from a consultation about their route with
the famous guide Mitchell Sabattis and "others acquainted with the region near Mt. Seward." Both Dunning, whom Colvin admired and appreciated as "born and bred a hunter and skilled in wood-craft," and
Sabattis lived in what became—just over two decades later—the
Adirondack Park. Their role in the Seward ascent was paradigmatic:
without their involvement Colvin, the visiting outsider, probably
would not have reached the Seward summit. Did Colvin want their

Long Lake guide Mitchell Sabattis. P. 9318.

residences to be within his Park? Did he want them erased? He does not say.[12]

Although Colvin emphasized the utilitarian argument for conservation, he closed with a ringing reminder that such an Adirondack Park, whatever the rationale behind its creation, would be of enormous recreational benefits: "a park for New York, as is the Yosemite for California and the Pacific States."[13] Colvin's acknowledgment of this argument for conservation mirrored similar pronouncements made by other writers. In 1872, guidebook author E. R. Wallace expanded on the anxieties articulated by Charles Brace and pleaded with the New York legislature to grant protection to "one of the world's most popular resorts," comparing Adirondack scenery to that of Yosemite.[14]

By citing the example of Yosemite, which had been ceded by the federal government to California in 1864 (the same year as Brace's editorial in the *Times*) "for public use, resort and recreation," both Colvin and Wallace helped to put Adirondack affairs into a national context. Whatever occurred in the Adirondacks did not happen in a vacuum; Easterners were profoundly aware of developments in other parts of the nation. Some hoped that the tentative step taken in Yosemite might be the beginning for similar action to protect scenic and natural wonders in the East. Samuel Bowles, for example, editor of the Springfield, Massachusetts, *Republican*, visited Yosemite Valley in 1864 and returned east full of enthusiasm for preserving important eastern natural sites. Among other places, including Niagara Falls and the lakes and forests of Maine, Bowles proposed setting aside "fifty miles square of the Adirondacks."[15]

In 1872 state efforts to protect some portion of Adirondack forests began. The New York Assembly appointed a citizen commission, including Colvin, to look into Adirondack matters and recommend steps for protecting the watershed as well as the open space of forests and lakes becoming increasingly popular with hunters, anglers, and other tourists. Significantly, this process began exactly two weeks after President Ulysses Grant signed legislation creating Yellowstone National Park (the world's first)—a federal act that undoubtedly inspired New York lawmakers. On March 15, 1872, the New York Assembly began consideration of a bill to appoint "Commissioners of Parks," whose chief mandate was "to inquire into the expediency of providing for vesting in the State the title to the timbered regions lying within the counties of Lewis, Essex, Clinton, Franklin, St. Lawrence, Herkimer and Hamilton, and converting the same into a public park."[16] The enabling legislation showed a combined interest in timber and recreation. Among the other appointees to the commission were former Governor Horatio Seymour and Franklin B. Hough of Lowville, a fierce champion of improved forestry practices.[17] Citing European examples of forests carefully cut, "affording supplies of valuable timber for house and ship building," the Commissioners asserted, "Should an Adirondack park be created, careful consideration should be given to the utilization of the forest."[18] But the chief reason for establishing an Adirondack Park was to protect watershed:

> Foremost among these considerations [for creating a park] is the question of water supply—of the maintenance of that quantity of water in the navigable rivers, in the streams that supply the canals and afford power to mills and manufactures, which has flowed in undiminished volume in their channels, and which only in these later days begins slowly to fail and disappear.

Invoking language and examples found in Marsh's *Man and Nature*, although that important book was not specifically cited, the Commissioners argued that the continuing destruction of Adirondack forests was a threat to the state's stability. "The State must apply the remedy, and, to protect [its] interests, preserve the forest." The Commissioners recommended protecting only the Hudson River watershed, in a park of some 834,000 acres, of which the state at the time owned only a small portion.[19]

Although the Park Commissioners were thus relentlessly utilitarian in their approach to Adirondack matters, they did not overlook entirely the recreational benefits that would follow the creation of an Adirondack State Park. They acknowledged the public interest in field sports and wild country and noted,

> Throughout this forest, game is still abundant; the deer, bear and panther, with smaller animals, find shelter and support and their presence gives to the magnificent scenery a strange, wild and romantic element,

which has contributed to make its more accessible portions a choice summer pleasure ground for those of our people who travel, and who admire
the natural splendor of their native land.[20]

Finally, anticipating an element in the conservation argument that
would be fundamental to the creation of an Adirondack Park two
decades later, the Commissioners declared that people from throughout the United States came to the Adirondacks to improve their health.
Anecdotes about the capacity of the Adirondack air to arrest the ravages of consumption had within only a few years become part of the
larger Adirondack story.

Buried among these reasons for establishing a park were scattered
references to the existence of the year-round residents, whom the Commissioners casually recognized as inhabiting "a few settlements only,"
and whose attempts to cultivate the land, declared the Report, had
been defeated by climate and soil—this despite the Commissioners' acknowledgment that Adirondack farmers produced excellent potatoes
and oats. The Commissioners, none of whom lived within the bounds
of the recommended park, explicitly maintained that Adirondack villages were marginal affairs, kept alive only by the growing presence of
tourists and the needs of the lumber camps.[21]

At the same time that the Commissioners were investigating the
possibility of a state Adirondack Park, others wanted to follow the
precedent of Yellowstone more precisely and establish an Adirondack
National Park, "dedicated," in the words of Charles Hallock, to "sports
of forest, lake and field." Hallock had in mind a park of some three million acres—about half the size of the current Park, but still "larger than
the state of Connecticut." The protection of watershed or a timber supply is conspicuously absent from Hallock's brief, as is the fact that
some of the landscape he proposed for a National Park was owned and
cultivated by people who lived on it year round. The requirements of
genteel sportsmen provided his sole rationale: "Let the disciples of the
rod and gun go up and possess the land."[22]

In the succeeding years, Colvin returned repeatedly to the need for
a park, reminding the legislature at every opportunity of its obligation
to provide protection for Adirondack forests. He did so in the report on
his survey work for 1873, for example, where he acknowledged resistance to the Park Commission proposal and suggested starting out

Powerful images of a ravaged landscape, as in these 1885 engravings by Julian Rix, titled (left), "A Feeder of the Hudson — As It Was" and (right), "A Feeder of the Hudson — As It Is," published in Harper's Weekly, *promoted public sentiment for protecting the Adirondacks. 77.196.2 (495).*

with a small park embracing only the high peaks and the surrounding region, a total of some 384,000 acres.[23] But the legislature was unwilling to move even this far, and Adirondack forests remained unprotected until 1883 when the state finally moved to withdraw its remaining Adirondack lands from public sale.[24]

On May 15, 1885, the New York legislature created the Adirondack Forest Preserve, comprised of scattered parcels totaling about 681,000 acres. The chief shortcoming of the forest preserve law was its lack of a clear indication of just what it was designed to protect. The Adirondack Forest Preserve was defined merely as state land within eleven Adirondack counties, with no provision for expansion or consolidation.[25] With its provision that "the forest preserve shall be forever kept as wild forest lands"—a phrase that has indelibly entered the discourse of Adirondack history—this legislation aimed high; it was seen as but a necessary preliminary toward effecting conservation for the entire region. But at least part of the result was just the opposite. By instituting such a rigorous clamp on state lands, it drew popular scrutiny away from the Adirondack lands that were not in the Forest Preserve.

What people in and near the Adirondacks thought about the creation of the Forest Preserve is hard to establish. For the most part, the lumber industry objected, arguing that if the state merely maintained the status quo, economic development would proceed and in any case the critical forest lands would eventually pass into state ownership, as they always had before—to which the New York *Tribune* acidly responded, "and without any trees!"[26] Conservation advocates included an Adirondack guide who testified before a legislative committee that twenty-five years of uncontrolled logging around the Saranac Lakes had led to a serious diminution of stream flow, up to one third of the pre-logging level. The solution, according to at least this one Adirondacker, whose livelihood depended on a healthy forest, was for the state to "reclaim the land at any reasonable cost." Other locals agreed.[27] But sentiment for protecting the forests largely came from outside the region, typified by a "Save the Adirondacks" convocation held at Delmonico's, an expensive New York City restaurant, in early 1884.[28]

A provision of the 1885 law established a state Forest Commission, mandated to manage the state-owned forests in both the Adirondacks and the Catskills. This Commission was expected to support itself and generate revenue for the state treasury through selective contracts with lumber companies. But from the start, the New York public cast a suspicious eye on the Forest Commission. Across the country, the 1880s was an era of rampant corruption, often involving collusion between government and corporate agents. In this climate, the public never trusted the Forest Commission to do its work honestly and fairly. Suspicions were hardly allayed when one of the first appointments to the Forest Commission was Theodore Basselin, a Lewis County lumber baron.[29]

Because the popular mind entertained various and occasionally conflicting hopes for the Adirondacks, the focus of media demands after 1885, as before, was diffuse. The editors of the influential *Garden and Forest*, for example, feared watershed deterioration and a timber famine, while *Forest and Stream*, the most popular journal of field sports in the late nineteenth century, worried about threats to Adirondack deer hunting. And doctors connected with the sanatoria clustered around Saranac Lake emphasized the claim for the curative qualities of

Adirondack air, depending entirely on the existence of a healthy forest. Combined, the calls of editors, sportsmen, doctors, and merchants, constituted an incipient environmental lobby, arguing that the protections provided by the Forest Preserve law of 1885 were inadequate.[30] In all cases, the positions of these groups depended on the image of the Adirondacks as a landscape of forests.

That the forest-preserve law and the administrative oversight of the Forest Commission were inadequate was the eloquent point of a series of articles appearing in the *New York Times* in the autumn of 1889. Whatever the goal of the law had been, wrote an unidentified but diligent reporter, environmentally catastrophic logging was continuing unchecked. He accused state officials of collusion with "pirates of the forest, lumber thieves and poachers." The front-page, above-the-fold headline for the lead article set the tone: "Despoiling the Forests—Shameful Work Going on in the Adirondacks—Everything Being Ruined by the Rapacious Lumbermen—State Employees Engaged in the Business."[31]

The Forest Preserve law provided neither definition nor prospects for consolidation. In his 1890 message to the legislature, Governor David B. Hill recognized this and renewed discussion of a park. With elegant simplicity, Hill suggested that the legislature spread out the map, and draw a line on it, identifying as a park the "wilder portion of this region covering the mountains and lakes, at and around the headwaters of the several rivers that rise in that locality, including the Hudson." Once thus defined, Hill hoped, this park could eventually become entirely public domain through exchange and purchase. By holding out the hope that the park would be made up entirely of state land, however, Hill sidestepped the question of what would happen if the state had a Forest Preserve, which was public domain, and a park, which included both private and public land. He also continued the by-now standard practice of ignoring the existence of Adirondack towns and villages. In the century since Governor Hill and his generation wrestled with what to do with the Adirondacks, the question of how much interest the state should have in the fate of private land has been divisive and increasingly unavoidable.[32]

The legislature was still not ready for a park, believing, for one thing, that it would be too expensive, but it did indicate that the establishment of an Adirondack Park might not be far off. It appropriated

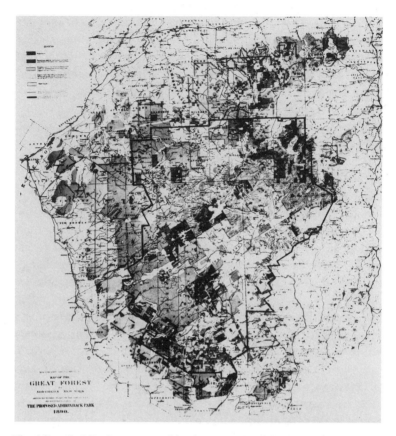

*The Adirondack Park, as proposed by the Forest Commission in 1890. Annual
Report for 1890, New York State Forest Commission. Adirondack Museum
Library.*

$25,000 for purchasing lands to be added to the Forest Preserve with
the vague suggestion that such lands "be available for the purposes of
a State Park."[33] This 1890 resolution to enlarge the Forest Preserve
through purchase was the true legislative origin of the Adirondack
Park. It constituted the first meaningful move toward the state's assuming responsibility to consolidate its holdings. So long as the Forest
Preserve was comprised simply of lands in which loggers or other entrepreneurs had showed no interest or lands acquired randomly
through tax default, the public domain was without any useful definition. But when the state declared its intention actively to enlarge and

enhance the Forest Preserve, the real promise of an Adirondack Park was born. That the amount appropriated was utterly inadequate does not diminish the importance of the act.

In its report to the legislature for 1890, the Forest Commission discussed in detail the possibility of creating an Adirondack Park; it was this report which first included a map of the proposed park with its boundary delineated in blue. To the Commissioners, the paramount goal was consolidating a contiguous public domain: "We deem it immaterial," declared the Commissioners, "whether the popular demand calls for a park or a preserve, provided the consequent legislation enables the State to acquire and hold the territory in one grand, unbroken domain."[34]

In a crucial statement, the Commissioners declared their expectation that if private clubs were allowed to continue their ownership of land within the proposed park's boundaries, "their exclusion of the public from the private preserve lands, can be, by negotiation and mutual concession, removed."[35] This prediction suggests two significant possibilities. First, it anticipates the use of scenic easements or other legal instruments whereby title to critical Adirondack property remains in private hands while public access or other considerations are granted to the state. Second, and even more important, it affirms the state's interest in private lands inside the Adirondack Park; it shows that state officials, as early as 1890, understood that private land in the Adirondacks enjoyed a status different from private land elsewhere and that what happened to it had statewide implications. It is essential to note, moreover, that the private property the commissioners had in mind was the large holdings of clubs and lumber companies, not the smaller town lots and farms of year-round residents.

In 1891 the Forest Commission moved the park effort closer to fruition. Following closely the 1890 suggestions of Governor Hill, it formally proposed that the legislature create an Adirondack Park of 2,847,000 acres within Essex, Franklin, Hamilton, Herkimer, and Warren counties—that it be a public park "forever reserved, maintained and cared for as ground open for the free use of all the people for their health and pleasure, and as forest lands necessary to the preservation of the headwaters of the chief rivers of the state, and a future timber supply." It asked that the Forest Commission be empowered to buy up all private land within designated towns for a price not to exceed a dollar and a half per acre. The possibility that some land might remain in private hands was not examined.[36]

Adirondack developments continued to reflect nationwide trends. In 1891, the United States Congress passed the Forest Reserve Act, which gave the President the power to identify critical parts of the federally owned public lands and set them aside, unavailable for settlement. Behind this was a growing fear of timber famine. The thirty-six million acres dedicated to Forest Reserves by Presidents Harrison and Cleveland over the next six years were the foundation of our National Forests. (The critical difference between the first National Forests and what New York state was considering for the Adirondacks was that the National Forests were carved out of lands already owned by the federal government.) State forestry programs, especially in the East, were also appearing. Moves to protect southern Appalachia, the White Mountains in New Hampshire, and what remained of the once extensive Pennsylvania forests were appealing to an increasingly concerned public.[37]

None of the maneuvering in New York was without its critics. In an age when natural resources were being boldly handed over to railroads and other corporations by both the federal and state governments, any effort to change the status of Adirondack lands raised eyebrows. The legislature was suspected of plotting to establish a park for corrupt reasons—either to create an exclusive hunting preserve for the wealthy or to provide a lucrative market wherein lumber companies could fleece taxpayers by selling worthless, cut-over lands to the state.[38] A Warrensburg newspaper editorialized that the argument for protecting watershed disguised a scheme hatched by wealthy land owners to prohibit the extension of railroad lines into the wilderness and "thus destroy at one fell swoop the chief business and source of wealth of northern New York." The paper raised the question of jobs:

> When we consider the amount of employment afforded by the lumber industry, the thousands of saw mills, tanneries, pulp and paper mills and factories of all kinds giving labor to hundreds of thousands of poor people and that all of this is to be stopped to afford a deer park and fishing ground for a few wealthy pleasure-seekers to air their smoke-dried anatomies is an injustice, the boldness of which is astonishing.[39]

Claims like this reflected a growing sense of alienation between Adirondackers and the downstate interests determined to settle the future status of the northern forests. Worried about their economic security, local residents feared that they had little influence on the fate of the region where they lived; such fears have been a significant part of the local culture ever since. At the time, they proved unpersuasive in Albany, and in 1892, after delicate maneuvering, the legislature finally sent Governor Roswell Flower a bill creating an Adirondack Park. The Forest Commission had been under attack for corruption, and the legislature took special interest in Adirondack matters that year. But the legislative documents reveal the same ambiguities and confusions that had dogged Adirondack conservation efforts throughout the preceding decades.[40]

The law defined the Park in by-now familiar language: "all lands now owned or hereafter acquired by the state" in specified Adirondack counties and towns "shall constitute the Adirondack park." It was to be dedicated to public use, watershed protection, and a "future timber supply."[41] The central thrust of this act was toward establishing a contiguous, useful public domain in the Adirondacks. It left to later legislatures the task of deciding what to do about the realities of vast private land holdings and the year-round residents. It did not say whether private land inside the blue line was legally in the Park.[42] An important implication of the expression "or hereafter acquired" is that private land within the blue line was understood as important to the state's welfare.

If we see the various Forest Commission reports and the legislative documents accompanying them as the Federalist Papers of the Adirondack Park, and if we search through them for something we might call the "original intent" of the Park's founders, we come across important lessons for how we should think about the Park. All of the evidence suggests that the chief reason the Park was needed was to provide adequate protection to forests and identity to a consolidated Forest Preserve. We find further that the state recognized that it had a special interest in what happened to private land in the Adirondacks, and this interest involved maintaining the forest character of the entire Adirondack region. The importance of this act is its clear statement that protection of this region, not just the state-owned Forest Preserve, was vital to the state of New York. How the state's interest has been demonstrated in the succeeding century is another story altogether.

The final step in this decade of conservation was the approval by New York voters of a new state constitution in November of 1894, one of the provisions of which, Article VII, Section 7, guaranteed that the lands of the Forest Preserve would "be forever kept as wild forest lands." Still in force today, this article makes the Forest Preserve one of the best protected landscapes in the world. The key element of the constitutional protection was the elimination of the option for logging on state land. Delegates to the constitutional convention became convinced that neither loggers nor the Forest Commission could be trusted on the Forest Preserve, and the consequence was a total ban on logging. But it is important to remember that it applies only to the Forest Preserve; the remainder of the Park, the privately owned lands, has never been subject to the forever-wild clause. At the time this provision was approved, most delegates believed that the state would eventually own all the land within the blue line.[43] It seemed a realistic and positive goal for a large, contiguous state domain to be "forever kept as wild forest lands."

Opponents of constitutional protection, chiefly lumber companies and the legislators they could influence, quickly went to work to reverse Article VII, Section 7. To amend the constitution required bills passed by two successive legislatures; this was done in 1895 and 1896. In November of 1896, New York voters had their first chance to confirm or change their views on the Forest Preserve. An amendment which would have permitted logging on state land in the Adirondacks was overwhelmingly rejected, with about 710,000 votes against, to only 320,000 votes for. The amendment failed in every New York county, including, significantly, all the Adirondack counties.[44]

But apparent widespread support for keeping loggers off state land could not disguise the fact that both the Park law and the 1894 Constitution were full of unfinished business. What was the state to do about private land inside the Blue Line? How was it to demonstrate its interest in that land? How important was the private land inside the Park to the people of New York?

A good illustration of this unacknowledged dilemma was the status of Mount Marcy—highest peak in the state and locus for stunning

"A HELPING HAND." From the New York Herald. March, 30. 1903.
Copyright. 1903, The New York Herald Co.

Even after the establishment of the Forest Preserve and Park, New Yorkers feared that corruption and collusion between state officials and logging barons remained a threat to Adirondack forests. New York Herald, *30 March 1903.*

views of mountains, lakes, and forest. One of the most common destinations for Keene Valley hikers, the summit of Mount Marcy was reached by a rough scramble of about ten miles and an elevation gain of some 4200 feet. By the time of the conservation activity of the 1880s and '90s, climbing in the high peaks was beginning to compete with boating and field sports as an attractive Adirondack recreation. The philosopher and psychologist William James, for example, who spent many summers hiking amid the spectacular mountain scenery of Keene Valley (which he called "one of the most beautiful things in this beautiful world"), enjoyed climbing Marcy and equally loved all the nearby high country.[45]

His affection for the Adirondacks appears with particular precision in a letter to his brother Henry, the novelist, who lived in England.

By 1900, as in this photograph by Norman S. Foote, the summit of Mount Marcy had become a popular destination for hikers. P. 23339.

William believed that Henry, on one of his infrequent trips to America, had made a great mistake in passing up a visit to the Adirondacks: "You missed it, when here, in not going to Keene Valley, where I have just been, and of which the sylvan beauty, especially by moonlight, is probably unlike aught that Europe has to show. Imperishable freshness!"[46]

But when James hiked in the high peaks, the unresolved status of much of the land he loved concealed a threat to the future capacity of the Adirondacks to provide the back-to-nature experience that was so important to him and many others. In 1898 James climbed Marcy on a strenuous hike of "10 1/2 hours of the solidest walking I ever made."[47] To James, as to countless other climbers of his day, the gray-green anorthosite of the Marcy dome was a sacred Adirondack destination. Yet when James stood on the summit of Mount Marcy, he was on private land; it had been sold by the state many years before the creation of the Forest Preserve and had not been reacquired through tax default or other means. Mount Marcy was in the Adirondack Park but not in the Forest Preserve.[48]

This was a pivotal moment in Adirondack history. William James and his generation could look back to an era when the Adirondack region was thought of as one big forest. Some of the land belonged to the state, some to lumber companies, some to individuals and families. (In the case of some parcels, no one knew *who* owned them, and this uncertainty kept Colvin and his crews busy trying to fix the location of occasionally century-old survey lines.) People had collected fire wood, hiked, hunted, and fished wherever they liked, blithely indifferent to the niceties of property lines. But the decade of the 1890s witnessed the division of the Adirondacks into two realms—public and private. Although William James was permitted to hike to the top of Mount Marcy, neither his right to do so nor the rights of the millions of New Yorkers who owned the Forest Preserve to do so were secure. At the same time, the constitution now forbade the traditional local practice of gathering fire wood on state land. Two decades of feverish conservation activity had aimed at protecting an entire region. The unanticipated result was splitting the region in two.

6

"The Havoc of the Years"

In 1892 New York created a park like no other park the world had ever seen—a park that was a complicated mix of private and public property. It had people living and working in it. It had land owned by individuals, families, clubs, and corporations. It had poor people dwelling in shanties, while down the road were millionaires who summered in mansions, where they played and postured like the European aristocracy they slavishly imitated. In between it had towns and villages where men and women worked at a host of occupations, raised families, went to church, and generally lived like many other Americans from coast to coast. It had land protected as forests forever and available to all for hunting, fishing, and camping and land where cut-and-run loggers savagely exploited the remaining resource in the name of a quick profit.

Over the next couple of decades, after the era of state conservation efforts, the Adirondacks slowly settled into the patterns that have dominated regional life for most of the twentieth century. The Adirondack story remained a story of nature, but just what nature meant continued to depend on what one demanded of nature, what one expected nature to be and do. The Adirondack Park occupied a landscape where recreation based on nature thrived alongside, sometimes right next door to, intensive exploitation of that same nature. Tourists came to the Adirondacks to camp out or stay at hotels, while companies owned by families or trusts based outside the region logged vast holdings of forest lands. Other large preserves were owned and exclusively used by private clubs, whose members came from the wealthy, elite circles of

106

eastern society. Local residents largely worked in the tourist industry, including various jobs at the great clubs and preserves, and in logging. Like the patterns of land ownership, the Adirondack story was complex; it was a fabric woven of many threads, a tale narrated by many voices.

Conversations among these various voices were equally complex and occasionally strained. The locals saw both the tourist and logging industries and the proprietors of the great preserves as their major sources of cash. Yet now and then they showed that their appreciation of this was colored by resentment. Meanwhile, a relatively sudden surge in logging, along with the railroads that were carrying increasing amounts of wood out of the forests, and a series of catastrophic fires, were exercising a profound impact on the land itself.

Despite the intensive conservation activity of the 1880s and '90s, logging in the Adirondacks reached its peak between 1890 and 1910. The constitutional prohibition on logging on the Forest Preserve did not obtain on private land, which continued to make up most of the Park. The harvest of Adirondack trees expanded because of a critical technological development. This was the invention of the process by which wood pulp could be made into paper. Until well into the nineteenth century, paper was made from rags, by means of a relatively expensive and time-consuming process. As demand for paper increased, with rising literacy and the growth of mass-circulation newspapers and magazines, entrepreneurs and inventors looked for new ways to manufacture paper. The answer to this demand was the cellulose fibers found in wood. Efficient processes for making paper from wood pulp were introduced into the United States from Europe at around the time of the Civil War and slowly began to take over the paper industry.[1]

Paper companies in New England and New York were among the leaders of the move from rag to wood pulp, and they began to purchase woodlands, often plots cut over once for lumber, to guarantee a steady supply of pulp. And companies that previously had been chiefly involved in logging for lumber expanded their focus to include pulp. In an age of consolidation and trusts, these gradually merged into a few giants controlling the industry. The International Paper Company, for example, formed in 1898 to consolidate sixteen smaller companies with twenty paper mills, was one of the earliest and largest of these new powerful combinations of capital and resources; at the time of its incorporation it owned 60,000 acres in the Hudson River watershed.[2] (It is now the largest owner of private land in the Adirondack Park, controlling in 1996 over 320,000 acres of forest lands. In Long Lake, International Paper owns over 59,000 acres, or just under 20% of the town.[3])

Beginning in about 1890, mills designed to manufacture paper from pulp appeared all around the Adirondacks, often built by companies with capital already invested in lumber mills and forest lands. With the introduction of pulp paper, these companies suddenly had new opportunities for making money on lands where the old-growth spruce and pine had been cut. Wood used for making paper did not need to be from long, clean logs; second growth and smaller trees that had been virtually useless for lumber were valuable for pulp. All this meant that loggers who had been harvesting for lumber and then abandoning their land now had reason to hold on to it. It was worth paying taxes while waiting for pulp harvests, which could profitably occur more often than could harvests for lumber.

New York quickly became a leader in the processing of wood pulp. In 1900 there were 293 pulp mills in the United States, of which over a third were in New York.[4] The consumption of wood at these mills was prodigious. In *The Great Forest* Barbara McMartin has gathered valuable data on the amounts of Adirondack wood turned into paper in the decades around the beginning of the twentieth century. She writes that in 1899, for example, the eight Adirondack mills owned by International Paper processed 103,000 cords of pulpwood, while "the entire north country region consumed 356,000 cords." At this time the species most used for pulp was spruce (though other softwoods were also logged for pulp), and the massive harvest of spruce, combined with the previous decades' cutting for lumber soon led to a severe shortage: "by 1910 more than half the pulpwood consumed in New York pulp and paper mills came from [Canada]."[5] The decline of sources of pulp occurred throughout the East and was part of a general eclipse of the entire regional logging industry. Vicious competition, overproduction, and the emergence of large-scale logging in the West and South all led to a near collapse of eastern logging in the years just before World War I.[6]

But before that there was a frenetic boom in felling Adirondack trees, a feverish, often ruthless drive to saw down the trees, get them to mills, and convert them to paper or lumber. Where loggers cutting

Logs cut for pulp near Tupper Lake, ca. 1900. Photograph by B. J. McCormick. P. 38312.

trees for lumber had cut only straight trees from which at least two thirteen-foot logs could be cut, pulp operations cut all the spruce, hemlock, or pine they could reach, including the giants. The largest spruce ever harvested in the Adirondacks, which left a stump forty-one inches across, was cut for pulp. Pulp logs were cut into four-foot lengths and either run down Adirondack rivers to mills or, as was increasingly the case, loaded onto spur railroad lines and shipped directly to mills.[7] Particularly in the northwestern Adirondacks, where immense tracts of forest remained largely untouched as late as 1890, railroad construction opened up new territory for rapid exploitation.[8]

Logging was the chief occupation for many Adirondack men. Over the course of the nineteenth century, the composition of the labor force had slowly evolved. At mid-century, when logging was just beginning to be a major employer, loggers were mostly born in the United States, with a few Canadians and native Americans, and they were usually men who identified farming as their primary occupation. By 1890, roughly a third of Adirondack loggers were foreign born, with nearly half of these German; within a decade after that French Canadians were the largest foreign-born group represented.[9]

In the fall men went into camps, cutting trees and dragging them to skidways, from which, after snow was on the ground, logs were moved on ice roads to banking grounds on frozen rivers or lakes to wait for the spring thaw. Ralph Hoy, who visited the logging camps operated by his father in the Chateaugay country in the years before World War I, recalled the pre-dawn work of getting logs to banking grounds: the work was dangerous and cold. One of the most perilous jobs was that of the teamsters, who negotiated huge sleds of logs "down steep pitches and around curves where the weight of previous loads had caused the sleigh tracks to freeze." One morning Hoy looked at the thermometer to discover a temperature of fifty-two below zero.[10]

Running logs down Adirondack rivers to mills was no less fraught with danger. One log stuck on a submerged boulder could almost instantly lead to a perilous jam, as more and more logs rushing downstream became hung up. Breaking up these logjams demanded expertise and courage and occasionally led to disaster. Jeanne Robert Foster described the "watery grave" of six "bold Shanty Boys" on the Hudson:

> It was on one Sunday morning
> As you are soon to hear,
> The logs were piled mountain high
> And we could not keep them clear.
> . . . .
> They had not rolled off many logs
> When the boss did hear them say—
> "My boys, you'd better be on your guard
> For the jam will soon give way."
> No sooner had he spoke those words
> When the jam did break and go.
> It carried away those six brave lads
> And their foreman, young Monroe.[11]

Loggers near Tupper Lake, ca. 1900. P. 62856.

But, as a resident of Wells recalled, despite the hardships and perils, "lumbering was practically the only industry of our village. . . . It was for many the only means of earning a livelihood."[12]

It was also a way of life that helped to define Adirondack culture. As Jeanne Robert Foster wrote,

> It was a clean hard life. Men went in when snow came
> And didn't take the hay road till the spring.
> There were some farmers too who hired out
> With regular lumberjacks when the crops had failed
> To earn a little cash to help the farm.
> . . . .
> It was a good clean life—the crash of falling trees,
> The smell of balsam and of spruce and pine,
> The chittering of the jays, the skidways piled
> With sappy logs, the resin on our hands.
> The cook house with its pans of pork and beans
> And johnny cake. . . . We had enough to eat.[13]

Not every observer agreed that it was a "good clean life." In the first decade of the twentieth century, Blue Mountain Lake remained a logging center, and many local men worked in the woods during the winter. Lester Stanton, a small boy then, who later became a Protestant minister, recalled that the village had "more saloons than churches" and that the bars were open for far more hours than the churches ever were. "A crowd full of tough men full of whiskey" led to the inevitable rowdiness and fights, which kept "genteel people" off the streets when the loggers were in town. Fights were so common and injuries so frequent that Stanton later wondered that more men had not been killed.[14]

Despite the tradition of "enough to eat," logging was not an ideal employment. Low pay and hard work were always part of the life, accidents were common, and life in the camps away from family was lonely. One logger's daughter described her father's life in camp as "a form of hibernation."[15] The logging companies, moreover, seldom paid much attention to the welfare of their workers. But Adirondack loggers never initiated serious efforts toward organizing themselves or demanding better conditions. Despite widespread discontent, Adirondack loggers resisted the notion of organizing; they preferred to maintain their image of rugged self-reliance and individualism.[16]

Those not actually laboring in the woods often found work in related industries. Wells had a bobbin and veneer mill, "our only industrial plant," which introduced to this small Hamilton County village its "first awareness of the industrial world." Children watched their neighbors heading off in the morning with dinner pails, "ready to begin the long day's work, and those same neighbors returning with steps less vigorous, as evening fell." In 1917, the mill burned, leaving many people jobless.[17]

The impact of logging on the landscape was profound; this impact was two fold. First, there was the intense harvest of a few valuable species (mainly spruce), which left other less valuable species (mainly hardwoods, especially beech) overrepresented.[18] Second, during the roughly twenty-five years after the establishment of the Forest Preserve, the Adirondack region was swept by a series of catastrophic forest fires. Neither lumberjacks nor their employers paid much thought to clearing away the vast amounts of slash and debris—bark, branches, needles—they left in their wake. This became tinder waiting for a

Packing fire-fighting supplies across a ravaged landscape, ca. 1902. Photograph by Abraham Knechtel. P. 22381.

spark. In the days before cutting for pulp, when harvests were more selective, thus producing less slash, and when the sparks commonly thrown off by locomotives were rare, this did not pose a major threat of fire. But once the demand for pulp revolutionized Adirondack logging and the mileage of railroad tracks increased, the menacing potential for fire was dramatically realized.

In 1899 and 1903 drought conditions in spring led to summers of fire in the Adirondacks. These were followed in 1908 by another cataclysmic fire season. In 1903 and 1908 fires burned about 800,000 acres in the Adirondack Park, or twenty-five percent of Park land, and smoke from these fires reached all the way to New York City. In 1908, May and June were especially dry, and small fires started in the spring before the new foliage could shade the ground. In July bad burns appeared across the Adirondacks. The real trouble came in September: locomotives, burning coal and without spark arresters, were still functioning, despite the obvious inevitability that they would make a menacing situation even more dangerous. The worst single fire was at Long Lake West (now Sabattis), where forty-four residents barely escaped by train to Tupper Lake before fire roared into the village; 30,000 acres burned in a single day, while other fires burned throughout the Park.[19]

One result of these conflagrations was a sudden interest in requiring loggers to take better care of their land. State foresters who studied the Adirondack forest fires saw quickly that the worst fires were in the slashes—the debris left by loggers on the ground. They proposed that loggers be required to practice "lopping," or cutting the branches off unused tops so they would lie close to the ground and rot quickly. If properly lopped, branches decompose within four years. In 1910 the Forest Fish and Game law required lopping on all cuts. And locomotives burning coal or wood were banned.[20] Once these measures were fully accepted, the threat of fire greatly diminished.

The fires of the early twentieth century also demonstrated how critically important the conservation efforts of the previous two decades had been. The threat to the watershed or to recreation posed by logging before the sudden demand for wood pulp may in fact have been overstated in the 1880s and '90s as the state was establishing the Forest Preserve and the Adirondack Park, but the horrible fires of 1903 and 1908 showed that uncontrolled exploitation of Adirondack forests could destroy everything that made the region vital to the state's welfare.

The forests that protected the watershed and offered recreational opportunities and a way of life like none other in New York were fragile and vulnerable, and the eloquent calls of S. H. Hammond, Verplanck Colvin, and others who argued so forcefully for conservation were shown by these fires to have been prescient. The state-owned Forest Preserve, where piles of slash were not awaiting a locomotive's spark, escaped the worst of the fires, which consistently broke out on recently logged land owned by lumber and pulp companies.[21] (On the private preserves, however, like the Adirondack League Club, which were well cared for, fires were infrequent.[22]) The decade of fire showed that the state had a pressing interest in what happened to forested land throughout the Adirondacks, and it proved the need for continuing and increased protection for Adirondack forests—public and private.

Because the state's forests were so vulnerable and because of lingering reservations about the capacity or willingness of the state bureaucracy to stick with a serious conservation agenda, an organized conservation lobby began to materialize. Established in 1902, the Association for the Protection of the Adirondacks was dedicated to encouraging state purchase of private lands for expanding the Forest Preserve, increasing the state's ability to fight forest fires, stopping the wide-spread and illegal practice of loggers' cutting trees on state land, and resisting efforts to dilute the force of the constitution's forever-wild provision.[23] One of the first concrete demonstrations of both state-wide concern about the Adirondacks and the involvement of the Association as an advocacy group occurred at the constitutional convention of 1915, where delegates, over strenuous objections from logging companies, approved a new constitution confirming the forever-wild protection of the Forest Preserve.

The debate over this provision in 1894 had shown that many delegates to that convention believed that the complete prohibition on logging on state land would be temporary, that once forestry had matured as a profession, logging on state land could resume. But in 1915, a majority of the delegates rejected this position. Chastened by the specter of apocalyptic fires sweeping across the north country summer after summer and intensely lobbied by the Association (some of whose officers were delegates), the convention re-inscribed protection for the Forest Preserve in the constitution, with no evidence that they thought this policy was subject to further review.[24]

The affirmation of the forever-wild clause at the 1915 constitutional convention and the interest in Adirondack matters showed by the Association served to re-emphasize a key element in the Adirondack narrative—that most of the people of New York wanted the Adirondacks to continue to be predominantly a place of nature. They remained unsure of how to go about protecting what was left of the once extensive nature of the north country, but the popular inclination to keep the Adirondacks as both recreational retreat and continuing protector of natural resources was clear.

Also clear was the continuing role of the wealthy classes in orchestrating and extending the protections—insufficient as they were. The Association for the Protection of the Adirondacks was the political arm of an entrenched and powerful Adirondack constituency. Its officers were mostly wealthy men who owned large Adirondack estates or were members of exclusive rod-and-gun clubs. Few lived in or even

near the Adirondacks: of twenty-eight trustees in office in 1912, eighteen lived in New York City, while only one, Dr. Edward L. Trudeau,
lived inside the blue line. Other early members included plutocrats like
William Rockefeller, Henry Harper, J. Pierpont Morgan, Harry Payne
Whitney, and Alfred G. Vanderbilt. New members had to be proposed
by current members and voted on by the trustees, annual meetings
were held on Wall Street, and the Association quickly "earned a reputation as a rich man's club."[25]

The Adirondacks continued to be the place where millionaires
hunted and fished. The wealthy members of the Association for the
Protection of the Adirondacks were interested in protecting nature in
the Adirondacks because it was the nature where they retreated from
the grime and competition of urban America. Among the affluent
classes of the eastern cities, it became axiomatic that when it came
to fashionable vacations July was for the shore and August for the
mountains. And while "mountains" to some might mean the Poco-
nos or the Catskills, no region possessed quite the same cachet as the
Adirondacks.[26]

In the years immediately following the Park's creation, both local
residents and middle-class outdoor enthusiasts from throughout the
eastern United States found themselves increasingly isolated from the
wealthy owners of the huge private preserves that popped up throughout the region. Class, economic, and ethnic distinctions had certainly
always existed in the Adirondacks, but they had seldom been overtly
acknowledged. Now they came painfully to the surface and have periodically reappeared to thwart reasonable debate ever since. Measures
calculated to protect the land ended up dividing both the landscape
and the people concerned about its future.

That American society at the end of the nineteenth century was divided into classes according to wealth and birth was a subject on which
most people had profoundly ambivalent feelings, particularly at a time
when rapid developments in industry, transportation, and commerce
were creating both an insular cadre of millionaires and a sprawling,
grindingly poor, barely employed working class. Americans had always liked to distinguish their ostensibly fluid, mobile society from
what they repeatedly told one another were the rigid, blood-bound
classes of Europe.

The Lake Placid Club. P. 15704.

Americans acknowledged their obvious distinctions of wealth and power, but these were understood to be the natural result of the talents of the winners and the sloth or bad habits of the losers in the competition of American life. It was a commonplace assumption that ample opportunities for material success existed for hard-working, clean living Americans and that they were available equally for all.[27] Adirondack enthusiast Theodore Roosevelt typified the views of many Americans, observing at one point, "There are really no classes in American life. . . . Our social and political systems do not admit of them in theory, and in practice they exist only in a very fluid state."[28] But Roosevelt's own more than comfortable position—possessed as a function of his inherited wealth, blue blood, and Harvard education—made this a disingenuous claim.

A well-worn anecdote in Adirondack history is the story about Roosevelt's being high on the slopes of Mount Marcy on a September afternoon in 1901 when word came that William McKinley was dying and that the young Roosevelt would soon be the twenty-third president of the United States. But he was not there as an ordinary New

Yorker, climbing the state's highest peak, which at the time was not even publicly owned but was instead jointly owned by two private preserves: he was staying for a month at the Tahawus Club, socializing with wealthy, aristocratic chums. Roosevelt was not a member of the Tahawus Club, but with his credentials of family, wealth, and power he could stay there whenever he wished—something neither a shopkeeper from Brooklyn nor a Newcomb lumberjack could ever do.[29]

The nation was divided into classes of rich and poor just as surely as the Adirondack Park was divided into the Forest Preserve and private land. And these were not unrelated divisions. One dilemma facing the state of New York, as it pondered what to do with its newly established Adirondack Park, concerned how to reconcile the resulting compromise of the goal of regional conservation. As it turned out, this goal— the original plan for one contiguous, consolidated and public park, what the forest commissioners of 1890 referred to as their hope for "the State to acquire and hold the territory in one grand, unbroken domain"—was, at least for the time being, abandoned.

A major consequence of the popularity of the Adirondacks around the beginning of the twentieth century had been the establishment of large private clubs. Wealthy sportsmen, eager to enjoy the benefits of the wilderness without rubbing shoulders with Murray's Fools and others lured to the Adirondacks by the hope of landing a trout or shooting a deer, banded together to purchase huge parcels of woods and waters. At these clubs—the Adirondack League Club near Old Forge is one of the best examples—men and women from prosperous families pursued the rituals of the outdoors. They hunted deer, angled for trout, picnicked in the woods, and plied their boats across lakes and rivers they owned and protected for their exclusive use.

For while New York as a collective polity may have been uncertain about what the best plan for the Adirondacks was, there were nonetheless plenty of individuals and small groups who knew precisely what they wanted: they wanted to own the place. And in the absence of a clearly conceived and forcefully implemented mandate by the state to expand its Adirondack holdings, these people seized the opportunity to do just that. The same era that saw the passage of conservation legislation for the Adirondacks and, slightly later, the consolidation of extensive lumber and pulp lands under the control of companies like International Paper, also witnessed the creation of most of the huge

The genteel life at the Adirondack Club, 1880s. P. 61013.

clubs and private preserves that still make up much of the contemporary Park.

Indeed, the establishment of these preserves undoubtedly was encouraged, though hardly intended, by the state's halting steps toward creating and protecting a public domain. Wealthy hunters and anglers, acutely alert to the state's inchoate hope for consolidation of a public park, wanted their own private playgrounds where they would not be forced to share their game with the hoi polloi. They decided that their only chance to protect their genteel notions of how deer should be shot and trout hooked was on their own property. Without meaning to, the activity of 1885, 1892, and 1894 created a sort of real-estate vacuum, into which the astute and opportunistic quickly rushed.

The first great private preserve, incorporated way back in 1876 and thus predating the conservation era, was the Adirondack Club, occupying the huge holdings of the McIntyre Iron Company and thus enjoying some of the most imposing scenery and valuable land in the region—Lakes Henderson, Colden, and Sanford, the Preston Ponds, and the southern slopes of Mount Marcy, among other bits of prime real estate. According to club historian Arthur H. Masten, the charter members were "well known men," including a couple of Roosevelts and other well-heeled, blueblooded scions of the New York aristocracy. (In 1897, the Adirondack Club was reorganized as the Tahawus Club.)[30] Other large preserves followed, especially as the state began actually to pursue a conservation agenda: the Adirondack Mountain Reserve, which purchased the Ausable lakes and most of the Great

Range, in 1887, and the Adirondack League Club, near Old Forge, in 1890—to name a couple of the largest and best known.[31]

The motives for creating these preserves varied. In the case of the Adirondack Mountain Reserve, the urge to control a spectacular private domain was coupled with a legitimate fear that if the land was not quickly bought from loggers it would be disastrously cut over and some of the region's finest mountain scenery would be destroyed for generations.[32] The founders of the Adirondack League Club began with a multiple-use philosophy, convinced that they could log their lands profitably though conservatively while nonetheless enjoying field sports and isolation from the urban world of office and factory. (As it turned out, the returns from logging seldom matched expenses.)[33] By the turn of the century, such preserves had bought and posted enormous chunks of the Adirondack landscape.

The often vicious exclusiveness of these clubs is well illustrated in the rules for membership in the Lake Placid Club, founded in 1895 by Melvil Dewey, New York State Librarian and inventor of the Dewey Decimal System:

> No one will be received as member or guest against whom there is a physical, moral, social, or race objection, or who would be unwelcome to even a small minority. . . . This invariable rule is rigidly enforced; it is found impracticable to make exceptions to Jews or others excluded, even when of unusual personal qualifications.[34]

The late nineteenth century was an age of intense racial anxiety. Americans of English or northern European heritage nervously feared that the current surge in immigration, especially from eastern Europe, would lead to destabilizing changes in American culture, to an end of Anglo-Saxon hegemony. The combination of immigration and what many observers were certain was a declining birth rate among "native" American stock (by which these writers most certainly did not mean Indians) was leading to "race suicide," to the "passing of this great Anglo-Teuton people" and their replacement by the "Latin and the Hun."[35] One of the many ways this anxiety was manifested was in the hope that the Adirondacks and other American enclaves of wild nature could be maintained as a retreat for the racially pure from the ethnic melting pot of the cities. The Adirondacks became infamous for the

WASPish racism of its expensive resorts, clubs, and hotels: advertisements blatantly expressing such ugly sentiments as "Hebrews need not apply" or "Hebrews will knock vainly for admission" were common.[36]

The impulse to lock up and post large tracts of forest quickly led to the establishment of preserves that were off limits to most New Yorkers. In 1904, the New York State Forest, Fish and Game Commission listed the major preserves and estimated their acreage. The Tahawus Club controlled nearly sixty thousand acres, the Adirondack League Club (whose trustees proudly proclaimed ownership of an "Adirondack empire") nearly eighty thousand, the Adirondack Mountain Reserve almost twenty-five thousand. Other major private parks included the Ampersand Preserve, carved out of the holdings of the Santa Clara Lumber Company; Brandreth Park, whose owners had been rusticating contentedly in the Adirondacks since before the Civil War; Whitney Park, in northern Hamilton County; railroad magnate Dr. William Seward Webb's Nehasane Park, in Hamilton and Herkimer counties; and

Trophy room at McAlpin Camp on Brandreth Lake, ca. 1916. Photograph by Harry M. Beach.

the more than fifty thousand acres owned by William Rockefeller in Franklin County. In all, sixty private preserves occupied nearly 800 thousand acres of the Adirondack Park.[37] Put another way, these preserves alone constituted over a third of all the private land in the Park, and there were many other prime parcels in private hands not quite big enough to make the Forest, Fish and Game Commission's list, not to mention the undeveloped lands of lumber and pulp companies.

Nearly all of these private preserves came into existence in direct response to the possibility that the state would put together a public domain in the Adirondacks. And their proprietors knew that they had a good thing going, whether they kept their land or eventually sold it to the state. The 1891 yearbook of the Adirondack League Club, for example, noted the renewal of legislative discussions of a park and smugly observed that no matter what happened the club could not lose:

> Whatever may be the action of the State in regard to the establishment of a State Park in the Adirondacks, the Club may view the situation with entire complacency. We have an absolute and indefeasible title to the most valuable tract in the Adirondacks, whether regarded as a productive forest or as a magnificent sporting preserve. It will become still more valuable if the State acquires title to the lands surrounding it.[38]

Even if the state moved to institute eminent-domain proceedings, the very existence of the Park would guarantee the club a handsome profit over the price originally paid for its land in 1889.

In discussing the significance of the private preserves, the Forest, Fish and Game Commissioners of 1904 noted that they "with a slight exception have been established within the last sixteen years—most within eleven years"—in other words, since the brief period between the creation of the Forest Preserve in 1885 and the Park law of 1892. The commissioners went on to observe that these preserves stirred up enmity between owners and those left out:

> the comparatively sudden exclusion of the public from its old camping-grounds has provoked a bitter hostility on the part of the hunters, fishermen and guides who formerly ranged over this territory. The sportsman who returns to some favorite haunt only to find himself con-

fronted with the words, "No Thoroughfare," turns back with a resentful feeling, while the guides, who were wont to conduct their patrons wherever game was plentiful, view with threatening looks the hired gamekeepers that guard the forbidden lands.[39]

Before the 1880s and 1890s, people in the Adirondacks—both locals and visitors—thought of the region as one big forest. Hunters hunted and anglers fished wherever they pleased. Working their way up a trout stream, anglers would fish from pool to pool, oblivious to the likely possibility of crossing a property line; hunters chased deer, hikers climbed mountains, and locals cut firewood equally indifferent to the details of boundaries and ownership.

In 1903 the potentially explosive character of relations between the owners of large holdings and their neighbors was demonstrated with tragic finality in the town of Santa Clara in Franklin County. Orrando P. Dexter, an eccentric and reclusive millionaire, maintained a palatial house on nearly 7,000 acres of posted and fenced land. His neighbors did not care for the relatively sudden appearance of no-trespassing signs on land they had been accustomed to using, and they continued routinely to hunt, fish, and collect firewood on it. He energetically prosecuted trespassers, and the neighborhood seethed in a climate of enmity and bitterness—to the point where violence seemed inevitable. One chilly September afternoon, as Dexter was driving a buggy down his seldom-traveled driveway, he was shot in the back and killed. According to historian Alfred Donaldson, even the local school children knew the name of the murderer, but no charges were ever filed.[40]

This murder increased the tension in a similar class-based conflict developing twenty miles south at Brandon. There William Rockefeller was engaged in a nasty feud with a few families possessing small inholdings in his huge Bay Pond estate. Rockefeller posted his land, hired gamekeepers and guards, and generally made life miserable for a handful of people whose land he wanted to buy and add to his own. He even pulled strings in Washington to have the local post office moved, just to make his antagonists' daily lives a bit more vexed. Though threatened with the same fate met by Orrando Dexter, Rockefeller kept up the pressure and, with nearly inexhaustible resources, outlived or outspent his foes. He ended up owning all the land he had wanted.[41]

Donaldson notes that the class hostility displayed at Brandon appeared throughout the Adirondacks, though generally in a less "virulent" form, and that it "existed more or less wherever similar conditions existed, and it began with the establishment of the first private park."[42] Despite this probably inevitable resentment, the preserves were appreciated for the jobs they created. In 1903 the Forest, Fish and Game Commissioners observed that even though the preserves posted their land and thus excluded many hunters and fishermen, the "owners of the preserves . . . furnish constant and lucrative employment [to] large numbers of guides and woodsmen"—not to mention caretakers, gardeners, cooks, housekeepers, and an assortment of other workers.[43]

This was all part of the dramatic transformation of the local culture and economy; the driving force of this change was tourism. The proprietors of the great preserves were not tourists in the strictest sense of the word, but they were seasonal residents who mostly pursued their lives and made their money outside the Park. Seasonal trade was also the hallmark of the hotel industry, which, argued the Commissioners,

> contribute[d] largely to the development and prosperity of Northern New York, fairly approaching in its magnitude that of the great industries which are dependent on the forest product of that region. In the management of this business employment is furnished to thousands of people, trade is stimulated by the large purchase of supplies, building operations increase the demand for skilled labor, while the railroad and steamboat lines reap the benefits accruing from the large passenger and freight traffic.[44]

Tourism was indeed an increasingly important factor in the north-country economy, especially as the pre-World War I collapse of the logging industry took hold. And it was about to become even more so as a transportation medium whose significance the Commissioners did not yet recognize began to appear. This was the automobile, the great democratizer of American vacations and leisure. The first car to reach the central Adirondacks careened into the village of Saranac Lake in July 1902. Driven by a honeymooning couple from Buffalo, it then puffed its way to Paul Smith's, frightening horses and exciting children along the road.[45] Four years later, a 1905 Winton operated by three col-

Inns and other accommodations along roadsides responded to the needs of tourists traveling by automobile. Lake Harris House, Newcomb, ca. 1915. P. 16257.

lege boys evoked amazed stares as it negotiated dirt roads all the way to Blue Mountain Lake.[46]

The arrival of the automobile was the latest element in the sequence of events that moved the Adirondacks closer to the mainstream of eastern American life and culture. The phenomenon of Murray's Fools was followed by affordable rail transport, which in turn was followed by moderately priced hotels. Once the automobile and reasonably passable roads opened up the Adirondacks to even greater throngs of tourists, the next step was campgrounds and motels. Even while millionaires reveled in their posted, rustic solitude, the Adirondacks appealed to the middle class.

During the earliest years of the automobile, families of moderate means could not afford cars, but this changed when the mass production of cheaper vehicles began, notably with Henry Ford's Model T's in 1908. Cars became available to middle-class families, who quickly proceeded to use them on vacations. By the 1920s, as lodging facilities and gas stations proliferated across the country, the image of the American

The Wonder Gift Shop, Newcomb, early 1920s. Eastern Illustrating & Publishing Co. postcard. P. 16271.

nuclear family, touring their country by car, had become a national institution.[47]

In the Adirondacks the emergence of a newly mobile vacationing class demanded a new look at the recreational uses of the Forest Preserve. The state conservation bureaucracy had been slowly expanding ever since the creation of the Forest Commission in 1885, and it began to see its chief function as popularizing and facilitating public use of state land. This was a marked change from its earlier posture, which had been one of general indifference to recreation and overt hostility to forever wild; for years, state foresters wanted to log state land, but after World War I, they suddenly showed significant interest in recreation.

During the first thirty years of the Forest Preserve, not a single new trail was marked by the state, not a lean-to or fireplace built, not a map or brochure published. In fact absolutely nothing was done by the state "to make this big vacation country more accessible, more interesting, more usable, and better known to those whose property it is."[48] This began to change in 1917 when the Conservation Commission, the successor agency to the Forest Commission, began marking trails to firetower summits. Tellingly, these trails began at points on highways where cars could be parked. Within two years, over twenty thousand hikers a summer were being greeted—and lectured on the need to prevent forest fires—by the fire observers. In 1920 the Conservation Commission opened roadside campgrounds designed exclusively for tourists traveling in cars. At the same time the state was ecouraging wilderness camping and issuing "Recreation Circulars," all this to respond to the increasing numbers of a new kind of tourist in the Adirondacks.[49]

The future for the Adirondacks and the people who lived there was clear. By 1920 the regional economy was becoming increasingly dependent on tourist dollars. The Conservation Commission, which saw its role in this development more as a Chamber of Commerce than as a state agency charged with protecting a natural resource, was well aware of this:

> Everywhere throughout the Forest Preserve region in both the Adirondacks and Catskills, the use of this great vacation ground is increasing at a tremendous rate, until now the most important business of the whole region is that of caring for vacationists. More money is invested in hotel and other properties, more people are employed, more wages are paid, and the annual turnover is greater, than in the entire lumber business, which once figured as the most important activity of the mountains. State roads and automobiles are largely responsible for this increase in the number of vacationists. As the State-built roads have brought vacationists to the threshold of the Forest Preserve, the Commission feels that it is now incumbent upon the State to receive them, make them welcome, and extend that assistance which will make vacations more profitable and enjoyable.[50]

The state developed facilities for tourists at the same time that new private businesses were appearing. By the 1920s, clusters or "courts" of cabins were providing accommodations for auto-tourists at towns throughout the Adirondacks.[51] For families unwilling or unable to pay for indoor lodging, camping was becoming an American obsession. Tourism historian John Jakle writes that after World War I tens of thou-

sands of American families pointed their cars to the highway, spending
their nights along the road or at designated campgrounds. Car camping satisfied a paradoxical pair of cultural impulses: it simultaneously
took a family back to nature and employed the latest in American
technology.[52]

One important consequence of the state's new-found commitment
to expanding recreational opportunities was its acknowledgment that
much of the prime hiking and camping territory in the Adirondacks remained posted and off limits to the public. Only a few years before, private preserves were viewed as appropriate stewards of Adirondack
forests, but with the remarkable surge in recreation of the early twentieth century, even this began to change. A bond issue with money ear-
marked for Forest Preserve acquisition was passed in 1916.

Although the Conservation Commission tried whenever possible to
negotiate purchase with willing sellers, it reserved the option of con-
demnation through eminent-domain proceedings. In 1919 the state acquired over 97,000 acres in the Adirondacks. These were mostly in the
high peaks, where lands that had been selectively logged once for lumber were threatened with ruinous pulpwood logging high on steep and
fragile slopes. As the Commissioners wrote in their annual report, jus-
tifying the high price paid for these lands, which included the summits
of mounts Marcy and Seward, "they are the forests of greatest value to
the people of the State of New York as protection forests for the sources
of some of the largest rivers, and as vacation grounds, including within
their boundaries the most beautiful and impressive scenery of the Empire State."[53]

The tilt of the state toward mass public recreational use of the
Adirondacks did not sit well with some of the members of elite clubs
and preserves. So long as the state managed the Forest Preserve in a
fashion calculated to protect watershed and prevent fires, the wealthy
members of these clubs saw the Conservation Commission as their ally
in their own efforts to enjoy their retreats in isolated splendor, but the
age of the automobile, with its democratization of access to the mountains set the state off in a new and unanticipated direction.

Arthur H. Masten expressed clearly the hostility of the old guard to
the arrival of people it considered unwelcome in the Adirondacks and
incapable of appropriate behavior. To Masten, the newcomers be-

longed more at Coney Island than in the Adirondacks; in his view (no doubt jaundiced by class prejudice), they littered, shot deer illegally, fished out the ponds, and left their campfires dangerously unattended. Perhaps part of Masten's pique derived from the fact that the state had exercised its right of eminent domain to condemn Tahawus Club lands around Lake Colden and add them to the Forest Preserve.[54] The notion that some people, because of birth, education, or wealth, "belong" in nature while others do not has seldom been absent from the Adirondack narrative.

What the ascendancy of the tourist economy and the concomitant expansion of the state conservation bureaucracy meant to the year-round residents is hard to say with precision. In many ways, although the local economy depended on dollars left in the Adirondacks by tourists or spent by state employees, people went about their daily lives in much the same way that small-town Americans were doing coast to coast. Life in Wells during the first decades of the twentieth century was portrayed by the Stanyon sisters in a way that would have

Village of St. Regis Falls, ca. 1912. Photograph by Harry M. Beach. P. 2202.

been familiar to millions of other Americans. This was small-town American life: Wells had a hardwood mill and a glove factory, where many of the men worked; a high school, where the girls studied Latin; and a Methodist church, where the Stanyons worshipped regularly every Sunday. Wells also boasted a general store, more churches, a dry goods store, an undertaker, a doctor and clinic, a weekly newspaper, a drug store, two hotels, three grocery stores, and two cemeteries. A Mrs. Perry "sold ladies' hats in one of her upstairs rooms."[55] In short, Wells was much more similar to than it was different from towns all over America.

Like most rural people, the Stanyon family lived in a house without plumbing or electricity. They heated the first floor with a wood stove and used kerosene lamps for light. Washing clothes was arduous, occupying both parents for two days of every week. The automobile revolutionized their lives just as it had those of other Americans and not just by bringing more tourists to Hamilton County; a memorable event for the Stanyon sisters was their father's purchase of a Model T Ford. After that, they could go to Gloversville to shop for clothes.[56]

Viewed in the light of later twentieth-century history, life in Adirondack towns was remembered as almost idyllic in its simplicity and sense of community. In the northern Adirondacks, Ralph Hoy recalled, neighbors always "looked after each other. . . . [A]s a community it was a grand place to grow up." Self-reliance was a way of life. Families raised their own vegetables for canning, stored potatoes and root vegetables in the cellar, made their own cider, and cut their own firewood.[57] Probably this image of such a perfect mix of self-reliance and neighborliness owes as much to the nostalgia that inevitably colors memory as to the reality of Adirondack town life, which undoubtedly had its share of conflict and woe, illustrated, for example, by recollections of brawling loggers in Blue Mountain Lake.

As it had been for their fathers and mothers, life for early twentieth-century Adirondackers was in many ways an outdoor life. Hunting and fishing were both recreation and a source of food. Ralph Hoy learned to hunt as a young boy, picking up "the woods lore that comes in handy when you are living off the woods or in the woods."[58] And the skill with which local people could bag a deer or land a trout was part of the way year-round residents distinguished themselves from the tourists they put up with all summer. Lester Stanton penned a series of verse reminiscences about his boyhood. In one, he recalled the "City Folks," who wondered how people got along without well-stocked food markets. Whenever his family needed meat, Stanton wrote, his father would take down his Winchester or a shotgun and head for the woods.

> If we don't have the cash for a T-bone steak,
> There's the game in the forest and fish in the lake.[59]

Despite the ways in which local life pursued its own rhythms, the tourist culture was omnipresent and unavoidable. Stanton recalled, "The whole Adirondack Mountains, 'The North Woods,' was one great summer resort. Vacationers left home from many cities for their own Summer cottages, or to some hotel. . . . Natives in the mountains were used to the annual influx of the Summer People. In fact, not only our village, Blue Mountain Lake, but every other place was almost entirely involved with them." For a little boy, the tourist trade could mean treats not otherwise available: Stanton worked as a messenger boy in the 1890s and was paid in chocolate sodas at the Prospect House, Blue Mountain Lake's great luxury hotel.[60]

The emergence of the state conservation bureaucracy and the protection of land in the Forest Preserve were new elements in the Adirondack picture. Like the growth of the tourist economy, they were changes that the year-round residents had to get accustomed to. Forests where locals had cut firewood or had logged for personal use were now declared "forever wild," and local guides were miffed when small hunting camps built on state land had to be removed.[61] Hunting led to an especially freighted encounter between old ways and new. Along with the Forest Preserve and the state conservation bureaucracy created to manage it came a series of game laws. Though such laws had been on the books since the eighteenth century, they were universally ignored in the Adirondacks—by tourist and local alike—until the era of conservation beginning in the 1880s. By the early twentieth century, game laws, nearly all concerned with seasons and limits for hunting white-tailed deer, were in place for all New York and were enforced in the Adirondacks by game wardens, who were occasionally obligated to arrest their neighbors—a situation loaded with dangerous potential.

In a poem by Jeanne Robert Foster, a game warden laments, "It's not the city sports, But folks right here who give me trouble." The warden goes on to report that while trying to stop some local men out jack-lighting illegally, he was fired upon. The bullet pierced his hat and "creased my head; I bled a bit." The next day, he finds a fresh killed haunch of venison at his front door with a note promising more of the same if he will "just keep your nose off Minnie Pond." He declines the offer, vowing to risk his life to "get those jackers."[62]

Tourist hunters undoubtedly hunted out of season as well, but the deer laws at this time were generally calculated by the legislature to make hunting legal during the late summer, when tourists were most likely to be in the Adirondacks, and illegal during the rest of the year, when the year-round residents had the woods to themselves. In Adirondack towns the game laws were widely seen as a state-sponsored intrusion into the daily lives of local hunters and a violation of their traditional reliance on the forest for food.[63] Game laws symbolized the changes introduced by the state's determination to protect the Adirondacks as nature for all New Yorkers. That this would in the long run help to bring downstate dollars into the local economy, spent by tourists who came to the Adirondacks for recreation, was not immediately apparent.

On the other hand, Forest Preserve lands were open to all. As was definitely not the case on the posted private lands, locals could hunt and fish, at least in season, on the Forest Preserve, continuing, at certain times of the year, their tradition of feeding their families with fish and game secured outside the cash economy. This allowed for the maintenance, though perhaps not with the degree of freedom most people would have preferred, of old ways under siege by the dramatic innovations enforced by modern tourism and corporate logging. The Forest Preserve, for locals no less than for tourists, was where some of the traditions of the frontier might persist, where both locals and transients might forestall the ravages of modernity.

Jeanne Robert Foster wrote poignantly of this in a poem entitled "State Land," where she described the benefits of having land in the Forest Preserve. A father is asked by his sons why he sold a timber lot to the state, rather than logging it for profit. He explains that dedicating this land to wilderness is his way of resisting

the tide of what to me is strange.
. . . .
I have watched the spoilers come and take away
So much I hardly know my township here.
I gave the mountainside to keep it wild,
Free for the life that it has had so long.

. . . .
I have looked down on the havoc of the years,
Dude ranches sprawling where the farmhouse stood.
I have no quarrel with what you call "our times,"
But my heart spoke: I must preserve this land.[64]

7

"The Roads Are Filled with Interest"

In the 1920s America truly surrendered itself to the horseless carriage. Improved roads, cheap gasoline, and widespread ownership of ever more affordable cars encouraged what quickly became the American love affair with the automobile.[1] Simultaneously, and to a large extent because of the dramatically increased mobility provided by the family car, America experienced yet another boom in outdoor recreation, and it was only to be expected that the Adirondacks would become an even more popular destination for vacationing families.

In an age when the automobile journey itself became an important part of the vacation experience, the rapidly expanding mileage of paved highways and scenic roadsides in the Adirondacks made the region all the more appealing to a nation infatuated with driving. As a writer for *Motordom* magazine, the publicity organ of the New York State Automobile Association, observed, "To whatever goal in the Adirondacks one may be seeking, the approach roads are filled with interest, running as they do constantly amid forest, mountain and lake scenes. Unlike other summer centers, the journey en route is not merely a matter of 'getting there'—it is something worth seeing in itself."[2]

The Adirondacks, observed the Conservation Commissioners in 1931, drew "a constantly increasing stream of tourists and campers in search of rest, health and recreation."[3] Or, as *Motordom* put it that same year, "Travelers from all over the world come to the Adirondacks, choosing one or another of the favorite spots for their rest and recreation. Some go to the secluded places, others to the great summer

*Accommodations and parking for auto-tourists at Blue Mountain Lake, 1940s.
P. 35918.*

colonies, but each finds in this great out of doors paradise the things
that bring the fullest health and most joyous recreation."[4]

The Conservation Commission was enthusiastically promoting public use of the Forest Preserve. In 1923, the Commissioners themselves
toured state facilities in the Adirondacks, found them insufficient to
meet surging demand from automobile tourists, and decided that the
state should begin developing large campsites offering bathrooms and
reliable water. Across the Adirondacks, existing campsites were enlarged and new ones built; these included, among others, the Sacandaga Public Campsite near Wells, one on the Schroon River near North
Hudson, and campsites at Wilmington Notch and Lewey Lake. These
were used both by families who seldom strayed far from their cars and
those interested in hiking, canoeing, hunting, and fishing in the back
country. Almost immediately, the Commissioners reported that these
facilities were overcrowded and new ones needed.[5]

The development of cheap, relatively lightweight canoes enabled
many people to head into remote country without the guides and
guideboats that had been essential elements of the classic nineteenth-

The state campsite at Fish Creek Ponds near Upper Saranac Lake quickly be-came one of the most popular Adirondack destinations. Postcard by Eastern Il-lustrating and Publishing Co. P. 12790.

century Adirondack camping experience. The canvas canoe has its roots in Maine in the mid-nineteenth century; by the early twentieth, it was sufficiently available and affordable to constitute an important new element in the way people encountered nature in the Adirondacks.[6] The image of the canvas canoe, paddled by tourists of any age, sex, or class became as essentially a part of the Adirondack story as the guideboat, rowed by a professional, hired guide, had been a generation or two earlier. After World War II, the canvas canoe was joined by the aluminum canoe. In 1946 the Grumman Corporation, whose contribution to the war effort had involved manufacturing lightweight airplanes out of aluminum, made over 10,000 aluminum canoes and a year later made more canoes than any other American manufacturer.[7]

Transportation connections provided by railroads, along with the improving highway system, allowed people to plan their own trips, camping with tents on the Forest Preserve or staying at lakeside hotels. The canoe route from Old Forge to Saranac Lake Village, passing up the Fulton Chain, through Raquette Lake, Forked Lake, Long Lake, and Stony Creek Ponds, was reaffirmed as one of the quintessential Adiron-

Aluminum canoes carried camp groups to popular lean-to's. Photograph by James Fynmore. P. 15934.

dack experiences. Train depots at either end and freight cars for canoes made it all possible and easy. Local businesses quickly identified a market, and rental canoes and camping gear became available on virtually every Adirondack lake with public access. At well-used carries, local entrepreneurs with wagons and horses would, for a price, transport canoe and gear from lake to lake. Although local people thus played an important part in making these canoe trips possible, the disappearance of the guide and the consequent reliance of tourists on their own skills in finding their way and establishing campsites constituted a major new twist in the story of Adirondack recreation.[8]

While water-borne recreation steadily grew in popularity, hiking and climbing also staked out a more prominent role. From the very beginnings of Adirondack recreation, the rivers and lakes had excited the most attention, but the appeal of the high peaks was always part of the picture. Spending most of their time on or near the lakes and rivers, both Charles Fenno Hoffman and Joel T. Headley had nonetheless responded to the allure of Mount Marcy. During the Murray era, the

lakes continued to provide the focus of most recreational activity, but
hotels and clubs around Keene Valley and Lake Placid emerged as
busy centers for mountain hiking. The nature that one climbed, often
precisely because it demanded more in the way of stamina and woodcraft, became just as much a part of the Adirondack narrative as the nature across which one rowed a guideboat or paddled a canoe.

The thick forests of the Adirondack high peaks made trail building
difficult, and through most of the nineteenth century, there was little
interest in developing a useful and extensive system of hiking trails. In
the latter decades of the nineteenth century, however, this slowly
changed, and by around 1910, many of the trails enjoyed by today's
climbers in the high peaks had been roughed out.[9] At first, these were
designed haphazardly by guides and climbers based in Keene Valley
and Lake Placid, but at about the same time the state began to build
public campsites, it also committed to developing hiking trails and
other facilities away from the waterways. The first state-built lean-tos,
loosely based on the rough shelters guides had traditionally con-

State lean-to at Marcy Dam, 1920s. P. 15098.

structed for their patrons, appeared on the Feldspar Brook trail to Mount Marcy in 1919.[10]

The combination of new trails and the post World War enthusiasm for the outdoors led to a greatly increased public interest in back country hiking. Among those eagerly seduced by the possibilities for solitude and adventure in the Adirondacks were two teenaged boys whose family summered on Lower Saranac Lake. In 1916 Robert and George Marshall, respectively sixteen and thirteen years old, climbed Ampersand Mountain, their first Adirondack peak. This was the beginning of an Adirondack climbing adventure that resonates to this day. Two

Robert Marshall, Herbert Clark, and George Marshall on summit of Marcy, ca. 1918. P. 61094.

years later, as they looked further afield for climbing opportunities, they were joined by a local guide, Herbert Clark, who had worked for their family for several years.

The Marshalls and Clark perused the then-current topographical maps and decided to identify and climb all the Adirondack summits over 4,000 feet above sea level. This they did, reaching their forty-sixth and last peak—Mount Emmons, a bump on the ridge radiating south from Mount Seward—in 1925. Word of their accomplishment circulated among Adirondack hikers, and it was not long before others set out to duplicate what the Marshalls and Clark had been the first to do. The result was the Adirondack 46-ers, a club of climbing enthusiasts and a sign of the enormous and steadily growing popularity of Adirondack hiking in the twentieth century.[11]

But most tourists, then as now, stayed close to the highways, venturing only a short distance away from the familiar and reassuring comforts of automobile or motel room. The car became a moving parlor, through the windows of which touring families admired the lake and mountain views, stopping for a picnic or eating at a roadside restaurant and spending the night either in a tent they carried or in a motel. Advertisements for diners around the Park periphery encouraged visits from families out for only an afternoon or evening drive.[12]

The idea of the road itself as an attraction for tourists led to the construction of a highway beginning at the village of Wilmington and winding almost to the very summit of Whiteface Mountain. This project required an amendment to the state constitution (because it involved cutting trees on the Forest Preserve), which was approved by voters in 1927 despite opposition from conservationists. In 1935 the eight-mile highway was finished, reaching a point within 300 vertical feet of the summit. Where the Marshall brothers and their disciples might sweat their way to the spectacular views in the remote back country in the high peaks, thousands of auto-tourists were able to pay a low toll and simply drive to the equally stunning panorama available on the summit of Whiteface.[13]

Partly because the Conservation Department was pushing recreation on state land, the public image of the Adirondacks was to a large extent crystallizing around the Forest Preserve. Since the private lands through which these climbers drove to get to trailheads remained mostly forested, and since the forest cover, recovering from the fires

The Whiteface Mountain highway. Photograph by Alfred Santway. P. 27657.

and overcutting of the years around the turn of the century, was in fact improving, the public paid little if any attention to the difference between the Park and the Forest Preserve.

Families in New York City might speak of a vacation in the "Adirondacks," thinking generically of the woods and waters north of the Mohawk River and east of Lake Champlain, but there was more than one "Adirondacks." For most people the word "Adirondack" evoked images of the Forest Preserve, protected by the state constitution and enjoyed by tourists from throughout the country. But there were also the huge private preserves like the Adirondack League Club or the Tahawus Club. There was the enormous acreage controlled by woods-products companies like International Paper. There was the growing number of smaller plots of a few acres, usually on a lake shore or the side of a river, owned by families from outside the region who built cabins for second homes. And there were the Adirondack towns and villages, ranging in size and character from small hamlets like Raquette Lake to larger towns like Saranac Lake or Tupper Lake. The Adirondacks continued to be a varied, complex place.

Throughout the first half of the twentieth century, the status of private lands inside the blue line remained largely unexamined. So long as they were mostly forested, the Adirondacks seemed safe. In an effort to keep the private lands aesthetically appealing to vacationers driving along Adirondack highways, the legislature passed a law in 1924 regulating billboards. This statute declared that no advertising sign could be erected on any land inside the blue line other than that on which the business being advertised was actually conducted. Calculated to protect "the natural beauty of the Adirondack Park," it acknowledged the importance of park-wide issues of aesthetics and naturalness.[14] And these it encouraged, preventing private land owners from selling space along roadsides for billboards hawking hotels and restaurants.

One further indication that state policy makers in Albany were thinking about the Adirondacks as a region, as opposed to promoting recreation on the Forest Preserve, came through expansion of the Park. The original blue line of 1892 enclosed just over 2.8 million acres of private and public land, and during the next century this area was expanded several times to embrace more and more of the forested part of northern New York in which the state considered it had an interest, although, as was repeatedly demonstrated, the reality of what this interest meant remained vague. The first expansion occurred in 1893, when the islands in Lake George were added to the Park.[15]

In 1912, the legislature enlarged the Park by some 1.25 million acres, mostly along the northern and eastern edges, to reach a total of over four million acres. More important, the Park legislation of 1912 addressed a major ambiguity of the original Park law of 1892. This was whether private lands inside the blue line were statutorily considered part of the Park; the 1912 law specifically said that they were. The law paid no attention to the fact that the types of private lands—small lots for houses and businesses in towns, lakeside vacation homes, giant preserves owned and guarded by the wealthy, and equally extensive holdings logged by pulp and lumber companies—were, to say the least, various. While this declaration that lands owned privately were part of a state park bore little significance for the time being, it was a crucial moment in Adirondack history. It prepared the way for the state to show, some six decades later, its understanding that what happened to private land inside the blue line mattered. In 1931, the blue line was extended again, adding another 1.1 million acres to the Park.[16]

During the 1920s and the succeeding decades, the Forest Preserve itself grew as the state slowly acquired important private lands for the public domain. State purchase of private lands was made possible by both legislative appropriation and a series of bond acts; bond acts including funds for enlarging the Forest Preserve were approved by New York voters in 1916 and 1924.[17] By 1950, the Forest Preserve, which had contained just over 681,000 acres at the time of its creation in 1885 (and which included some parcels outside the blue line), had more than tripled in size to over 2.1 million acres.[18]

One way the public was paying attention to private land in the Adirondacks was through the growth of a second-home culture. The freedom provided by the automobile meant that families could come and go when they pleased, slipping up to the Adirondacks for a weekend, staying for a month in the summer or a week at Christmas. Middle-class travelers who spent their first night in the Adirondacks at a state campsite or a roadside motor court, perhaps aware that wealthy families were rusticating comfortably at the great camps, wanted their own private corner of New York's remaining wild country.

In 1916 logging baron Ferris Meigs began developing a colony of vacation homes on Santa Clara Lumber Company property on Big Wolf Lake near Tupper Lake. Throughout the Adirondacks similar clusters of second homes followed. Raquette Lake, Long Lake, the Saranacs, the St. Regis lakes, the Fulton Chain—these and hundreds of miles of lake or river shore privately owned and accessible by car, and some accessible only by boat, entered a slow process of subdivision and development.[19] Lake shores that had been completely forested or punctuated only rarely by cabins or more elaborate great camps began to present a monotonous profile of vacation homes, docks, and boat houses to passing canoeists.

The appeal of owning one's own lot in the Adirondacks arose from both the wish to get back to nature privately, unmolested by the crowds of strangers at the public campsites, and the prospect of profiting from a good investment. In 1924 a developer on Otter Lake, pointing out that the completion of a state-constructed paved road established accessibility, trumpeted the benefits of his lots: "Why not buy a lot in this restricted section of Otter Lake, readily accessible by auto or train and where property values have increased from 100 per cent to 1,000 per cent within the last five years. . . . Drive up and let us show you these

*These illustrations from a 1919 advertising booklet
for a second-home development near Old Forge
typify the early appeal to middle-class buyers.
Adirondack Museum Library.*

lots."[20] In the 1930s Lewis County realtor Charles Z. Mihalyi circulated
a "Million Dollar Real Estate Catalog," offering hundreds of "summer
resort properties, cottages and camp sites" on lakes and rivers throughout the Adirondacks.[21]

   Promotions like these typified the land-boom hucksterism that has
been a thriving part of Adirondack culture ever since the time of
Ebenezer Emmons. It acquired a relatively new face after World War I
in the guise of vacation-home development, which brought together
major, perhaps contradictory threads of the Adirondack story: the lure

of nature for recreation and personal redemption, the appeal of nature to a large constituency financially able to reach and enjoy it, the wish to appreciate nature away from the crowds of other people attracted by the same nature, and the desire to make a profit exploiting nature. The ineluctable conundrum of the second-home phenomenon—at what point does the number of second homes irretrievably efface the nature or diminish the experience of nature that appealed to people in the first place?—has been an increasingly pressing and contentious issue.

For the time being, the threat posed by vacation homes to the integrity of the Adirondack landscape seemed remote. A more immediate menace came in the form of various efforts to dilute the strictures

of the forever-wild provision of the state constitution. The 1927 refer-
endum on the Whiteface highway was but one of several assaults on
the Forest Preserve in this period. This was quickly followed by de-
signs on the Forest Preserve emanating from the organizers of the 1932
Winter Olympic Games scheduled for Lake Placid. In 1929 an Essex
County Assemblyman maneuvered a bill through the legislature permitting the construction of a bobsled run on state land. The Association
for the Protection of the Adirondacks identified this as a foot in the
door for all sorts of unacceptable mischief and resolved to take the matter to court.

The case went first to the Appellate Division in Albany, where Justice Harold J. Hinman, agreeing with the Association's strict interpre-
tation of forever wild, issued an opinion that ever since has helped to
steer the debate over what level of manipulation of the Forest Preserve
the constitution allows:

> We must preserve it in its wild nature, its trees, its rocks, its streams. It
> was to be a great resort for the free use of the people, but it was made a
> wild resort in which nature is given free rein. Its uses for health and plea-
> sure must not be inconsistent with its preservation as forest lands in a
> wild state. It must always retain the character of a wilderness.[22]

In Justice Hinman's view any activity that violated this definition of
how the Forest Preserve should be managed, including cutting trees for
a bobsled run, required an amendment to the constitution. This is exactly what had happened in 1927 with the Whiteface highway, and it
reoccurred in 1941, when New York voters approved a constitutional
amendment permitting the state to cut trees to build ski slopes on Forest Preserve land on Whiteface. The Conservation Department took the
bobsled case to the New York State Court of Appeals, which affirmed
the lower court ("The Adirondack Park was to be preserved, not destroyed"), and the Olympic planners opted to accept an easement
arrangement with the Lake Placid Club and build the bobsled run on
private land.[23]

The bobsled case was but one battle among many as the state conservation bureaucracy throughout the decades of mid-century tried to
expand its authority to develop and manage the Forest Preserve. It was
an ideological struggle over how the publicly owned nature of the

The bobsled run, built, after contentious litigation, on private land.

Adirondacks was to be defined and how it was to be used. Representatives of the Association for the Protection of the Adirondacks and other preservationists argued that the constitution said just what it meant: the language of the clause "nor shall the timber thereon be sold, removed or destroyed" unambiguously said that trees on state land could not be cut.

The only exceptions, constructed mostly through opinions issued by state attorneys general, were minimal cutting for primitive recreational purposes, as in the case of campsites (and even here strict constitutionalists maintained that this was not legal), and for protection of the forest from fire, as with safely sited lean-tos and fireplaces.[24] These rulings did not prevent an almost continual effort from various factions in the Conservation Department to test the limits of the constitution with plans for greatly expanded public campsites and an extensive system of dirt roads for fire trucks.[25]

In the dispute over the constitutionality of the truck trails, waged in the 1930s, one of the most articulate, forceful voices for strict protection

of the Forest Preserve was that of Robert Marshall, who had moved
from his adolescent enthusiasm for Adirondack peak bagging to a life-
long commitment to the American wilderness. In addition to earning a
Ph. D. in Plant Physiology from Johns Hopkins, he worked in the
United States Forest Service, helped found the Wilderness Society,
wrote several books and dozens of articles on America's remaining
wilderness, and never failed to come to the defense of his beloved
Adirondacks.[26]

On the truck trails, however, which Marshall and others considered
unnecessary intrusions in the wilderness that would inevitably be
opened up to public use, Marshall was unable to persuade the Association for the Protection of the Adirondacks to take the Conservation
Department to court. But his efforts made a compelling case for the importance of maintaining the constitutional safeguards for the Forest
Preserve. The arguments advanced for the sanctity of the Forest Preserve, for its recreational and spiritual value in a rapidly modernizing
country, helped to inspire a dedicated corps of wilderness advocates
who worked tirelessly to defend the forever-wild provision.[27]

When a new state constitution was proposed in 1938, efforts to dilute the protections of Article VII, Section 7 (which became Article XIV,
Section 1, in the new document) were unsuccessful. The Convention
Committee charged with examining Forest Preserve issues carefully
studied the recent history of disputes between the Conservation Department and preservationists like Marshall and tried to gauge public
sentiment. What did the people of New York want of their Forest Preserve? Were they content to leave it alone as much as possible, using it
for wilderness recreation, interfering minimally, if at all, with natural
processes? Or did they want further developments like the road up
Whiteface, projects that might allow greater access to and more diverse
uses of the Forest Preserve, but at the expense of the integrity of the forest itself and of the wilderness experience considered so vital by preservationists like Robert Marshall? With the tight language of the 1894
forever-wild provision specifically in mind, the Committee concluded
that the public wanted the Forest Preserve to remain largely undeveloped, with its constitutional protections maintained: "A prepon-
derant public opinion appreciates the wisdom of this section and its
continuation."[28]

The last major effort of the state conservation bureaucracy to find ways around the constitution followed a great windstorm, the Big Blowdown, that swept through the Adirondacks on November 25, 1950. Some or all of the timber was knocked down on over 400,000 acres, including many merchantable trees on state land, and the threat of fire and insect infestation loomed. The Conservation Commission requested and received an opinion from the Attorney General permitting salvage operations and the right to sell dead trees to cover the costs of the cleanup.[29]

With this foot in the door, the Conservation Commission decided to go all the way and ask once and for all whether New Yorkers wanted to maintain the strict, hands-off policy of the constitution. A year after the great storm, the editor of the *Conservationist*, the chief public-relations organ of the Conservation Commission, asked his readers to ponder a series of questions, the main thrust of which was to suggest that New York's Forest Preserve would be much better managed—the wildlife would be more abundant, the state would receive more revenue, the forests would be healthier, recreation opportunities would expand—if the constitutional prohibition on logging were lifted. This initiated a furious response that has been known ever since as the Big Blowup.[30]

The most energetic defender of the forever-wild principle was Paul Schaefer of Schenectady, who wrote eloquently of the need in a modern, bustling state like New York of a place where bulldozers and chain saws were absent. "Today, in both the Adirondacks and the Catskills," observed Schaefer, "we have mountain, lake and river regions where primitive conditions have returned and where one can walk among forest giants and sense that tranquillity obtainable only in the wild forest, away from the sights and sounds and hustle of this mechanized civilization." Rather than weaken the constitution, wrote Schaefer, what New York needed was more land similarly protected for people "attracted to these magnificent regions by their wild forest character, an element which is vanishing from the American landscape with appalling rapidity."[31] Arguments like these won the day, and, reluctantly, the conservation bureaucracy abandoned its half-century effort to change the constitution.

But the constitution protected only the Forest Preserve. The need for region-wide conservation to keep the Adirondack region the kind of nature that New Yorkers apparently wanted surfaced in a controversy surrounding the plans of the Black River Regulating District to dam the South Branch of the Moose River. First proposed in 1919, the dam remained an engineer's dream until after World War II, when the Regulating District's aggressive effort to see it built resulted in a major environmental brawl and an alliance between defenders of the Forest Preserve and private land owners.

Although the stated purpose of the dam was to control flooding outside the Park, the generation of hydroelectric power for business and municipal use was a generally well understood outcome. The dam, moreover, would have required the flooding of several thousand acres of both public and private land inside the blue line. Climaxing in 1955, the battle eventually involved the legislature, the governor, the courts, and three separate attempts to amend the New York constitution. The dam was not built. In addition to demonstrating the ability of citizen environmentalists, led by Paul Schaefer, to stand up to and defeat the combined might of government bureaucracy and business, this struggle showed that what happened to private land had implications for the entire region.[32]

For the most part what was happening on private land was that it was being logged. But, slowly, the attitudes of forest land owners were evolving away from the cut-and-run mentality that had dominated Adirondack logging in the nineteenth century. The abuses—and the reaction against them—that led to the conservation activity of the 1880s and '90s, coupled with the catastrophic fires of the early twentieth century, gradually led to improved forestry practices. As early as the 1890s, Gifford Pinchot, the first American to work as an academically trained, scientific forester, was arguing for conservative cutting that could both protect the resource and provide profits and jobs. Hired by millionaire W. Seward Webb to design a logging plan for the 40,000 acre Nehasane Park in the western Adirondacks, Pinchot studied the land and its forest and wrote up a detailed proposal for a harvest that would save young growth and minimize the fire hazard.[33]

It was many decades before such an attitude could be said to characterize Adirondack logging in general, although as early as 1912 the New York legislature empowered state foresters to inspect logging operations on private land and advise the owner on appropriate management and harvest. In 1923, forester A. B. Recknagel, in a book on the forests of New York state, observed that the state was at a crossroads: the case for conservative, sustained-yield forestry was well established, but too many loggers ignored it to pursue short-term profits.[34] By mid-century, the argument was still going on.

The problems confronting even a land owner with the best of intentions are well illustrated by the case of the Adirondack League Club. Established in 1890 with an explicitly declared intention to serve as a model of conservative forestry, showing other Adirondack forest owners that forest health, recreation, and scientific logging could peacefully coexist, the League Club encountered decades of internal controversy, unfulfilled expectations, and occasionally sloppy logging. Loggers sometimes cut more than their contracts stipulated or left a scarred landscape. And when prices for lumber or pulpwood were high and money was needed for maintenance of Club facilities, paying taxes, or retiring debts, there was a temptation to let market forces rather than forest health dictate the harvesting policy.[35]

Between World War I and 1950, actual practices in the Adirondack logging industry experienced major changes, which had profound implications for local life, both in the nature and availability of work and in the daily lives of Adirondack people. The internal combustion engine, which in the form of the automobile had revolutionized tourism, had a similarly profound impact on logging. Trucks and tractors, which began chugging about in Adirondack forests in significant numbers in the 1920s, completely altered the nature of Adirondack logging. The development of the chainsaw was equally important. By 1950, the patterns of seasons and work that had prevailed in the age of the horse had largely disappeared.[36]

Before the gasoline engine arrived, all heavy logging work was done with draft horses, which were used to skid logs from stump to loading station and to haul wagon loads of logs either to a banking ground or to a logging railroad. The arrival of gasoline-powered trucks and tractors meant that moving logs became much easier and was not restricted to the winter when smooth, iced roads were best for horse-drawn wagons or sleds. It also meant that loggers could move relatively quickly back and forth between home and the woods.

In the age of the horse, loggers lived in logging camps deep in the woods, often spending the entire winter there, cutting, skidding, and banking logs for the spring river drives. Once roads were built for trucks, loggers could commute between village and work. Finally, the combination of trucks, tractors, and the new chain saws meant that fewer loggers were needed. In 1915 some one hundred and fifty Adirondack logging camps employed between seven and eight thousand people. During the Great Depression, Adirondack logging suffered along with the rest of the country, and only about twenty camps were operating. Even as the industry recovered, moreover, changes in technology meant that fewer loggers were working and living in camps: in 1940 sixty camps provided work for three thousand loggers and their support crews.[37]

The ascendancy of the truck and tractor also meant the end of Adirondack river drives. Getting logs from stump to mill was quicker and cheaper with trucks, and rivers carried fewer and fewer logs out of the region. The last drive on the Moose River occurred in 1948, while the last logs went down the Hudson in 1950.[38] The switch from river to truck meant changes in harvesting as well. Only softwood logs, which float well, left the Adirondacks via the rivers; hardwoods were left alone. But trucks could carry anything, and hardwoods, which had been mostly ignored by loggers, except for local uses like charcoal or heating fuel, were harvested by the thousands of cords.[39]

Changes in the logging industry affected local laborers and their work, often negatively, and most logging companies continued to pay little heed to human welfare issues like consistent wages, benefits, retirement, and safety. Employers often conspired among themselves to keep wages low. An industry with high rates of accidents and turnover, logging had difficulty attracting younger workers. Yet the tradition of an absence of labor strife in Adirondack logging persisted; discontent and hardship did not lead to the organization of a union.[40]

Trends in Adirondack logging indicated how the Adirondacks was increasingly part of the national economy and culture. The other major Adirondack industry, tourism, was also merging into the larger culture. At the Higby family's Big Moose resort, changing tastes demanded constant attention. Tourists had once been content with wooden bunks, straw mattresses, a "thunder jug" under the bed or a privy out back, and no light other than a candle. By the 1920s, even in a moderately

Logjam on the Moose River, 1940s. Photograph by James Fynmore. P. 15904.

priced establishment, they expected box springs, private bathrooms and electric lights. At around the time of World War I, many hotels were generating their own electricity with small, independent plants; regional utilities like Niagara Mohawk took over in the early 30s.[41]

It was all part of a process whereby life for Adirondackers and their tourist clients was a mix of the modern and the traditional. The Higbys tapped maple trees for syrup, hunted and fished for food and recreation, and trudged through the winter woods on homemade snowshoes. During the same years, they added dance bands and tennis courts to their resort and promoted the construction of golf courses. Deep in the woods, on remote Big Moose Lake, one encountered the sights and sounds of the Roaring Twenties: "jazz, bobbed hair, and short skirts." Tourists interested in overnight backpacking trips were willing to sleep on the ground with one blanket; they also wanted a golf course and a cocktail lounge. In houses across the Adirondacks, people who only a few years earlier seldom read a paper less than three days old tuned in their radios for the evening news, and they talked to one another on the telephone exchanges that were widespread by the 1920s.[42]

Minnie Stanyon remembered the installation of the first phones in Speculator; the original central office was located in a private home, where the mistress of the house and her daughters operated the switchboard.[43] Telephones connected house to house and region to nation and symbolized how the central Adirondacks was both a part of a busily modernizing, technologically sophisticated nation and a rural culture holding on to its own traditions and idiosyncrasies. Roy Higby recalled that for people stuck in isolated homes during bad weather the telephone became a much-appreciated source of entertainment. In the days of rural exchanges, everyone shared lines with the rest of the village and "listening in on telephone conversations was the vogue": when gossip got out of hand, "it resulted in some rather unhappy situations."[44] In Elizabethtown, listening to someone else's phone conversation was known as "rubbering in."[45]

In the 1920s, another national issue, Prohibition, became part of the Adirondack story. Route 9, running from Plattsburgh to Albany, was known as the "Rum Trail," as bootleggers ran Canadian whisky from Quebec to downstate New York along the Lake Champlain corridor. To avoid a trap routinely set up by State Police near Pok-O-Moonshine Mountain, rum-runners cut over from Keeseville to Ausable Forks and rejoined route 9 below Elizabethtown. But the Police quickly caught on to this stratagem and moved their traps from place to place.

It was hardly a picturesque affair. In 1924, for example, at North Hudson, State Police had just stopped four cars traveling together when a Cadillac approached. Its driver tried to turn around, but one of the officers put a bullet in its gas tank. After stopping yet another vehicle, the policemen found themselves surrounded by an angry crowd, which began snatching beer bottles. Then one bystander leapt into a seized truck and roared away, while the rest of the crowd, armed with loaded revolvers, moved in on the outnumbered cops and liberated the remaining vehicles. No one was shot, but it was a day of humiliation for the police.[46]

Prohibition appears to have had little effect on local hotels and inns. At Big Moose Lake, recalled Roy Higby, "Prohibition was in force, but there was just as much drinking as ever." Roy always kept a supply of Canadian ale on hand. When he bought the ale from a local bootlegger, it was usually wrapped in "wet and mouldy cloth feed bags." Canadian dealers dropped bags with bottles of ale in them into the St. Lawrence River at a point where the current would steer them to the New York side; there they were picked up for distribution.[47] Sam Spain, who ran a hotel near Benson in St. Lawrence County, made his own liquor, a product of such high quality that it acquired a state-wide reputation.[48]

The era of Prohibition and flappers, which had nearly as much impact on the Adirondacks as in the cities and was a period of growth and development in local tourism, was followed by the lean years of the Depression. As it was on rural cultures throughout the country, the Depression was hard on the Adirondacks. The tourist economy depended on outside cash, and families in the eastern cities that typically supplied the tourists were themselves suffering. Despite continuing use of state campsites by auto-tourists, the economy floundered, as family vacations, especially those spent at a hotel or resort, became a luxury that many could no longer afford. Hoping both to lure to the central Adirondacks those families still able to travel and to provide employment for local workers, the Hamilton County Board of Supervisors put county money into an elaborate series of public recreation facilities. Bonds were approved to finance toboggan runs, ski jumps, town parks, beaches, and water impoundments. Public relief funds were annually exhausted, and genuine deprivation and hardship prevailed throughout the county, despite the arrival of federal assistance in the form of the Civilian Conservation Corps and the Works Projects Administration.[49]

It was more than the tourist economy that suffered. Those parts of the Adirondacks directly tied to the nexus of American industry and commerce underwent wrenching convulsions. International Paper Corporation, for example, supported a flourishing town at Piercefield Falls on the Raquette River, a few miles west of Tupper Lake. There a population that peaked at nearly a thousand people enjoyed the amenities of two churches, a modern school, a stylish hotel, and a community center which housed a movie theater, a dance hall, and a bowling alley. In 1933, International Paper suddenly shut down its Piercefield operations, and the town was devastated. People moved

Town of Piercefield, in prosperous times. Photograph by Harry M. Beach.
P. 2626.

away, houses were razed, churches closed, and the population shrank
to less than half of its pre-Depression level.[50]

But Adirondack traditions of community and neighborliness helped
people to struggle on. At Big Moose, people "worked together. . . . We
had days when a group of us would take our teams, axes, and saws to
cut and haul a supply of wood to some friend whose supply was exhausted and who could not afford to buy fuel. Another time we would
collect food and take it to some needy family."[51] Living off the land
helped many families; there were venison and berries in the woods,
and Adirondackers depended on wild food to keep their children fed
and to trade or sell in the local economy.[52] As was the case through
most of the country, it was only with the beginning of World War II
that the crisis atmosphere of the Depression came to an end in the
Adirondacks.[53]

After World War II, with the memories of the Depression gradually
fading and with yet another boom in outdoor recreation beginning, the
Adirondacks entered the present era. The first half of the twentieth cen-

Haying near Indian Lake. Local agriculture persisted through the Great Depression, providing both food and jobs. P. 60418.

tury lacked dramatic events like the rush to the wilderness of Murray's Fools or the momentous conservation measures of 1885 or 1892. It was, rather, an era of consolidation and gradual change. By 1950 the Adirondack Park was known as a place of nature set aside by the people of New York. It was a major tourist destination, with a Forest Preserve managed by a state bureaucracy. Surrounding the Forest Preserve, and still largely ignored by the cultural mechanisms that defined the region's meaning in the popular mind, were the private forest lands.

And interspersed among the publicly and privately owned forests were the towns and villages where, at mid-century, roughly 100,000 people lived. For these people, living in the Adirondacks was a complicated affair. They lived in a place that was in many ways profoundly different from the places where the tourists they saw every summer lived; many Adirondackers could literally step out the back door in deer season and bag the winter's venison. At the same time, as they were across the country, regional distinctions, especially those surviving in rural areas, were slowly eroding as the national culture tended toward homogenization and uniformity. In addition to living among scenes of spectacular mountains and crystalline lakes, Adirondackers watched television, attended public schools with curricula established by the state, and endured the same economic uncertainties well understood by working- and middle-class Americans from coast to coast.

The Adirondacks offered a landscape in a natural condition rare in the eastern United States; in much of the region, the forest at mid-century, recovering from fires and irresponsible overcutting, was in better shape than it had been only fifty years earlier. And the Adirondacks had a variety of constituencies intensely interested in the region's future—from preservationists who wanted to maintain and extend protections, to local businessmen trying to support their families and entrepreneurs looking for a way to make a quick buck. As always, people constructed meanings of the land and what it was good for out of their own experiences and needs. A Tupper Lake lumberjack, a 46-er from Troy, an affluent member of the Association for the Protection of the Adirondacks, a restaurant owner in Warrensburg, a deer hunter from Syracuse—these and many others knew and appreciated the Adirondack Park. But, outside a shared knowledge of the location of the blue line, could they ever agree on what this place was?

8

"A Crisis Looms"

Recent Adirondack history has been a series of conflicts, all revolving around disputes over the best way to protect, use, or enjoy the Adirondack landscape. Profoundly different visions of what the Adirondack Park should be have led to rancorous debates in the New York legislature, a sense of beleaguered isolation among many year-round residents, and even violence. Development, property-rights, and business interests have lined up against environmentalists—in the courts, in the legislature, and in the arena of public opinion—to determine the future of the Adirondacks. Against this political backdrop, Adirondackers go about their daily lives, sharing in the national culture of work, play, and family and simultaneously living in and loving a unique region with very specific opportunities and challenges.

The same dilemma that first appeared a century and a half ago in the reports of Ebenezer Emmons continues to dog New York's efforts to understand and appreciate the Adirondacks: is this a place of nature to be treasured and protected for its difference from the cultivated, urbanized eastern United States? Should it be statutorily *kept* different— even if this means challenging the almost sacred doctrine, subscribed to by many Americans, that people can do whatever they want with private property? Or is this a region like all others, subject to and eventually to be governed by the same pressures for landscape change, for the replacement of nature by culture, that have characterized so much of the history of the American land?

The Adirondack conflicts of recent years have been the inevitable result of the failures of the conservation legislation of the 1880s and '90s.

159

Contemporary conservationists, politicians, business interests, nature-lovers—these and all people concerned about the present and future status of the Adirondacks—have been forced to wrestle with two stubborn legacies of 1892 and 1894. When the Park was established, little notice was paid to the fact that people lived here. And after constitutional protection was granted to the Forest Preserve, the idea of a contiguous Park began to recede. It was left to the late twentieth century to address the need to think about the Adirondacks as one region, a region that over 125,000 people now call home.

As it had been for most of the twentieth century, the automobile was a primary agent in pushing New Yorkers to face the social and economic forces converging on the Adirondacks. After World War II, the nearly complete domination of the Adirondack economy by auto-tourism led to the appearance of strange new constructions on the local landscape. Where the wilderness and scenery of the Adirondacks had been sufficient to attract tourists and vacationers throughout the nineteenth and early twentieth centuries, beginning around mid-century, for many (but hardly all) Americans, nature was no longer enough. Individual entrepreneurs, corporations, and local chambers of commerce competed with one another to dream up tourist attractions—theme parks, amusements, and consumer palaces—designed to lure tourists and their dollars.

In 1949 New York City businessman Julian Reiss opened Santa's Workshop on a slope of Whiteface Mountain near Wilmington. The first of a rapidly built succession of such tourist attractions—places conceived and constructed with no purpose other than to provide a destination for vacationers on the move—Santa's Workshop made only the most tenuous stab at a connection with the Adirondack landscape. American children grow up hearing that Santa Claus lives at the North Pole, and the community of "North Pole" that Reiss designed for Whiteface occupied a spot further north and generally colder than were the homes of most of his visitors.[1]

Similar concoctions popped up across the Adirondacks. In 1952 Frontier Land in North Hudson opened and was soon entertaining tourists in a mock western town where the stage coach was held up at gun point every day. Animal Land, a commercial zoo in Lake George (which quickly acquired a reputation as the gaudiest, most commercial town in the Adirondacks), offered tourists the opportunity to stroll past cages of exotic animals like kangaroos, ostriches, and alligators. The Land of Make Believe opened in Upper Jay in 1955 (the same year that Disneyland opened in California). Here a former Hollywood set designer, Arto Monaco, achieved the quintessence of mid-century tourist hype, offering, all on a child's scale, plaster-and-wood depictions of fairy tales, including Hansel and Gretel's candy house, Peter's pumpkin, and a cottage for Lewis Carroll's Queen of Hearts. Not to be outflanked, the western Adirondacks entered the fray with the Enchanted Forest in Old Forge in 1956.[2] The predictions of Ebenezer Emmons that the Adirondacks offered promising opportunities to the shrewd capitalist were coming true in new and unexpected ways.

Increasing auto-tourism and the proliferation of destinations led to efforts to attract even more automobiles to the Adirondacks. The 1950s, moreover, was an era of extensive highway construction across the nation, especially of high-speed, limited-access roads, culminating in the Interstate Highway Act of 1956.[3] As part of an effort to secure some of the federal highway funds established by this act, New York voters ap-

Automobile tourism changed the landscape near Lake George, 1960s. Photograph by James Fynmore. P. 21053.

proved an amendment to the New York State Constitution in 1959 permitting the alienation of some 300 acres of the Forest Preserve for a super highway running north from Albany to the Canadian border.[4]

The approval and construction of this highway was a pivotal event in Adirondack history. Conservationists wanted to keep it out of the Park altogether or at least as close to Lake Champlain as possible, while business interests in the central Adirondacks lobbied strenuously for a route west of Schroon Lake; the towns of the central Adirondacks believed their future prosperity depended on easy tourist access. The battle over this highway rekindled a conflict that has been raging in the Adirondack Park ever since. It has generally involved two main camps: business interests promoting one form or another of development—from theme parks to clusters of vacation homes or, more recently, such temples of the consumer culture as a Wal-Mart store in Lake Placid—and conservationists arguing that such developments destroy the natural integrity of the Park.

Where environmental disputes earlier in the twentieth century had largely focused on the Forest Preserve and how best to use or protect it, the public disagreement about the Northway, as this stretch of Interstate 87 came to be known, involved the very idea of the Adirondack Park, and it quickly expanded to a fight over what should happen to private land in the Park. The highway was completed in 1967; it made getting into the region easier and quicker than ever before, and it is part of a combination of events that brought unprecedented pressures on the Adirondacks along with contentious efforts to address these pressures.

The '60s was a decade of a renewed interest in nature. One of the unexpected consequences of this was a startling jump in the number of campers, hikers, and other tourists in the Adirondacks. Thousands signed registers at trailheads, climbers swarmed the high peaks (leading quickly to charges that they were destroying the sense of remoteness that lured them there in the first place), and auto-tourists lined up at the increasingly crowded state campsites. A writer noted in 1962, "One of the most unforgettable spectacles of the Adirondacks is an evening view of Fish Creek Pond Campsite. . . . The site accommodates 600 campers; there may be as many as fifty cars lined up, with people sleeping in them, waiting for vacancies the next morning."[5] In 1968 nearly a million campers spent 2,270,560 "camper days" at the

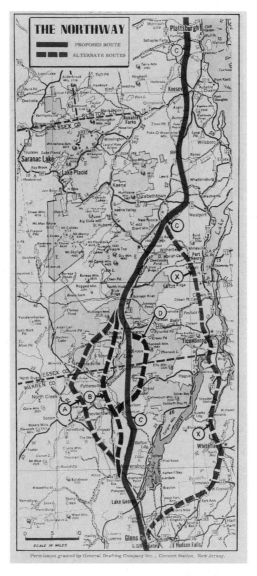

*Planners offered a variety of possible routes for
the Northway; the one marked "B" here was
adopted. Map accompanied brochure presented to
Governor Averall Harriman by State Department
of Public Works. Adirondack Museum Library.*

*When the Northway was finished, it offered easy access to the central Adiron-
dacks and effected dramatic changes on the landscape. Photograph, New York
State Department of Commerce. Adirondack Museum Library.*

state's forty-two large public campgrounds, and thousands were
turned away for lack of space.[6] Many of these hikers and campers decided that the Adirondacks would be a pleasant place to have a summer cottage. There were millions of acres of Adirondack land in private
hands and hundreds of miles of undeveloped lake and river shore. A
new highway penetrating the region and a population both interested
in getting closer to nature and able to afford it added up, ironically, to
a potential environmental catastrophe.

In the 1960s, the Adirondack region, despite a century and a half of
logging, the existence of towns and a tourist-industry infrastructure,
and the gradual merging of the local economy and culture into the national picture, remained largely undeveloped when compared to the
rest of New York. Roughly the size of Vermont, the Adirondack Park

was home to about 100,000 year-round residents. Hamilton County, with a population of under 5,000, was (and is) larger than the state of Rhode Island yet did not have an intersection sufficiently busy to require a stoplight. Of the nearly six million acres of the Park (expanded again, by about 100,000 acres, in 1956), the Forest Preserve, owned and protected by the State of New York, constituted just under forty percent. The remaining three fifths of the Park continued to be controlled by a variety of types of owners, but most of the critical back-country forested lands were owned by a relatively small number of logging companies, private clubs, and wealthy families. Nearly two million acres of largely undeveloped forest land were controlled by only 626 owners. It was clear that decisions made by a small number of individuals and corporations could alter forever the wild character of the Adirondack Park.[7]

And the forested nature of the Park already seemed threatened by theme parks and a host of currently permissible developments. Across Lake Champlain, in Vermont, a booming vacation-home industry was turning open space into concentrations of population that often looked more like Boston suburbs than the traditional New England countryside. Would the completion of the Northway mean that the Adirondack Park was next?[8] The need to find some way to prevent inappropriate development of private lands seemed especially pressing in light of the ineluctable fact that the dream of 1892, state purchase of all the private land inside the blue line, was by now and forever utterly out of reach.

In 1967 a group of planners associated with Laurance S. Rockefeller stunned New Yorkers with a proposal that the Federal Government create in the central Adirondacks an Adirondack Mountains National Park, to be comprised of some 1,120,000 contiguous acres of land from the Forest Preserve and 600,000 acquired from private holdings. The National Park proposal constituted one reaction to the widely shared fear that the special character of the Adirondacks could never be reliably safe so long as the fragmented Forest Preserve was surrounded by millions of acres of private land over which the people of New York had no effective control. In other words, New Yorkers had to begin thinking about the Adirondacks in Park-wide terms: the conceptual split between the Park and the Forest Preserve had to be overcome.[9] The National Park proposal was not taken seriously as an answer to Adirondack problems, but it stimulated further thinking.

The next chapter in this saga began in 1968 when Laurance Rocke-feller's brother, Nelson, the current governor, appointed a board of distinguished citizens to study the Adirondacks, consider what threatened the region's character, and make recommendations for its future. Chaired by millionaire businessman Harold K. Hochschild, whose family had purchased William West Durant's Eagle Nest near Blue Mountain Lake in 1904 and who had founded the Adirondack Museum, the Temporary Study Commission on the Future of the Adirondacks was charged to examine the Adirondack Park as a whole.

Temporary Study Commission Chairman Harold K. Hochschild and New York Governor Nelson Rockefeller at the Adirondack Museum, 1960s.

Other members of the Commission represented various state-wide constituencies, but Adirondack politicians and business interests asserted from the start that their point of view was excluded from the Commission's deliberations. They maintained that the Commission was stacked to reflect the views of wealthy conservationists and that input from ordinary, working-class Adirondackers was not invited.[10]

The most pressing issue the Commission confronted was the possibility that private land owners would convert their holdings from forests to developments of second homes. Governor Rockefeller asked the Commission to address this basic question: "What measures can be taken to assure that development on private land is appropriate and consistent with long-range well-being of the area?"[11] The Commission found that corporate and individual land owners were actively looking for new ways to subdivide and develop their land and that, consequently, a "crisis looms in the Adirondack Park." With the Forest Preserve guarded by Article XIV, the Commission decided that some protection for private land was also needed: "Unguided development on the 3,500,000 acres of private land will destroy the character of the entire Park if immediate action is not taken."[12] The Commission also recommended a further expansion of the Park's boundaries. When this was approved by the legislature in 1973, the Park reached its present size of 5,927,600 acres.[13]

Even the existence of a crisis was disputed by local interests who hoped to maintain the state's laissez-faire attitude toward private lands. Many Adirondackers argued that environmentalists eager to extend state power were exaggerating the threat, painting an unrealistic, nightmarish picture of cluster homes and destruction of the forest. But there was plenty of evidence that developers were eagerly contemplating their options. In June of 1970, for example, the *New York Times* reported that a developer from Toronto, the Great Northern Capital Corporation, was buying 10,000 acres of prime forest northwest of Old Forge in Herkimer County, with plans to dam the North Branch of the Moose River, build marinas and golf courses, and sell off up to 5,000 "leisure properties." This project was Great Northern's second Adirondack venture: in 1967 it began developing a 280-acre site near Indian Lake, where it was selling 300 lots, the smallest only a quarter of an acre. Conservationists, unimpressed by Great Northern's claims of commitment to environmentally sensitive planning, saw developments like these as precisely the reason why land-use controls were essential to saving the Adirondack Park.[14]

Although late twentieth-century government reports lack the stylistic vigor of earlier writers like Hammond and Colvin, the theme remains the same. Where Colvin anxiously condemned the "chopping and burning off of vast tracts of forest" by loggers, his descendants of this century have warned of the possibility that the Adirondack region could lose forever its characteristic expanses of that same forest. The Temporary Study Commission proposed that the legislature establish an Adirondack Park Agency, with two main charges: first, to draw up a State Land Master Plan, which would serve as the chief guide for the Department of Environmental Conservation in its management of the Forest Preserve; second, and infinitely more controversial, to exercise "planning and land use control powers over private land in the Park." After lengthy debate in the legislature and after significant diminution of the powers proposed for this Agency, it was established in 1971. The State Land Master Plan was approved by Governor Rockefeller a year later, and the Agency submitted its Private Land Use and Development Plan in 1973.

The key feature of the Private Land Plan, which was essentially an exercise in regional zoning, was a map of the entire Adirondack Park, whereon every acre of private land was color coded and assigned to a land-use category establishing the permissible level of development. The bases for evaluating land included, among a long list of criteria, proximity to Forest Preserve, presence of wetlands, suitability for wildlife habitat, previous use, slope and elevation, quality and depth of soils, and accessibility. In the towns and villages, development was largely unrestricted, but the further one moved from the population centers, the more limited the allowable development.

The lands for which the lowest level of development was permitted, categorized as Resource Management in the plan, constituted fifty-three percent of the Park's private land, or some 1.9 million acres. Here development was limited to ten units (which meant houses, particularly vacation houses) per square mile, or an average lot size of just under sixty-four acres. This was a plan designed to protect open space, to keep the Adirondack Park largely a forested place.

Opposition to the Private Land Plan came mostly from Adirondack residents and their representatives. Year-round residents believed that

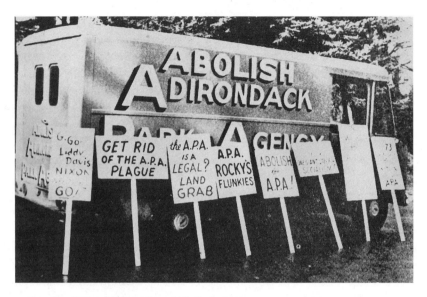

Local resistance to the Adirondack Park Agency.

their interests had been ignored by both the Temporary Study Commission and the Park Agency, which, in their view, were dominated by downstate conservationists who valued a narrowly defined nature more than the livelihoods of the people who lived and worked year-round in the Park. The Private Land Plan was seen as an unnecessary imposition of bureaucratic red tape in local affairs, an assault on the local business climate, and an unconstitutional abridgment of property rights. At a public meeting in Indian Lake, a Long Lake businessman, wearing a faux Indian headdress and carrying a spear, declared that the Private Land Plan was "the first government financed land grab since the Cherokees were forced to walk across the mountains."[15]

During the legislative debate local politicians again argued that there was no crisis, that the Private Land Plan violated the tradition of home rule and had been dreamed up just to placate environmental alarmists. But the plans announced in 1972 by the Horizon Corporation for developing 24,000 acres in St. Lawrence County helped to persuade the legislature that immediate action was demanded. Horizon officers foresaw up to 10,000 houses on their land, along with an extensive system of roads, golf courses, and several dams on the Grass River. Such a prospect was unpalatable to many members of the legislature (but not including those representing year-round residents), who saw the Private Land Plan as just what the Adirondacks needed. After further and often acrimonious debate and after feverish wrangling over details, it was approved by the legislature in 1973; one of the main compromises was raising the allowable density of development on Resource Management lands from ten units per square mile to fifteen, or to an average lot size of just under forty-three acres.[16]

Behind the antagonism was the old debate, argued via conflicting stories about what the Adirondack land was: was the Adirondack Park, including lands privately owned, to be understood as nature, protected as such for the people of New York? Or was this just another American region where land was viewed as an asset to be developed for profit according to individual need or whim?

Even in the case of the Forest Preserve, the simultaneous existence of different narratives, different ideas about how state land should be defined and understood, led to division and conflict. The State Land Master Plan divided the Forest Preserve into several different categories, with roughly half of the Forest Preserve set aside in Wilderness Areas. Wilderness was defined in terms of ecosystems, as a place "where the earth and its community of life are untrammeled by man— where man himself is a visitor who does not remain."[17] Such a view, which today we might call biocentric, struck many of the locals as misanthropic and unsympathetic to historic recreational use of the Forest Preserve. The very notion of prohibiting logging in the Forest Preserve still seemed economically wasteful to some people.

The story of state land had two distinct threads. In one version the Forest Preserve was wilderness, the most pristine form of nature, protected as tightly as possible for its spiritual, recreational attributes, for its existence as a place outside or beyond the social, cultural, human world. In the other version, preferred by many Adirondackers, the Forest Preserve was an outdoor park, managed for a wide variety of human uses. In the more extreme version of this narrative, all of the Forest Preserve should be opened up for intensive uses like snowmobiling and even logging.

These distinctly different understandings of the reality of the Forest Preserve came into head-on conflict in the Pharoah Lake Wilderness

Area. This rugged parcel of some 43,000 acres in the southeastern Adirondacks, between Lake George and Schroon Lake, was classified as Wilderness in the State Land Master Plan. A mixed coniferous and hardwood forest, with many small ponds and streams, it had been logged and partially burned over the course of the preceding century. In the north-central section is Crane Pond, reached by a dirt road maintained by the Town of Schroon, about two and a half miles of which pass through the Wilderness Area. In 1971 the Temporary Study Commission recommended both that this road be closed and that the fire tower on Pharoah Mountain be removed, in order to eliminate "nonconforming uses." The Park Agency agreed and so indicated in the State Land Master Plan, but nothing was done for nearly twenty years.[18]

In December of 1989, the Department of Environmental Conservation closed the Crane Pond road, but local residents, offended from the start by the wilderness designation, removed the barriers the following May and continued to drive up and down the road for picnicking and fishing at Crane Pond, as, they insisted, they and their parents and grandparents had been doing for generations. When the radical environmental group Earth First! attempted to set up a new barrier to motorized vehicles, a brawl—caught by the camera of a local TV station on footage that eventually made its way to CBS's *60 Minutes*—ensued, wherein a local politician physically assaulted an Earth First! representative.[19]

That same spring Earth First! announced that it had cut the support cables for the Pharoah Mountain fire tower. An Earth First! spokesperson told a reporter that cutting these cables was but the beginning of local "monkey wrenching" and that more would follow: "We're taking a radical stand to defend what's left," he said.[20] Meanwhile, some locals repaired the cables on the fire tower. Cal Carr, President of the Adirondack Solidarity Alliance, a citizens organization opposed to the Park Agency, Wilderness Areas, and the entire state conservation bureaucracy, declared, "The fire tower is a symbol of the resistance of the Adirondack people. Those cables being reattached to the fire tower will be tantamount to the raising of the flag by our servicemen on Iwo Jima." Carr argued that Adirondackers had been pushed too far by state regulations, zoning of private land, and the State Land Master Plan.[21]

Some conservationists argued that the real threat to the Forest Preserve came not from fire towers or dirt roads but acid precipitation. Despite a New York State law passed in 1984 and amendments to the Federal Clean Air Act, approved by Congress in 1990, the lakes and forests of the Adirondacks, far from beginning the slow process of healing, are continuing to deteriorate. Wafting from the tall smokestacks of the Midwest and settling on the Adirondacks in the form of rain, sleet, fog, snow, and even dry particles, acid precipitation affects every living organism it touches, from the dwarf spruces of the high peaks to the mammals on the land, the insects in the air, and the fish and amphibians of lakes and wetlands. Many of these plants and creatures, exposed to enough of the effects of acid pollution, will eventually die.[22]

The threat to Adirondack forests and lakes posed by acid precipitation was one issue friends and foes of the Park Agency could agree on, but it was just about the only one. When it came to the Private Land Plan the acrimony was even more intense than the feud over the Crane Pond Road. The primary local version of the Adirondack narrative acknowledged that the Park was a place of beauty and natural splendor but insisted that local governments elected by local people were perfectly capable of protecting the Park. This narrative frequently cast the story of the Park Agency and the Private Land Plan into a class-based contest between two groups. On one side were politically powerless blue-collar Adirondack families whose love of the land, based on experience and history, was deep and genuine. On the other were effete, wealthy, politically powerful conservationists from outside the region who were indifferent to the lives and well-being of the year-round residents and aimed only to "use the Adirondacks for their greedy enrichment and elitist pleasure." As Anthony D'Elia, one of the most strident opponents of the Private Land Plan, put it, "It was the age old scenario of the powerful against the powerless, the rich against the poor."[23]

This insider-versus-outsider narrative possessed dramatic political appeal, but it left out at least one important third party—the cadre of developers and real estate lawyers who stood to make fortunes if no restraints were placed on the development of private land in the Adirondacks. There were, moreover, Adirondackers whose families had lived in the Park for generations who supported the Private Land Plan and hoped it would protect a way of life that they felt was threatened by uncontrolled development. Finally, the oversimplified story of rich-versus-poor also failed to note that virtually all of the land in the Resource Management classification, the land most restricted by the Private Land Plan, was owned by corporations, clubs, and wealthy families with bases outside the blue line.

The case of Anthony D'Elia illustrates how recent conflict in the Adirondacks cannot be neatly reduced to a simple story. A leader of the resistance to the Park Agency, D'Elia was anything but a poor Adiron-dacker oppressed by indifferent conservationists. He was himself an outsider, a successful, college-educated businessman and teacher from New York City, who moved to the Adirondacks in 1972 at the age of fifty-two with plans to develop vacation homes around the Loon Lake golf course. When the Park Agency found his scheme to be in violation of the Private Land Plan and denied him a development permit, he took up the banner of home rule and fought the Park Agency, with an energetic combination of zeal and bitterness, until his death in 1990.[24] Far from being the subject of a simple tale of class conflict, the Adiron-dack Park was becoming a focal point in a debate of national signifi-cance: to what extent does a society have an interest in what happens to private property? And what power does it have to demonstrate and protect that interest?

The first years of the administration of the Private Land Plan by the newly established Adirondack Park Agency did nothing to reduce the level of local resistance. The staff was young and dedicated but came from outside the region. Overworked, they had trouble keeping up with permit applications, the guidelines for which appeared cumber-some and legalistic. Local builders, indisposed from the start to accept the very idea of zoning, grew increasingly impatient with the Private Land Plan and with the Agency, some of whose staff, according to one account, were "perceived as young, insensitive, and arrogant."[25]

Behind much of the local hostility to the Park Agency and the Pri-vate Land Plan were the realities of the local economy. Politicians and business leaders believed that development—meaning, for the most part, construction of vacation homes—would lead to the creation of jobs and the infusion of outside capital into the local economy. And the Adirondack economy definitely appeared to be in trouble. The Tempo-rary Study Commission found an Adirondack economy characterized by relatively low labor force participation rates, high dependence on government jobs, and high unemployment. What jobs there were in the Adirondacks tended to be less skilled and more oriented toward service sectors than in the rest of New York. In 1960, the unemployment rate for New York State was 5.2 percent, while in the Adirondack Park it was more than twice that, at 11.2 percent. Many Adirondack jobs, moreover, were tied to the seasonal tourist economy and were thus unable to provide year-round employment. The median family income in the Park was only 82 percent of that of the rest of New York.[26]

Even though these figures reflected conditions obtaining before the creation of the Park Agency, after 1971 the Agency itself and its restrictions on development were routinely blamed for any sluggishness perceived in the Adirondack economy.[27] But after two decades of the Private Land Plan, a study conducted by the Nelson A. Rockefeller Institute of Government for the New York Department of Labor found that the economy of the Adirondacks was in certain respects faring better than that of either New York state or the nation as a whole. In particular, the Rockefeller Institute observed that both employment and payrolls rose faster in the Adirondacks during the recession of 1989–92 than in the state or the nation. Between 1985 and 1992 employment rose by twenty-five percent in the Park; during the same period, it actually decreased slightly in the rest of New York.

None of this meant that the Adirondack economy was exactly thriving. As in many parts of rural America, public sector jobs and lower-paying service industries were overrepresented, while higher-paying service jobs were less common than in New York as a whole. But it was clear that during the first two decades of the existence of the Private Land Plan the Adirondack economy, far from losing ground as compared with New York state, had in fact narrowed the gap.[28] Whether this was a direct function of the environmental protections enforced by the Adirondack Park Agency is impossible to say. But environmentalists insisted that it was illogical to lay regional economic disappointments at the feet of the Park Agency.

The Adirondack economic picture is indeed a complicated one. The local tax base illustrates how different local finances are from those of most of the rest of New York. In many Adirondack towns, the state owns a significant portion of the real estate, in some cases as much as half of the town. Taken out of the base of land available for logging or other substantial development, the Forest Preserve might appear to be unproductive and a drag on the tax base. But, argue defenders of the Forest Preserve, this is not necessarily the case. The Forest Preserve attracts thousands of visitors from outside the region, in all seasons of the year, who leave their dollars with local merchants. So long as the lands of the Forest Preserve remain undeveloped, moreover, they create no demands for municipal services such as police protection, roads, sewers, and the like. Finally, since the very establishment of the Forest Preserve, in order to alleviate any negative impact on the tax base, the state has paid taxes on it to Adirondack counties and school districts.[29] As the Forest Preserve grew, this funding source evolved into a virtual state subsidy of local economies; by 1964 a Joint Legislative Committee on Assessment and Taxation of State-Owned Land could declare, "Taxation of state lands has become a source of 'state aid' for the support of local governments and schools."[30]

One consequence of this (and of the existence of large holdings in private hands that also contributed significant tax dollars to Adirondack counties) was that, despite an economy that still lagged behind that of the rest of the state in terms of employment and income, some Adirondack school districts were among the best funded in the state. Small populations coupled with major sources of tax dollars coming from outside the town led to high per-student school budgets. For example, in 1993–94, the average number of students per teacher in all of New York state's public schools was 14.3; in New York City it was 15.9; in Long Lake it was 6.[31] During the two decades after the establishment of the Park Agency, the average student-teacher ratio in all Adirondack school districts improved by better than a third. In 1992, a State Education Department study found that Adirondack school districts, with a few exceptions, had more library books per student than did districts across the state. The same study showed that per-student expenditures averaged higher in the Adirondacks than in New York state as a whole: $7,624 for Adirondack school districts, $6,908 statewide, with some Adirondack districts way above the statewide average—for example, Newcomb at $18,586 and Long Lake at $11,660. Even though both average household and per capita incomes were significantly lower in these towns than in New York state as a whole, because of the tax payments made by the state and land owners not living in the town, they constituted relatively rich school districts. At the same time, it must be noted, some of the larger Adirondack districts spent considerably less per student than the statewide norm: e.g., Tupper Lake spent $5,414 and Saranac Lake $5,630.

The complexities and paradoxes of the Adirondack economy, if anything, only increased local hostility to the environmental agenda. And environmentalists, in fact, were often themselves disappointed with the Private Land Plan, which reflected a series of compromises demanded by the exigencies of legislative politics and was thus unable to provide the level of protection that they had hoped for.[32] While these compromises may have been politically necessary, they weakened a plan designed from the start to permit (while controlling) development, not stop it altogether. Throughout the 1970s and '80s conservationists warned repeatedly that the forested character of the Park was slowly eroding as developments perfectly legal under the Private Land Plan popped up throughout the region.

In 1989 a powerful article in the *New York Times Magazine*, illustrated with shocking before-and-after photographs, pointed out that during the previous two years alone more than 100,000 acres of forest had passed into the hands of speculators eager to subdivide and resell. The problem was rooted in the economics of the logging industry. Holding onto forest lands and periodically realizing what profits could be derived from conservative logging was beginning to seem much less appealing to many of the owners of the still-undeveloped back country than selling off for immediate profits.[33] Conservationists wondered what would happen to the Adirondacks if the big land owners, woods products companies like International Paper or Finch, Pruyn and Co. (based in Glens Falls, with a history of over a century of Adirondack logging and holdings of some 154,000 acres), under pressure from stock holders to maximize income, simply decided to get out of the business of logging and into the business of selling lots for vacation homes.[34] Even if interpreted in the strictest way possible, the Private Land Plan could not prevent what seemed to many to be a potential environmental disaster.

That same year Governor Mario Cuomo, responding to a growing conviction among downstate conservationists that the Private Land Plan did not provide adequate protection, appointed another special commission to study the Park and recommend changes in policy. As with the Temporary Study Commission, locals argued that this new body was set up from the start to advance a radical environmental agenda with little regard for property rights or regional business interests. After holding hearings throughout the state, the Commission on the Adirondacks in the Twenty-First Century reported to the governor in the spring of 1990. Reflecting the views of many of the New Yorkers who had testified before the Commission, the Report concluded that without serious modification of the Private Land Plan, the Adirondack Park could lose forever the character of forested open space that had defined the region in the popular mind since early in the nineteenth century.

Among other things, the Twenty-First Century Commission called for an immediate one-year moratorium on building in the back country, tighter controls on development along all lake and river shores, and further state acquisition of key parcels of privately owned forests and waters.[35] The initial response from Adirondackers, already exasperated by what they saw as endless attacks on local autonomy, was almost universally hostile, repeating the claim that conservationists were callously indifferent to the economic travails of local residents.[36] Opposition to the Report quickly became a rallying cry for home rule in the Adirondacks. Citizen organizations issued press releases condemning the Report and arguing that if the legislature adopted its recommendations the local economy would be devastated. The Adirondack Fairness Coalition, based in Chestertown, declared that any evidence of a "crisis" was invented by environmentalists.[37]

To demonstrate opposition to the Report, another group, the Adirondack Solidarity Alliance, organized a dramatic protest. On May 11, 1990, vehicles driven by Alliance members and sympathizers conducted a "freedom drive" that snarled traffic and created near total gridlock on the Northway between exits 20 and 28.[38] Supported by several local politicians, including Republican State Senator Ronald Stafford of Plattsburgh, who rode in the lead vehicle, opponents of the Report organized another motorcade on May 25. One thousand cars and trucks caravanned from Exit 34, near Elizabethtown, all the way to Clifton Park, where they turned around before heading north again for a rally near Frontiertown. The sentiments of the drivers were acidly expressed on one of many large banners: "Take this Report and Shove It."[39] Meanwhile, Donald Gerdts, one of the Report's shrillest opponents, declared of the Twenty-First Century Commission, "They want our blood, they want our land, and they want us out of here."[40]

Conservationists struggled to protect at least some of the Report's recommendations, and a local group supporting tighter development controls, the Residents' Committee to Protect the Adirondacks, emerged to counter the claims of the Solidarity Alliance and other groups. The Residents' Committee argued that groups like the Solidarity Alliance did not represent the views of all Adirondackers, many of whom believed that overdevelopment threatened their traditions and way of life but, because of the virulence of the Twenty-First Century Report's foes, were afraid to speak out in its favor.[41] The efforts of the Residents' Committee and others notwithstanding, however, the Report was dead on arrival. Governor Cuomo appeared not seriously committed to its recommendations, and after several months of acrimony, accusations, and the absence of substantive discussion, the Report faded into regional memory, another chapter in the story of New Yorkers' trying to decide what to do with the Adirondacks. Although the Report's specific recommendations were not adopted, some local moderates hoped that the furor it generated might lead to new efforts to establish better relations between local government and the Park Agency. Whether this hope will become reality remains one of the crucial uncertainties of the contemporary Adirondack drama.[42]

Conservationists lamented the failure of the legislature to implement tighter controls on development, and the slow but steady erosion of the Park's open space continued. A pattern of development and construction that began with the completion of the Northway in 1967 was continuing and even accelerating. Between 1967 and 1987, the Park saw an average of 1,000 new houses built each year; the Private Land Plan appeared to have little affect on new housing starts. Indeed, after 1987, the number of new houses grew to roughly 1,200 per year.[43] In 1995 Park Agency Chair John Collins (himself a fourth-generation native Adirondacker who fervently supported the Private Land Plan) observed that in 1992 the Park had sixty-two percent more dwellings than it had had in 1967. In his view, the open space of the back country and the remaining undeveloped shores of lakes and rivers were woefully vulnerable to inappropriate development.[44] Indeed, in the two decades after the initial approval of the Private Land Plan, 135 miles of roads and sixty-five miles of shoreline that had been lined only with trees had been turned over to real estate development.[45]

A current example of the potential for substantial environmental change in the Adirondack Park is Whitney Park, in northern Hamilton County. First acquired in 1897 by millionaire William C. Whitney, designer of the lucrative New York City streetcar lines, this tract of 52,000 acres and some forty lakes and ponds, incorporated as Whitney Industries, has been owned, enjoyed, and logged by Whitney's descendants for nearly a century. Though heavily logged and crisscrossed with dirt roads, Whitney Park remains largely forested and would make an in-

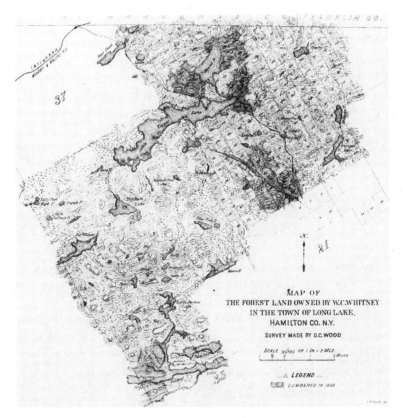

A map of 1899 showing Whitney Park. Henry S. Graves, of Practical Forestry in the Adirondacks (Washington: U. S. Department Agriculture, Government Printing Office, 1899).

valuable addition to the Forest Preserve. W. C. Whitney's grandson, Cornelius Vanderbilt Whitney—socialite, co-founder of Pan American Airways, backer of the film *Gone With the Wind*, breeder of fine race horses—died in 1992.[46] And his widow and children were faced with the expense of maintaining an Adirondack empire and retiring Whitney Industries' debt of nearly $4 million. If they opt to subdivide the property to pay their taxes, a devastating blow will have been dealt to the forested character of the very center of the Adirondack Park. The state cannot afford to buy the property for the Forest Preserve, and conservationists are frantically trying to piece together schemes involving easements or some other mechanism to protect the undeveloped open space of Whitney Park.[47]

Meanwhile, the Whitney family, interested in subdividing and developing their land for profit, is expressing a hostility to the Park Agency and the Private Land Plan that further belies the characterization of recent Adirondack history as a conflict between working-class locals and wealthy, downstate conservationists. Tightly aligned with the eastern, elite establishment of prestige and affluence—precisely that element of American society identified by some locals as the sinister power behind the Private Land Plan—C. V. Whitney's aristocratic widow and her son from an earlier marriage complain that "eco-socialists" are interfering with their right to develop their property and hope that Republican Governor George Pataki, elected in 1994, will force the Park Agency to tilt toward property-owning developers and away from regional conservation.[48] In the summer of 1996, when the Whitney family announced plans to re-assign title to four large lots on Little Tupper Lake, conservationists feared that this might be the beginning of a gradual dismemberment of Whitney Park.[49]

The Adirondack political scene continues to be one of paradox, a chief example of which is an uneasy alliance between the forest-products industry and conservationists, both of whom hope that tax policies and other instruments can be devised to keep currently forested lands producing trees and not turned over to developers. The chief legal mechanism, viewed positively but cautiously by both conservationists and forest owners, is the easement, whereby a land owner might trade development rights for lower taxes. Such an arrangement might help keep a woods-products company in business, save the jobs of its loggers, and keep the land from being sold off in small lots.[50]

In the late nineteenth century avaricious loggers threatened the landscape loved by vacationers and vital to a healthy watershed; today the logging interests—the modern equivalent of the transportation lobby of the 1880s and '90s—line up with conservationists to protect the forest from uncontrolled second-home development. "The state," declared Twenty-First Century Commission Chair Peter A. A. Berle (who subsequently became President of the National Audubon Society), "must not let the Park be overwhelmed by the short-sighted interests that would destroy the forest industry and treat the Park as a mere piece of saleable real estate."[51]

Berle's muted acknowledgment of the importance of logging to the local economy is a tentative step toward bringing the year-round residents and their fate into discussions of what the Adirondack Park is and can be. While not all Adirondackers are loggers (or developers), they all need jobs and a viable community life if the Adirondack Park is to be a good place for both people and nature. Like rural towns across the country, Adirondack communities face a dilemma of monumental dimensions. As a resident of Essex County put it, "How can we preserve the positive rural environment that we call 'home' and at the same time improve our economic condition so that we and our children can remain here?"[52] Can the economic picture be brightened without sacrificing the rural features that make the Adirondack Park appealing?

While there is no single "Adirondack" identity, no such thing as the typical "Adirondacker," people throughout the Park share a culture that makes their lives distinct. Adirondackers live in a region where the state owns almost half the land and where the Private Land Plan and the Adirondack Park Agency constitute a layer of bureaucracy that many other rural Americans never confront. More important, they live surrounded by millions of acres of forests and trees. Many Adirondackers treasure the life of the outdoors; they hunt and fish, they climb the peaks. As William Bibby of North Creek told photographer Mathias Oppersdorff, "I feel a part of these mountains, and I feel the mountains are part of me."[53]

Equally important, they are profoundly aware that they enjoy a rural life that is threatened by a host of problems. The Adirondack economy remains relatively unstable, and young people are often unable to find work in the communities where they grew up. The stock of affordable, year-round housing is inadequate. While some towns, like Keene Valley or Lake Placid, attract swarms of tourists and their dollars, others, off the main tourist corridors, appear dilapidated and unkempt.[54] Adirondackers deal with driving distances—to grocery stores, medical facilities, movies, visits with friends—that seem more typical of the West than of a densely settled state like New York. But most Adirondackers like their rural life and want it preserved. Both those whose great-grandparents struggled with the uncooperative soil and climate to make a living as farmers and those who have recently moved here, fleeing the crime, pollution, and chaos of the cities, value a life whose rhythms are still largely dictated by nature.

But they also want a healthy economy, and the fundamental dilemma of trying to improve economic conditions without obliterating the mix of the rural and the wild that makes the Adirondack Park unique remains. For a century and a half, the Adirondack region has appealed to people because it seems so different from the settled, developed remainder of New York. The antimodernism of Joel Headley and William James, the environmental concerns of Verplanck Colvin and David Hill, and the current drive to protect forested open space all depend on a certain image of the Adirondacks—an image of nature as either antidote to modern ills or fragile reservoir of valuable resources.

And the difficulties involved in protecting both human and natural values reflect the continuing power of narratives to define the land and influence people's understandings of the land's meaning. Conservationists have their story of what the Adirondack Park is, what its problems and opportunities are, and what should be done for it. Summer mountain climbers, November deer hunters, January skiers, and white water rafters in the spring have their version of the Park's meaning. Local business interests and developers have another. And thousands of Adirondack families, allied with neither environmentalists nor developers, cherishing the rural life next to the East's last great wilderness but anxious about their economic security and their children's futures, have yet another.

The gap between these distinct and, one hopes, not mutually exclusive understandings recalls the equally profound difference between John Todd and Joel Headley of a century and a half ago. The question of Adirondack history is, whose narrative of the land will prevail? Or, to look at it more optimistically, can a new narrative be constructed that seeks accommodation, that sees the Adirondacks as a cultural landscape, with people and nature, and thriving, healthy opportunities and protections for both?

If we return to the conservation era of the 1880s and '90s and recall the failure of the legislature to resolve the dilemma posed by private land in the Park, we may find just the unifying narrative we need to forge a hopeful story for the future of the Adirondacks. The realities of the twentieth century have made public ownership and management of the entire Park impossible. Although it is an accident of history, the unintended mix of private land, villages, and state-owned wilderness can itself be seen as *the* Adirondack story, a source of conflict but also a great opportunity.

In the Adirondacks we have a landscape that could be a model for the world. It is a place where people live and where nature matters, where it is just this combination, this interrelationship between people and nature, that defines the place, provides its meaning, constructs its narrative. If we think of the Adirondack Park as one big place rather than in terms of distinct landscapes within it—the villages and private land on the one hand and the Forest Preserve on the other—then we have a place that can be both functional and protected. If we can say that the failure of the New York legislature over a century ago to decide just what it wanted in the Adirondacks is the beginning of what has become the latest and most promising Adirondack narrative, then the irresolution of 1892 might be seen as a stroke of incredible good fortune.[55]

Notes

Bibliography

Index

Notes

Introduction

1. [Farrand N. Benedict], "The Wilds of Northern New York," *Putnam's Monthly Magazine* 4 (July–Dec. 1854): 263, italics in original. The article appears without a byline, but the *Adirondack Bibliography* (entry 956) identifies Benedict as the author. On Benedict and his many Adirondack connections, see Barbara McMartin, *To the Lake of the Skies: The Benedicts in the Adirondacks* (Canada Lake, N.Y.: Lake View Press, 1996), 15–36.

2. The European account of this episode is Samuel de Champlain, *Voyages of Samuel de Champlain, 1604–1618,* ed. W. L. Grant (New York: C. Scribner's Sons, 1907), 163–66. See also Bruce G. Trigger, *The Children of Aataentsic: A History of the Huron People to 1660* (Montreal: McGill-Queens Univ. Press, 1976), 1: 247–56. The authors of an exhibit catalog concerning the native inhabitants of the Champlain Valley dispute Champlain's version of the battle, arguing that the Mohawks were not part of a war party and were attacked without cause by Champlain and his allies; see *The Original People: Native Americans in the Champlain Valley* (Plattsburgh, N. Y.: Clinton County Historical Museum, 1988), 26.

3. See the discussion of myth in Richard Slotkin, *The Fatal Environment: The Myth of the Frontier in the Age of Industrialization, 1800–1890* (Middletown, Conn.: Wesleyan Univ. Press, 1986), 13–32, and William Cronon, "A Place for Stories: Nature, History, and Narrative," *Journal of American History* 78 (March 1992): 1347–76.

4. J. Donald Hughes, "Ecology and Development as Narrative Themes of World History," *Environmental History Review* 19 (Spring 1995): 1–16.

5. Bill McKibben, "The People and the Park," *Sierra* 79 (March–April 1994): 139.

1. "A Broken Unpracticable Tract"

1. Lynn Woods, "A History in Fragments: Following the Trail of Native Adirondack Cultures," *Adirondack Life* 25 (Nov.–Dec. 1994): 30–37, 61, 68–71, 78–79. William A. Ritchie, *The Archaeology of New York State,* rev. ed. (New York: Doubleday, 1980), xxx–xxxi, figure 1. John H. Thompson, ed., *Geography of New York State* (Syracuse: Syracuse Univ. Press, 1966), 114–16. Lawrence Hamilton, Barbara Askew, and Amy Odell, *Forest History:*

New York State Forest Resources Assessment, Report No. 1 (Albany: New York State Department of Environmental Conservation, 1980), 8. Evidence for an argument against this position is suggested by John Todd, *Long Lake* (Pittsfield, Mass., 1845), 27–28, 48, where the author claimed to have seen the remains, including vestiges of houses and corn fields, of a permanent Indian settlement on the Raquette "opposite the mouth of Stony Brook."

2. See Roderick Nash, *Wilderness and the American Mind,* 3rd ed. (New Haven: Yale Univ. Press, 1982), 23–43.

3. Lewis Evans, "Analysis," Lawrence Henry Gipson, *Lewis Evans* (Philadelphia: Historical Society of Pennsylvania, 1939), 11.

4. *The Papers of Sir William Johnson* (Albany: Univ. of the State of New York, 1921–62), 12: 814–15.

5. Thomas Pownall, *Topographical Description of the Dominions of the United States of America,* ed. Lois Mulkearn (Pittsburgh: Univ. of Pittsburgh Press, 1949), 51. The name "Couchsachraga" (as it is spelled today) has been bestowed on a remote Adirondack peak in Essex County.

6. Jeptha Simms, *Trappers of New York* (Albany: J. Munsell, 1850).

7. Ted Aber and Stella King, *The History of Hamilton County* (Lake Pleasant, N.Y.: Great Wilderness Books, 1965), 19.

8. On the establishment and function of the Natural History Survey, see Michele Alexis La Clerque Aldrich, "New York Natural History Survey" (Ph.D. diss., Univ. of Texas, 1974); Philip G. Terrie, *Forever Wild: A Cultural History of Wilderness in the Adirondacks* (Syracuse: Syracuse Univ. Press, 1994), 27–43.

9. Ebenezer Emmons's reports to the legislature were printed as follows: "First Annual Report of the Second Geological District of New York" (Assembly Document 161, 1837), "Report of E. Emmons, Geologist of the 2d Geological District of the State of New York" (Assembly Document 200, 1838), "Third Annual Report of the Survey of the Second Geological District" (Assembly Document 275, 1839), "Fourth Annual Report of the Survey of the Second Geological District" (Assembly Document 50, 1840), and "Fifth Annual Report of Ebenezer Emmons, M.D., of the Survey of the Second Geological District" (Assembly Document 150, 1841). These were followed by the final report, *Geology of New-York, Part II: Comprising the Second Geological District* (Albany: Carroll and Cook, 1842–44). On the naming of the region and Mount Marcy, see Russell M. L. Carson, *Peaks and People of the Adirondacks* (Garden City, N.Y.: Doubleday, Page, 1927; reprint, Glens Falls, N.Y.: Adirondack Mountain Club, 1973, 1986), 8–10, 55–58.

10. Henry David Thoreau, *The Maine Woods* (Princeton: Princeton Univ. Press, 1972), 82. The Adirondack reference comes near the end of Thoreau's essay "Ktaadn," which originally appeared in *Union Magazine* in 1848; the trip to Katahdin (the modern spelling) took place in 1846. The Emmons episode to which Thoreau refers is described in the report for that year (Assembly Document 150, 1841, 117–18). See Harold K. Hochschild, *Township 34* (New York: privately printed, 1952), 42–43, where Hochschild incorrectly suggests that the Indian was Mitchell Sabatis of Long Lake; Emmons, at the end of his report, identifies him as "Elijah Benedict, of the St. Francois, or Paleseegantuck tribe" (128). This was Lewis Elijah, who lived on Indian Lake. I am grateful to Warder H. Cadbury for help in identifying this Indian guide.

11. Nash, *Wilderness and the American Mind,* 44–66.

12. Emmons, *Geology of New-York*, 36–37.

13. Warder Cadbury, "The Improbable Charles C. Ingham," *Adirondac* 51 (August 1987): 23–25.

14. Nash, *Wilderness and the American Mind*, 67–83. Barbara Novak, *Nature and Culture: American Landscape Painting, 1825–1875* (New York: Oxford Univ. Press, 1980).

15. Emmons, "Fifth Annual Report," 114–15.

16. Emmons, "Fifth Annual Report," 120.

17. In "Nature" (1836), Emerson had written, "In the wilderness, I find something more dear and connate than in streets and villages," advancing the familiar romantic distinction between nature and civilization. Ralph Waldo Emerson, *The Complete Works of Ralph Waldo Emerson* (Centenary Edition, Boston: Houghton, Mifflin, 1903–4), I: 10.

18. See Hans Huth, *Nature and the American: Three Centuries of Changing Attitudes* (Berkeley: Univ. of California Press, 1957), 102–28.

19. Emmons, "Fifth Annual Report," 128.

20. Emmons, "Report of E. Emmons, Geologist of the 2d Geological District," 242–43. On previous names for the region, see Carson, *Peaks and People*, 7–13.

21. See Robert F. Berkhofer, Jr., *The White Man's Indian: Images of the American Indian from Columbus to the Present* (New York: Alfred A. Knopf, 1978), 88, 90.

22. Charles Lanman, *Adventures of an Angler in Canada, Nova Scotia and the United States* (London: Richard Bentley, 1848), 91–92. Much of the confusion about Indian names in the Adirondacks originated with Charles Fenno Hoffman, who suggested some Iroquoian words as suitable names for Adirondack sites, including the word "Tahawus" for Mount Marcy. Hoffman knew that these names had no local authenticity, but subsequent writers, including Lanman, misunderstood Hoffman's intent and inferred that the names had been used by Indians. See Carson, *Peaks and People*, 57.

23. Arthur A. Ekirch, Jr., *Man and Nature in America* (New York: Columbia Univ. Press, 1963), 35–41.

24. See, among others, Ray A. Billington, *Westward Expansion: A History of the American Frontier* (New York: MacMillan, 1982); Frederick Merk, *Manifest Destiny and Mission in American History* (New York: Knopf, 1963); Henry Nash Smith, *Virgin Land: The American West as Symbol and Myth* (Cambridge: Harvard Univ. Press, 1950), 35–43.

25. Benedict, "The Wilds of Northern New York," 269.

26. Ross F. Allen, et al., "An Archaeological Survey of Bloomery Forges in the Adirondacks," *IA: The Journal of the Society for Industrial Archaeology* 16 (1990): 3–20; Arthur H. Masten, *The Story of Adirondac* (New York: privately printed, 1923), 16–22, 41–42; Harold K. Hochschild, *The MacIntyre Mine—From Failure to Fortune* (Blue Mountain Lake, N.Y.: The Adirondack Museum, 1962), 1–4.

27. Emmons, *Geology of New-York*, 250.

28. Emmons, "Third Annual Report," 227. The idea that agriculture is the best use to which any land can be put is a much-discussed feature of American culture. See, for example, Smith, *Virgin Land*, 123–83; John Stilgoe, *The Common Landscape of America, 1580–1845* (New Haven: Yale Univ. Press, 1982), 135–208.

29. See Michael Williams, *Americans and their Forests: A Historical Geography* (Cambridge: Cambridge Univ. Press, 1989), 144–45.

30. Emmons, "Third Annual Report," 226.

31. See, among others, Leo Marx, *The Machine in the Garden: Technology and the Pastoral Ideal in America* (New York: Oxford Univ. Press, 1964), 73–144.

2. "Long Lake Was a Hard Place to Live"

1. Alfred L. Donaldson, *A History of the Adirondacks* (New York: Century, 1921; reprint, Harrison, N. Y.: Harbor Hill Books, 1977), 1: 51–61.

2. Donaldson, *A History of the Adirondacks,* 1: 62–74

3. Donaldson, *A History of the Adirondacks,* 1: 78–79.

4. Thompson, ed., *Geography of New York State,* 146–47.

5. Robert Shaw, "Second Section," in George and Robert Shaw, "Tahawus—Newcomb and Long Lake, 1842–1900," ed. Howard Becker (privately printed, 1955; typescript, Adirondack Museum Library), 10.

6. Aber and King, *The History of Hamilton County,* 15.

7. Manuscript Census Schedules for Hamilton County, 1850 (Adirondack Museum Library), microfilm. See also George and Robert Shaw, "Tahawus—Newcomb and Long Lake," where all the antebellum settlers of Long Lake are identified and discussed.

8. Franklin B. Hough, *A History of St. Lawrence and Franklin Counties, New York* (Albany: Little & Co., 1853), 484.

9. Thompson, ed., *Geography of New York State,* 170–71.

10. William Cronon, *Changes in the Land: Indians, Colonists, and the Ecology of New England* (New York: Hill and Wang, 1983), 155–56; Carolyn Merchant, *Ecological Revolutions: Nature, Gender, and Science in New England* (Chapel Hill: Univ. of North Carolina Press, 1989), 193–97; Patricia Anderson, *The Course of Empire: The Erie Canal and the New York Landscape* (Rochester: Memorial Art Gallery of the Univ. of Rochester, 1984), 13–15; Peter D. McClelland and Richard J. Zeckhauser, *Demographic Dimensions of the New Republic: American Interregional Migration, Vital Statistics, and Manumissions, 1800–1860* (London: Cambridge Univ. Press, 1982), 50–51.

11. William Reed, *Life on the Border Sixty Years Ago* (Fall River, Mass., 1882; reprint, Saranac Lake, N.Y.: Saranac Lake Free Library, 1994), 5.

12. Henry Conklin, *Through Poverty's Vale: A Hardscrabble Boyhood in Upstate New York, 1832–1862* (Syracuse: Syracuse Univ. Press, 1974), 82.

13. "Second Section" of the Shaw ms. The story of the Shaw family's travails is touching, especially in the light of contemporary America's continuing failure to resolve its racial problems: once the typhus set in, "Short of money, sick with fever, there was no place for the poor Irishman or his family. The case became desperate, the children delirious, mother homesick, two children, one five the other two years old crying. . . . Finally, a Mr. David Green, a colored man, commonly called a Nigger, learning of our sad condition, came forward and took the whole family into his own home . . . [and] shared his cabin til spring" (1).

14. John Todd, *Long Lake* (Pittsfield, Mass., 1845; reprint, Harrison, N.Y.: Harbor Hill Books, 1983), 30.

15. Reed, *Life on the Border,* 7.

16. Consider the case of hunter and hermit Alvah Dunning, evicted from several parcels of property belonging to others (Donaldson, *A History of the Adirondacks,* 2: 113–14).

17. Livonia Stanton Emerson, "Early Life at Long Lake, N. Y." (typescript, Adirondack Museum Library, n.d.).

18. Shaw, "Second Section," 2.

19. Conklin, *Through Poverty's Vale*, 94.

20. Conklin, *Through Poverty's Vale*, 188–89.

21. Conklin, *Through Poverty's Vale*, 101–2.

22. Emerson, "Early Life at Long Lake, N. Y.," 33; see also Conklin, *Through Poverty's Vale*, 194, 208.

23. Emerson, "Early Life at Long Lake, N. Y.," 7.

24. Reed, *Life on the Border*, 6.

25. Shaw, "Second Section," 46.

26. Todd, *Long Lake*, 20.

27. Reed, *Life on the Border*, 10–14.

28. Conklin, *Through Poverty's Vale*, 100, 106. Reed, *Life on the Border*, also wrote of the interminable labor of "felling the forest," 19.

29. Emerson, "Early Life at Long Lake, N.Y.," 7.

30. Martin John Byrne, "Life in the North Country 100 Years Ago," (Adirondack Museum Library, n.d.), microfilm 4.26, 1–3.

31. Shaw, "Second Section," 8.

32. Byrne, "Life in the North Country," 5–6.

33. Conklin, *Through Poverty's Vale*, 86, 93, 99, 121, 202

34. Conklin, *Through Poverty's Vale*, 100–1.

35. Byrne, "Life in the North Country," 17, 19.

36. Shaw, "Second Section," 48–50.

37. Conklin, *Through Poverty's Vale*, 96–97.

38. Todd, *Long Lake*, 13.

39. Reed, *Life on the Border*, 106–7.

40. Conklin, *Through Poverty's Vale*, 126, 129.

41. Shaw, "Second Section," 3–5.

42. Manuscript Census Schedules for Hamilton County, 1850.

43. Shaw, "Second Section," 16.

44. Byrne, "Life in the North Country," 13.

45. Emerson, "Early Life at Long Lake, N. Y.," 9, 26–30.

46. Byrne, "Life in the North Country," 20.

47. Conklin, *Through Poverty's Vale*, 205–6, 210.

48. Conklin, *Through Poverty's Vale*, 102–3.

49. Conklin, *Through Poverty's Vale*, 161; Emerson, "Early Life at Long Lake, N.Y.," 15.

50. John Richard Moravek, "The Iron Industry as a Geographic Force in the Adirondack-Champlain Region of New York State, 1800–1971" (Ph.D. diss., Univ. of Tennessee, 1976), iv–v, 104–5.

51. Moravek, "The Iron Industry," 102–03. Arthur H. Masten, *The Story of Adirondac* (New York: privately printed, 1923; reprint, Blue Mountain Lake, N.Y.: The Adirondack Museum; Syracuse: Syracuse Univ. Press, 1968), 131–32, 143.

52. Moravek, "The Iron Industry," 104.

53. Barbara McMartin, *Hides, Hemlocks and Adirondack History* (Utica, N.Y.: North Country Books, 1992), 133, 233. Aber and King, *The History of Hamilton County*, 69.

54. Conklin, *Through Poverty's Vale*, 190. McMartin, *Hides, Hemlocks and Adirondack History*, 5–6, 12–18.

55. Aber and King, *The History of Hamilton County*, 69, 905, 907, 967–68.

56. Conklin, *Through Poverty's Vale*, 154–55. The brother, Abiah, died of yellow fever on a ship between Panama and California, and the money earned logging, over $200, was stolen.

57. William F. Fox, *History of the Lumber Industry in the State of New York* (Harrison, N.Y.: Harbor Hill Books, 1976), 35–36; Barbara McMartin, *The Great Forest of the Adirondacks* (Utica, N.Y.: North Country Books, 1994), 26–27.

58. Hamilton, Askew, and Odell, *Forest History*, 13–14.

59. Conklin, *Through Poverty's Vale*, 123–24.

60. Todd, *Long Lake*, 31.

61. Charles Brumley, *Guides of the Adirondacks: A History* (Utica, N.Y.: North Country Books, 1994), 26.

62. Emerson, "Early Life at Long Lake, N.Y.," 15.

63. Quoted in Aber and King, *The History of Hamilton County*, 74.

64. Seneca Ray Stoddard, *The Adirondacks: Illustrated* (Albany: Weed, Parsons, 1874), 83.

65. Emerson, "Early Life at Long Lake, N.Y.," 20.

66. Conklin, *Through Poverty's Vale*, 107–8.

67. Philip G. Terrie, *Wildlife and Wilderness: A History of Adirondack Mammals* (Fleischmanns, N.Y.: Purple Mountain Press, 1993), 96–112.

68. Conklin, *Through Poverty's Vale*, 147–48.

69. Conklin, *Through Poverty's Vale*, 107.

70. Conklin, *Through Poverty's Vale*, 216.

71. Conklin, *Through Poverty's Vale*, 125.

72. Emerson, "Early Life at Long Lake, N.Y.," 26.

73. Aber and King, *The History of Hamilton County*, 173, 751.

74. Terrie, *Wildlife and Wilderness*, 54–55, 92–93, 115–16.

3. "The Freedom of the Wilderness"

1. Edward Halsey Foster, *The Civilized Wilderness: Backgrounds to American Romantic Literature, 1817–1860* (New York: Free Press, 1975), 4.

2. Novak, *Nature and Culture*; Foster, *The Civilized Wilderness*, 4–5.

3. Philip G. Terrie, "Urban Man Confronts the Wilderness: The Nineteenth-Century Sportsman in the Adirondacks," *Journal of Sport History* 5 (Winter 1978): 7–20.

4. Redfield's letters to the *New York Journal of Commerce* appeared on Sept. 21, 24, and 25, 1837; these became the basis of "Some Account of Two Visits to the Mountains in Essex County New York, in the Years 1836 and 1837; With a Sketch of the Northern Sources of the Hudson," *American Journal of Science and Arts* 33 (July–Dec. 1837): 301–23. On Hoffman, see Homer Francis Barnes, *Charles Fenno Hoffman* (New York: Columbia Univ. Press, 1930).

5. Cheney told the story of Hoffman's disappointment to sporting writer Charles Lanman, who recorded it in *Adventures of an Angler*, 93–94.

6. Hoffman's letters appeared in the *New York Mirror* on Sept. 23, 30; Oct. 7, 14, 21, 28; and Dec. 16, 1837. They were reprinted in his *Wild Scenes in the Forest and Prairie* (London: Richard Bentley, 1839). On the rituals, values, and aesthetics of the romantic travelers, see Terrie, *Forever Wild,* 44–67.

7. Joel T. Headley, *The Adirondack; or, Life in the Woods* (New York: Baker and Scribner, 1849; reprint, Harrison, N.Y.: Harbor Hill, 1982), 167–68. On the publishing history and popularity of this book, see my Introduction to the Harbor Hill reprint. The last edition to appear in Headley's lifetime was published by Charles Scribner's Sons in 1882. Evidence of Headley's nervous disorder may be found in his introduction (p. i), where he declares, "An attack on the brain first drove me from the haunts of men to seek mental repose and physical strength in the woods."

8. Donaldson, *A History of the Adirondacks,* 1: 292–304.

9. Kenneth Durant and Helen Durant, *The Adirondack Guide-Boat* (Camden, Maine: International Marine Publishing Co., 1980; reprint, Blue Mountain Lake, N.Y.: The Adirondack Museum, 1986), 17–36; Hallie E. Bond, *Boats and Boating in the Adirondacks* (Blue Mountain Lake, N.Y.: The Adirondack Museum; Syracuse: Syracuse Univ. Press, 1995), 40–45.

10. Ralph Waldo Emerson, "The Adirondacs: A Journal Dedicated to My Fellow Travellers in August, 1858," *The Complete Works of Ralph Waldo Emerson* (Centenary Ed., Boston: Houghton Mifflin, 1903–4), 6: 182–94. For a first-hand account of Emerson's Adirondack experience, see William James Stillman, *The Autobiography of a Journalist* (Cambridge, Mass.: Houghton, Mifflin, 1901) 1: 239–81. For a scholarly analysis, see Paul F. Jamieson, "Emerson in the Adirondacks," *New York History* 39 (July 1958): 215–37.

11. Samuel H. Hammond, *Hills, Lakes and Forest Streams* (New York: J. C. Derby, 1854), 143–44.

12. Emerson, "The Adirondacs," 184.

13. Edmund Burke, *A Philosophical Enquiry into the Origin of Our Ideas of the Sublime and Beautiful* (London: Routledge & Keagan Paul, 1958). The introduction to this edition by James T. Boulton is an excellent account of the composition and importance of Burke's *Enquiry.*

14. Thomas Bangs Thorpe, "A Visit to 'John Brown's Tract,'" *Harper's New Monthly Magazine* 19 (June–Nov. 1859): 170.

15. Todd, *Long Lake,* 22–23.

16. Louis Legrand Noble, *The Life and Works of Thomas Cole* (Cambridge: Harvard Univ. Press, 1964), 177.

17. Hoffman, *Wild Scenes in the Forest and Prairie,* 50.

18. Alfred B. Street, *The Indian Pass* (New York: Hurd and Houghton, 1869), 23–24.

19. Patricia C. F. Mandel, *Fair Wilderness: American Paintings in the Collection of the Adirondack Museum* (Blue Mountain Lake, N.Y.: The Adirondack Museum, 1990), 58–60.

20. Headley, *The Adirondack,* 174.

21. Paul Schullery, *American Fly Fishing: A History* (New York: Nick Lyons Books, 1987). See also Charles Eliot Goodspeed, *Angling in America* (Boston: Houghton Mifflin, 1939), and Kenneth M. Cameron, "Adirondack Fancies," *Adirondack Life* 3 (Spring 1972).

22. See, for example, Alfred B. Street, *Woods and Waters; or, the Saranacs and Racket* (New York: M. Doolady, 1860), 190.

23. W. W. Ely, "A Trip to the Wilderness," *Moore's Rural New Yorker* 11 (1860): 273.

24. Street, *Woods and Waters*, 194.

25. Hammond, *Wild Northern Scenes; or, Sporting Adventures with the Rifle and the Rod* (New York: Derby and Jackson, 1857), 35. See also Hoffman, *Wild Scenes in the Forest and Prairie*, 29–30, where John Cheney is compared to Cooper's Natty Bumppo.

26. E. g., Nash, *Wilderness and the American Mind;* Max Oelschlaeger, *The Idea of Wilderness* (New Haven: Yale Univ. Press, 1991).

27. Governor William Bradford wrote of his party's first encounter with Massachussets, in 1620: "Besides, what could they see but a hideous and desolate wilderness, full of wild beasts and wild men," *Of Plymouth Plantation, 1620–1647* (New York: Modern Library, 1981), 70.

28. Henry Adams, *The Education of Henry Adams* (Boston: Houghton Mifflin, 1973), 38.

29. *New York Observer*, Oct. 19, 1844, 66; quoted in Warder H. Cadbury, Introduction, Todd, *Long Lake*, xiv–xv.

30. Todd, *Long Lake*, 46–54, 71–81.

31. Hammond, *Hills, Lakes and Forest Streams*, 175.

32. *New York Observer*, Jan. 23, 1847, quoted in Cadbury, Introduction, xxi.

33. Ely, "A Trip to the Wilderness," 273.

34. Hammond, *Wild Northern Scenes*, 83.

35. Hammond, *Wild Northern Scenes*, 33–34.

36. Headley, *The Adirondack*, 29–30, 36–43.

37. Samuel H. Hammond and L. N. Mansfield, *Country Margins and Ramblings of a Journalist* (New York: Baker and Scribner, 1849), 317–17; Street, *Woods and Waters*, 99–101, 106–17.

38. William James Stillman, "Sketchings," *The Crayon* 2 (July–Dec. 1855): 280–81, 296, 328–29.

39. T. Addison Richards, "A Forest Story," *Harper's New Monthly Magazine* 19 (June–Nov. 1859): 319.

4. "The Genius of Change Has Possession of the Land"

1. William H. H. Murray, *Adventures in the Wilderness; or, Camp-Life in the Adirondacks* (Blue Mountain Lake, N.Y.: The Adirondack Museum; Syracuse: Syracuse Univ. Press, 1970).

2. Warder H. Cadbury, Introduction to *Adventures in the Wilderness*, 11–75.

3. Cadbury, Introduction to *Adventures in the Wilderness*, 13–18.

4. Thomas R. Dunlap, *Saving America's Wildlife* (Princeton: Princeton Univ. Press, 1988), 9. Donna R. Braden, *Leisure and Entertainment in America* (Dearborn, Mich.: Henry Ford Museum & Greenfield Village, 1988), 204.

5. Braden, *Leisure and Entertainment in America*, 205.

6. Paul Russell Cutright, *Theodore Roosevelt: The Making of a Conservationist* (Urbana: Univ. of Illinois Press, 1985), 34–37.

7. David Strauss, "Toward a Consumer Culture: 'Adirondack Murray' and the Wilderness Vacation," *American Quarterly* 39 (Summer 1987): 270–286. Ann Douglas, *The Feminization of American Culture* (New York: Avon Books, 1977). T. J. Jackson Lears, *No*

Place of Grace: Antimodernism and the Transformation of American Culture, 1880–1920 (New York: Pantheon, 1981).

8. *First Annual Report of the Commissioners of State Parks of the State of New York. Transmitted to the Legislature May 15, 1873* (Senate Document 102, 1873; Albany: Weed, Parsons, 1874), 21. The members of the Commission were former governor Horatio Seymour, William A. Wheeler, Franklin B. Hough, Patrick H. Agan, William B. Taylor, George Raynor, and Verplanck Colvin. Colvin is generally thought to have been the primary author of the report.

9. See Lears, *No Place of Grace*, 47–58.

10. Verplanck Colvin, *Seventh Annual Report on the Progress of the Topographical Survey of the Adirondack Region of New York* (Albany: Weed, Parsons, 1880), 8.

11. Murray, *Adventures in the Wilderness*, 12–15.

12. Donaldson, *A History of the Adirondacks*, 1: 243–65. Frank Graham, Jr., *The Adirondack Park: A Political History*, (New York: Alfred A. Knopf, 1978), 46–52. Sheila Rothman, *Living in the Shadow of Death: Tuberculosis and the Social Experience of Illness in American History* (New York: Basic Books, 1994), 159–60, 189–206.

13. See Peter J. Schmitt, *Back to Nature: The Arcadian Myth in Urban America* (New York: Oxford Univ. Press, 1969), and Ralph H. Lutts, *The Nature Fakers: Wildlife, Science, and Sentiment* (Golden, Colo.: Fulcrum Publishing, 1990).

14. Harold K. Hochschild, *Doctor Durant and His Iron Horse* (Blue Mountain Lake, N.Y.: The Adirondack Museum, 1961), 1–6.

15. Charles Hallock, *The Fishing Tourist: Angler's Guide and Reference Book* (New York: Harper & Brothers, 1873), 70–74.

16. Harold K. Hochschild, *An Adirondack Resort in the Nineteenth Century* (Blue Mountain Lake, N.Y.: The Adirondack Museum, 1962), 25–42.

17. Murray may have been the first so to designate Paul Smith's: *Adventures in the Wilderness*, 44. Stoddard, *The Adirondacks: Illustrated*, 80, 3. William Crowley, *Seneca Ray Stoddard: Adirondack Illustrator* (Blue Mountain Lake, N.Y.: The Adirondack Museum, 1982). Hallock, *The Fishing Tourist*, 75.

18. Quoted in Hallock, *The Fishing Tourist*, 67.

19. Colvin, *Seventh Annual Report*, 8.

20. Hallock, *The Fishing Tourist*, 74–75.

21. Crowley, *Seneca Ray Stoddard*, 5.

22. S. S. Colt, *The Tourist's Guide through the Empire State, Embracing All the Cities, Towns and Watering Places* (Albany: privately printed, 1871), 158.

23. Hallock, *The Fishing Tourist*, 76.

24. See John F. Sears, *Sacred Places: American Tourist Attractions in the Nineteenth Century* (New York: Oxford Univ. Press, 1989), 3–11.

25. Harold K. Hochschild, *Life and Leisure in the Adirondack Backwoods* (Blue Mountain Lake, N.Y.: The Adirondack Museum, 1962), 1–32. Craig Gilborn, *Durant: The Fortunes and Woodland Camps of a Family in the Adirondacks* (Utica: North Country Books, 1981), passim. Harvey H. Kaiser, *Great Camps of the Adirondacks* (Boston: David R. Godine, 1982), 71–94.

26. Gilborn, *Durant*, 19–23; the Stoddard quotation is on 19.

27. Kaiser, *Great Camps of the Adirondacks*, 115–167.

28. Hamlin Garland, *Main Traveled Roads* (New York: New American Library, 1962), 72.

29. Donaldson, *A History of the Adirondacks,* 2: 102–3. Hochschild, *An Adirondack Resort* 2–3. *Summerings Among the Thousand Islands. . . .* (Syracuse: Boyd, 1882), 109.

30. Delaware and Hudson Rail Road, *A Summer Paradise* (Albany: Delaware and Hudson Rail Road Passenger Department, 1898).

31. Moravek, "The Iron Industry," iv–v, 115–17, 183–88, 225–28.

32. Minnie Patterson Stanyon, *The Quiet Years* (privately printed, 1965; reprinted, 1994), 20, 32.

33. Juliet Baker Kellogg, Diary (ms. 61–83, Adirondack Museum Library), entries for Feb. 19 and April 27, 1864.

34. Noel Riedinger-Johnson, "Introduction," Jeanne Robert Foster, *Adirondack Portraits: A Piece of Time,* ed. Noel Riedinger-Johnson (Syracuse: Syracuse Univ. Press, 1986), xxi–xli.

35. Jeanne Robert Foster, "The Boiled Shirt," *Adirondack Portraits,* 91.

36. Jeanne Robert Foster, "Mis' Cole," *Adirondack Portraits,* 28.

37. Kellogg, Diary, entries for May 3, 1865, and Feb. 19 and April 27, 1866.

38. Stanyon, *The Quiet Years,* 34, 9.

39. Jeanne Robert Foster, "Letter to Ruth Riedinger," *Adirondack Portraits,* 5.

40. Jeanne Robert Foster, "The Old Log House," *Adirondack Portraits,* 17.

41. Jeanne Robert Foster, "Jackson Balls," *Adirondack Portraits,* 20.

42. Jeanne Robert Foster, "Wax-on-Snow," *Adirondack Portraits,* 21–22.

43. Jeanne Robert Foster, "Neighbors," *Adirondack Portraits,* 13.

44. Jeanne Robert Foster, "Wax-on-Snow," *Adirondack Portraits,* 22.

45. Jeanne Robert Foster, "My First Journey," *Adirondack Portraits,* 42–43.

46. Stanyon, *The Quiet Years,* 108. Foster, "The Old Village," *Adirondack Portraits,* 49–50.

47. Foster, "The Old Village," *Adirondack Portraits,* 50.

48. Foster, "The Old Village," *Adirondack Portraits,* 49.

49. H. M. Clark, Diary, 1897–1901 (Adirondack Museum Library), microfilm 4.51.

5. "One Grand, Unbroken Domain"

1. Thomas Cobb, "The Adirondack Park and the Evolution of its Current Boundary," *The Adirondack Park in the Twenty-First Century: Technical Reports* ([Albany, N.Y.]: State of New York, 1990) 1: 24, notes that the Park of 1892 consisted of 2,807,760 acres, of which 551,093 were owned by the state. On subsequent additions to the Park, see Cobb. Basic histories of legislative and constitutional conservation in the Adirondacks in this era are the following: Donaldson, *A History of the Adirondacks,* 2: 163–96; Graham, *The Adirondack Park,* 65–132; Terrie, *Forever Wild,* 92–108.

2. Thomas R. Cox, et al., *This Well-Wooded Land: Americans and their Forests from Colonial Times to the Present* (Lincoln: Univ. of Nebraska Press, 1985), 113–15.

3. William F. Fox, *History of the Lumber Industry in the State of New York* (Harrison, N.Y.: Harbor Hill, 1976; originally published in *6th Annual Report of the New York Forest, Fish and Game Commission,* 1901); Donaldson, *A History of the Adirondacks,* 2: 150–58; Barbara McMartin, *The Great Forest,* 21–28.

4. Cox, et al., *This Well-Wooded Land*, 120–21.

5. McMartin, *The Great Forest*, 64–65.

6. George Perkins Marsh, *Man and Nature; or, Physical Geography as Modified by Human Action*, David Lowenthal, ed. (Cambridge: Harvard Univ. Press, 1965), 43. On Marsh, see David Lowenthal, *George Perkins Marsh: Versatile Vermonter* (New York: Columbia Univ. Press, 1958).

7. McMartin, *The Great Forest*, 38–50, 35–37.

8. Graham, *The Adirondack Park*, 68. The editorial appeared in the *Times* on August 9, 1864, and is quoted in Graham, 68–69.

9. For a thorough discussion of the intricacies of tax defaults and auctions, see McMartin, *The Great Forest*, 76–83.

10. Verplanck Colvin, "Ascent of Mt. Seward and Its Barometrical Measurement," *Twenty-Fourth Annual Report of the New York State Museum of Natural History* (Albany: Argus, 1872), 179.

11. Colvin, "Ascent of Mt. Seward," 180 (small caps and italics in original). Colvin gets credit for first using the term "Adirondack Park" by a narrow margin. The New York State Museum *Report* is dated 1872, but it is in fact a Senate Document (No. 68) of April, 18, 1871, and thus takes precedence over another use of the term reaching print in 1872. This appeared in E. R. Wallace, "A Reliable and Descriptive Guide to the Adirondacks," an appendix to H. Perry Smith, *The Modern Babes in the Wood; or Summerings in the Wilderness* (Hartford: Columbian Book Co., 1872), 243: "if our state authorities will but wisely take counsel of the increasing hosts of [tourists], the science of Geography must soon add to its best vocabulary, this euphonious designation of one of the world's most popular resorts:—'THE NEW YORK STATE ADIRONDACK PARK!'" (small caps in original).

12. Colvin, "Ascent of Mt. Seward," 172.

13. Colvin, "Ascent of Mt. Seward," 179–80.

14. Wallace, "A Reliable and Descriptive Guide to the Adirondacks," 243–44.

15. Quoted in Nash, *Wilderness and the American Mind*, 112.

16. *First Annual Report of the Commissioners of State Parks*. Graham, *The Adirondack Park*, 76–77. On Yellowstone, see Alfred Runte, *National Parks: The American Experience* (Lincoln: Univ. of Nebraska Press, 1979), 46.

17. *First Annual Report of the Commissioners of State Parks*, 5.

18. *First Annual Report of the Commissioners of State Parks*, 20.

19. *First Annual Report of the Commissioners of State Parks*, 13, 19.

20. *First Annual Report of the Commissioners of State Parks*, 6.

21. *First Annual Report of the Commissioners of State Parks*, 6–7.

22. Hallock, *The Fishing Tourist*, 69.

23. Verplanck Colvin, *Report of the Topographical Survey of the Adirondack Wilderness of New York for the Year 1873* (Senate Document 98, 1874; Albany: Weed Parsons, 1874), 155–56.

24. *Laws of the State of New York, 1883* (Albany: Weed Parsons, 1883), Chapter 13. Marvin Wolf Kranz, "Pioneering in Conservation: A History of the Conservation Movement in New York State 1865–1903" (Ph.D. diss., Syracuse Univ., 1961), 147.

25. *Laws of the State of New York, 1885* (Albany: Weed Parsons, 1885), chapter 283. The Adirondack counties were Clinton (from which the towns of Altona and Dannemora

were excepted), Essex, Franklin, Fulton, Hamilton, Herkimer, Lewis, Saratoga, St. Lawrence, Warren, and Washington; a twelfth, Oneida, was added in 1887. The law also designated three Catskill counties. See Graham, *The Adirondack Park*, 96–106; Terrie, *Forever Wild*, 96–97.

26. Kranz, "Pioneering," 160, 167–70. *New York Tribune,* Jan. 30, 1984, cited in Kranz, 168.

27. *Plattsburgh Republican,* Feb. 9, 1984, cited in Kranz, "Pioneering," 170; see also 177–78.

28. *New York Times,* Feb. 20, 1884, cited in Kranz, "Pioneering," 171.

29. McMartin, *The Great Forest,* 93; Graham, *The Adirondack Park,* 108, 123–24; Terrie, *Forever Wild,* 100.

30. *Forest and Stream* 19 (Jan. 25, 1883): 502, and 21 (Dec. 13, 1883): 381; *Garden and Forest* 3 (March 12, 1890): 121; Donaldson, *A History of the Adirondacks,* 1: 273–88.

31. *New York Times,* Sept. 16, 18, 23, and 25, and Oct. 4 and 6, 1889.

32. New York State Forest Commission, *Annual Report . . . for 1890* (Assembly Document 84, 1891; Albany: James B. Lyon, 1891), 67–68.

33. Kranz, "Pioneering," 333. Norman J. VanValkenburgh, *The Adirondack Forest Preserve: A Narrative of the Evolution of the Adirondack Forest Preserve of New York State* (Blue Mountain Lake, N.Y.: The Adirondack Museum, 1979), 48–49. New York State Forest Commission, *Report for 1890,* 70.

34. New York State Forest Commission, *Report for 1890,* 57, 77.

35. New York State Forest Commission, *Report for 1890,* 87–88. Kranz, "Pioneering," 335–37. VanValkenburgh, *Adirondack Forest Preserve,* 50.

36. New York State Forest Commission, *Report for 1891* (Assembly Document 34, 1892; Albany: James B. Lyon, 1892), 22, 30.

37. Harold K. Steen, *The U.S. Forest Service: A History* (Seattle: Univ. of Washington Press, 1976), 26–46, 123–24; David Clary, *Timber and the Forest Service* (Lawrence: Univ. Press of Kansas, 1986), 3–28.

38. Kranz, "Pioneering," 321–30.

39. *Warrensburgh News,* Feb. 27, 1890, quoted in Kranz, "Pioneering," 330–32.

40. Kranz, "Pioneering," 358–67. Norman J. Van Valkenburgh, *The Adirondack Forest Preserve: A Narrative of the Evolution of the Adirondack Forest Preserve of New York State* (Blue Mountain Lake, N.Y.: Adirondack Museum, 1979), 52–53.

41. *Laws of the State of New York, 1892,* chapter 707, 1459–60. See also New York State Forest Commission, *Report for 1890,* 57, 70, 77, 87–89; New York State Forest Commission, *Report for 1891,* 22, 25. 30; New York State Forest Commission, *Report for 1893* (Senate Document 85, 1894; Albany: James B. Lyon, 1894). Kranz, "Pioneering," 333, 335–37; VanValkenburgh, *Adirondack Forest Preserve,* 48–50.

42. *Laws of the State of New York, 1892* (Albany: Banks & Brothers, 1892), chapter 707, 1459–60. See also New York State Forest Commission, Annual Report for 1893.

43. On the Constitutional Convention of 1894 and the passage of Article VII, Section 7, see Donaldson, *A History of the Adirondacks,* 2: 187–96; Graham, *The Adirondack Park,* 126–32; Terrie, *Forever Wild,* 104–8.

44. Louise A. Halper, "'A Rich Man's Paradise': Constitutional Preservation of New

York State's Adirondack Forest, A Centenary Consideration," *Ecology Law Quarterly* 19 (1992): 260.

45. *Letters of William James,* ed. Henry James (Boston: Atlantic Monthly Press, 1920), 2: 261. The editor was William James's son.

46. *Letters of William James,* 2: 259.

47. *Letters of William James,* 2: 75–78.

48. The Marcy massif belonged to two owners: the Adirondack Mountain Reserve, a private club based around the Ausable Lakes and with which William James was on good terms, owned the east half, while the successors to the McIntyre iron works owned the west half. See Edith Pilcher, *Up the Lake Road: The First Hundred Years of the Adirondack Mountain Reserve* (Keene Valley, N.Y.: Adirondack Mountain Reserve, 1987), 53.

6. "The Havoc of the Years"

1. David C. Smith, "Wood Pulp Paper Comes to the Northeast, 1865–1900" *Forest History* 19 (April 1966): 13–25.

2. Smith, "Wood Pulp Paper Comes to the Northeast, 1865–1900," 22. McMartin, *The Great Forest,* 193. International Paper Corporation, "A Tradition in New York" (Albany: n.d.), inside front cover.

3. Figures on International Paper from telephone conversation, April 8, 1996, with Robert Steggeman, Regional Manager for Public Affairs, International Paper Corporation, Albany, New York. Figures on Long Lake from telephone conversation, April 9, 1996, with Joe LeBlanc, Long Lake Assessor.

4. Fox, *History of the Lumber Industry in the State of New York,* 77.

5. McMartin, *The Great Forest,* 121.

6. William G. Robbins, *Lumberjacks and Legislators: Political Economy of the U. S. Lumber Industry, 1890–1941* (College Station: Texas A&M Univ. Press, 1982), 5–7, 14–16.

7. Fox, *History of the Lumber Industry in the State of New York,* 77–78.

8. McMartin, *The Great Forest,* 128–38, 146–47.

9. Nelson T. Samson, "Woods Labor in the Adirondacks" (Ph.D. diss., State Univ. College of Forestry, Syracuse, 1952), 55.

10. Ralph L. Hoy, *An Adirondack Boyhood Remembered* (Santa Barbara, Calif.: Mendicus Press, 1978), 12.

11. Foster, "Garron's Rock," *Adirondack Portraits,* 135. This poem is "based on an old Adirondack ballad."

12. Gladys Stanyon and Mildred S. Colvin, *Reflections: Wells on the Sacandaga* (privately printed, 1975), 84–87.

13. Foster, "Shanty Days," *Adirondack Portraits,* 131–32. In the passage quoted, the first ellipsis represents lines I have not included, while the second is in the original.

14. E. Lester Stanton, "Memories," *Souvenirs of the Adirondack Mountains* (Batavia, Ill.: privately printed, 1982), 80.

15. Sadie E. Canton, "My Father, a Lumberjack," in Sadie Canton, Melba Wrisley, Marilyn Cross, and Sonja Aubin, *Growing Up Strong: Four North Country Women Recall Their Lives* (Elizabethtown, N.Y.: Pinto Press, 1995), 13.

16. Samson, "Woods Labor in the Adirondacks," 2–3, 9. For a summary of early efforts to organize workers in the woods products industry, see Cox, et al, *This Well-Wooded Land*, 170–74.

17. Stanyon and Colvin, *Reflections*, 84–88.

18. McMartin, *The Great Forest*, 127–28.

19. James Lord, "Another Centennial Celebration," *The Conservationist* 39 (May–June 1985): 26–28. William G. Howard, *Forest Fires* (Albany: J. B. Lyon, 1914; State of New York Conservation Commission, Bulletin 10). Robert Bernard, "Years of Fires," *Adirondack Life* 20 (March–April 1981): 43–46. McMartin, *The Great Forest*, 139–42.

20. Raymond S. Spears, "State Forest Fire Service," *The Angler and Hunter* 2 (March 1910): 143–48. McMartin, *The Great Forest*, 141.

21. McMartin, *The Great Forest*, 141.

22. New York State Forest, Fish and Game Commission, *Eighth and Ninth Annual Reports* (Albany: J. B. Lyon, 1904), 37.

23. Kranz, "Pioneering," 498–99; Graham, *The Adirondack Park*, 147; Donaldson, *A History of the Adirondacks*, 2: 210–13.

24. On the importance of the deliberations of the 1915 convention, see Philip G. Terrie, "Forever Wild Forever: The Forest Preserve Debate at the New York State Constitutional Convention of 1915," *New York History* 70 (July 1989): 251–75.

25. Graham, *The Adirondack Park*, 147. Association for the Protection of the Adirondacks, miscellaneous minutes, papers, and correspondence (Adirondack Museum Library), microfilm, April 14, 1903, April 17, 1912, March 31, 1902.

26. Stephen Birmingham, *The Right People: A Portrait of the American Social Establishment* (Boston: Little, Brown, 1958), 260.

27. The literature on class and wealth and popular attitudes about them in late nineteenth-century America is vast. See, for example, Stephan Thernstrom, *Poverty and Progress: Social Mobility in a Nineteenth Century City* (Cambridge: Harvard Univ. Press, 1964).

28. Theodore Roosevelt, "Fellow-Feeling as a Political Factor," *The Century* 59 (Jan. 1900): 467.

29. Donaldson, *A History of the Adirondacks*, 1: 155–56.

30. Masten, *The Story of Adirondac*, 175–89.

31. Edith Pilcher, *Up the Lake Road*. Philip G. Terrie, "'The Grandest Private Park': Forestry and Land Management" in Edward Comstock, Jr., ed., *The Adirondack League Club, 1890–1990* (Old Forge, N.Y.: The Adirondack League Club, 1990), 73–111.

32. Pilcher, *Up the Lake Road*, 27–32.

33. Terrie, "'The Grandest Private Park,'" 74.

34. Quoted in Birmingham, *The Right People*, 266. Born "Melville," Dewey, a proponent of a system of simplified spelling, signed his name "Melvil."

35. Quoted in John Higham, *Strangers in the Land: Patterns of American Nativism, 1860–1925* (New Brunswick: Rutgers Univ. Press, 1955), 147.

36. Quoted in Birmingham, *The Right People*, 266.

37. New York State Forest, Fish and Game Commission, *Eighth and Ninth Annual Reports*, 37–43. *Adirondack League Club Yearbook* (New York: Adirondack League Club, 1893), 52–53.

38. *Adirondack League Club Yearbook* (New York: Adirondack League Club, 1891), 39.

39. New York Forest, Fish and Game Commission, *Eighth and Ninth Annual Reports,* 36.

40. Donaldson, *A History of the Adirondacks,* 2: 142–43. Neal Burdick, "Who Killed Orrando P. Dexter?," *Adirondack Life* 12 (May–June, 1982): 23–26, 48–49.

41. Donaldson, *A History of the Adirondacks,* 2: 143–48.

42. Donaldson, *A History of the Adirondacks,* 2: 148.

43. New York Forest, Fish and Game Commission, *Eighth and Ninth Annual Reports,* 36.

44. New York Forest, Fish and Game Commission, *Eighth and Ninth Annual Reports,* 44.

45. Donaldson, *A History of the Adirondacks,* 2: 296.

46. Hochschild, *Life and Leisure,* 97–98.

47. Donna R. Braden and Judith E. Endelman, *Americans on Vacation* (Dearborn, Mich.: Henry Ford Museum & Greenfield Village, 1990), 44. Foster Rhea Dulles, *A History of Recreation: America Learns to Play* (Englewood Cliffs, N.J.: Prentice Hall, 1965), 316–17.

48. New York State Conservation Commission, *Ninth Annual Report for the Year 1919* (Albany: J. B. Lyon, 1920), 105.

49. VanValkenburgh, *Adirondack Forest Preserve,* 126–31.

50. New York State Conservation Commission, *Ninth Annual Report,* 116–17.

51. Bond, *Boats and Boating in the Adirondacks,* 199.

52. John A. Jakle, *The Tourist: Travel in Twentieth-Century America* (Lincoln: Univ. of Nebraska Press, 1985), 152. Warren James Belasco, *Americans on the Road: From Autocamp to Motel, 1910–1945* (Cambridge, Mass.: MIT Press, 1979), 3–69.

53. New York State Conservation Commission, *Ninth Annual Report,* 101. VanValkenburgh, *Adirondack Forest Preserve,* 127. According to Edith Pilcher, *Up the Lake Road,* 53, the purchase of Marcy was not completed until 1923.

54. Masten, *The Story of Adirondac,* 186–88.

55. Stanyon and Colvin, *Reflections,* 10.

56. Stanyon and Colvin, *Reflections,* 17–22.

57. Hoy, *Adirondack Boyhood,* 2, 16.

58. Hoy, *Adirondack Boyhood,* 10–11.

59. Stanton, "Memories," *Souvenirs,* 6–7.

60. Stanton, *Souvenirs,* 20–21.

61. E.g., Stanyon, *The Quiet Years,* 80.

62. Foster, "The Game Protector," *Adirondack Portraits,* 113–14.

63. See Terrie, *Wildlife and Wilderness,* 96–108.

64. Foster, "State Land," *Adirondack Portraits,* 142–43.

7. "The Roads Are Filled with Interest"

1. Jakle, *The Tourist,* 121–26; Kathryn Grover, "The Automobile Tourist in the Adirondacks" (unpublished report submitted to Adirondack Museum, Feb. 11, 1996), 34–35.

2. *Motordom* 24 (June 1931), n. p.

3. New York State Conservation Commission, *Twenty-First Annual Report . . . 1931* (New York: Burland Printing Co., 1932), 22.

4. "World Famous Recreation," *Motordom* 24 (June 1931), n.p.

5. Van Valkenburgh, *Adirondack Forest Preserve*, 135–36, 142–43.

6. Bond, *Boats and Boating*, 151, 154, 157.

7. Bond, *Boats and Boating*, 207–8.

8. Bond, *Boats and Boating*, 158–61.

9. Laura and Guy Waterman, *Forest and Crag: A History of Hiking, Trail Blazing, and Adventure in the Northeast Mountains* (Boston: Appalachian Mountain Club, 1989), 209–19.

10. Paul Jamieson, "Camping on State Lands Through the Years: The Adirondack Lean-to and the Forest Preserve," *The Conservationist* 19 (Feb.–March 1965): 5.

11. Laura and Guy Waterman, *Forest and Crag*, 514–17.

12. Grover, "The Automobile Tourist," 39.

13. Van Valkenburgh, *Adirondack Forest Preserve*, 144. Grover, "The Automobile Tourist," 46–48. Graham, *The Adirondack Park*, 185.

14. Van Valkenburgh, *Adirondack Forest Preserve*, 137.

15. Thomas L. Cobb, "The Adirondack Park and the Evolution of its Current Boundary," *The Adirondack Park in the Twenty-First Century: Technical Reports* (Albany: State of New York, 1990), 1: 25–30.

16. Cobb, "The Adirondack Park and the Evolution of its Current Boundary," 28. Norman Van Valkenburgh, "The Blue Line of the Adirondack Park, Part V—Expansion," *Adirondac* 59 (Jan.–Feb. 1995): 15–17. Two further expansions of the Park boundary were adopted, in 1956 and 1973; these are discussed in the next chapter.

17. James C. Dawson, "Adirondack Forest Preserve Acquisition: Policies and Procedures," *The Adirondack Park in the Twenty-First Century: Technical Reports* (Albany: State of New York, 1990), 1: 112.

18. Van Valkenburgh, *Adirondack Forest Preserve*, 303–6.

19. Grover, "The Automobile Tourist," 38.

20. *Utica Daily Press*, "Summer Resort Guide, 1924" (Adirondack Museum Library, "Description and Travel, 1920–1929"), quoted in Grover, "The Automobile Tourist," 38.

21. Charles Z. Mihalyi, "Million Dollar Real Estate Catalog" (Glenfield, N.Y.: n.d.; Adirondack Museum Library, "Real Estate [Adirondack—Earlier]"); internal evidence establishes the publication of this brochure in the late 1930s.

22. Quoted in Van Valkenburgh, *Adirondack Forest Preserve*, 150.

23. Van Valkenburgh, *Adirondack Forest Preserve*, 151; Graham, *The Adirondack Park*, 184–87.

24. Graham, *The Adirondack Park*, 188.

25. On the frequent ideological clashes between the Conservation bureaucracy and preservationists, see Terrie, *Forever Wild*, 109–35.

26. James M. Glover, *A Wilderness Original: The Life of Bob Marshall* (Seattle: The Mountaineers, 1986), esp. 194–95.

27. Graham, *The Adirondack Park*, 195.

28. Van Valkenburgh, *Adirondack Forest Preserve*, 175–76. See also New York State Conservation Commission, *Twenty-Ninth Annual Report . . . 1939* (Albany: J. B. Lyon, 1940), 47; Graham, *The Adirondack Park*, 196.

29. Van Valkenburgh, *Adirondack Forest Preserve*, 197.

30. Van Valkenburgh, *Adirondack Forest Preserve*, 201–4.

31. Paul Schaefer, "Wild Forest Land," *The Conservationist* 6 (Feb.–March 1952): 3–4.

32. Roscoe C. Martin, *Water for New York: A Study in State Administration of Water Resources* (Syracuse: Syracuse Univ. Press, 1960), 147–68. Graham, *The Adirondack Park*, 197–200. Terrie, "'The Grandest Private Park,'" 93–101.

33. Harold T. Pinkett, *Gifford Pinchot: Private and Public Forester* (Urbana: Univ. of Illinois Press, 1970), 36–38.

34. A. B. Recknagel, *The Forests of New York State* (New York: Macmillan, 1923), 52, 77–78.

35. Terrie, "'The Grandest Private Park,'" 73, 77–82, 101–7.

36. Peter C. Welsh, *Jacks, Jobbers and Kings: Logging in the Adirondacks, 1850–1950* (Utica, N.Y.: North Country Books, 1995), 1–5.

37. Welsh, *Jacks, Jobbers and Kings*, 67; Frank Reed, *Lumberjack Sky Pilot* (Lakemont, N.Y.: North Country Books, 1976), 29.

38. McMartin, *The Great Forest*, 160.

39. McMartin, *The Great Forest*, 162–63.

40. Samson, "Woods Labor," 2–3; Welsh *Jacks, Jobbers and Kings*, 68–70.

41. Roy C. Higby, *A Man from the Past* (Big Moose, N.Y.: Big Moose Press, 1974), 31, 39, 43.

42. Higby, *A Man from the Past*, 19–21, 28–32. See also Stanyon, *The Quiet Years*, 108.

43. Stanyon, *The Quiet Years*, 108.

44. Higby, *A Man from the Past*, 19.

45. Canton, "The Telephone," *Growing Up Strong*, 34.

46. Allan S. Everest, *Rum Across the Border: The Prohibition Era in Northern New York* (Syracuse: Syracuse Univ. Press, 1978), 24, 106–7.

47. Higby, *A Man from the Past*, 28–29.

48. Herbert Keith, *Man of the Woods* (Blue Mountain Lake, N.Y.: The Adirondack Museum; Syracuse: Syracuse Univ. Press, 1972), 140–41.

49. Aber and King, *The History of Hamilton County*, 231–37.

50. Louis J. Simmons, *Mostly Spruce and Hemlock* (Tupper Lake, N.Y.: privately printed, 1976), 343–44.

51. Higby, *A Man from the Past*, 98.

52. Cross, "A Way of Survival," *Growing Up Strong*, 104–5.

53. Cross, "Is Bigger Better?" *Growing Up Strong*, 138.

8. "A Crisis Looms"

1. Grover, "The Automobile Tourist," 69.

2. Grover, "The Automobile Tourist," 69. Grover writes that Animal Land was begun by Paul Lukaris in 1953; Art Smith, the current owner, in a telephone conversation with me (June 4, 1996), asserts that Lukaris first opened in 1948. Arthur L. Benson, *Adirondack Mountain Adventure* (North Hudson, N.Y.: Frontier Town Productions, n.d.), 50–55.

3. Donna R. Braden, *Leisure and Entertainment in America*, 328. Belasco, *Americans on*

the Road, 171. Mark Rose, *Interstate: Express Highway Politics 1941–1956* (Lawrence: Univ. Press of Kansas, 1979), 85–94.

4. VanValkenburgh, *Adirondack Forest Preserve,* 218; Graham, *The Adirondack Park,* 212.

5. Harold Burton, "Holiday Handbook of Escape," *Holiday* 32 (July 1962): 101–6, quoted in Grover, "The Automobile Tourist," 64. On the rising number of 46-ers, see Tim Tefft, ed., *Of the Summits, Of the Forests* (Morrisonville, N.Y.: Adirondack 46-ers, 1991), 14.

6. Temporary Study Commission on the Future of the Adirondacks, *The Future of the Adirondacks,* (Blue Mountain Lake, N.Y.: The Adirondack Museum, 1971), 2: Technical Report 5, 6.

7. Richard A. Liroff and G. Gordon Davis, *Protecting Open Space: Land Use Control in the Adirondack Park* (Cambridge: Ballinger Publishing Co., 1981), 14–15. Cobb, "The Adirondack Park and the Evolution of its Current Boundary," 28.

8. Liroff and Davis, *Protecting Open Space,* 14.

9. Graham, *The Adirondack Park,* 219–22.

10. Liroff and Davis, *Protecting Open Space,* 21.

11. Temporary Study Commission on the Future of the Adirondacks, *The Future of the Adirondacks,* 2: Technical Report 1, 5.

12. Temporary Study Commission on the Future of the Adirondacks, *The Future of the Adirondack Park* (vol.. 1 of *The Future of the Adirondacks*), 6.

13. Cobb, "The Adirondack Park and the Evolution of its Current Boundary," 29.

14. Paul J. C. Friedlander, "Blueprint for Lesiure in the Adirondacks," *New York Times,* June 21, 1970, Travel.

15. *Hamilton County News,* Jan. 25, 1973.

16. Temporary Study Commission on the Future of the Adirondacks, *The Future of the Adirondack Park,* 25. Graham, *The Adirondack Park,* 242–46, 248–53. The State Land Master Plan, since it did not involve any change of New York law, required only executive approval before becoming state policy. The Private Land Plan required approval from the legislature before it could become effective.

17. Temporary Study Commission on the Future of the Adirondacks, *The Future of the Adirondacks, Technical Reports: Private and Public Lands,* vol. B (Blue Mountain Lake, N.Y.: The Adirondack Museum, 1971), 25.

18. Temporary Study Commission on the Future of the Adirondacks, *The Future of the Adirondacks, Technical Reports: Private and Public Lands,* B: 38.

19. Jeff Elliott, "Adirondack Vigilantes Assault EF!ers—Police Refuse to Halt Mob Violence," *Earth First! Journal* 10 (Sept. 22, 1990): 1, 13. Linda Laing, "The Open Road: Wilderness, Politics and the Way to Crane Pond," *Adirondack Life* 27 (Annual Guide 1996): 26–32.

20. *Hamilton County News,* May 22–28, 1990.

21. Larry Maxwell, "Group Sets Out to Make Repairs," *Glens Falls Post Star,* Oct. 29, 1990.

22. The literature on acid precipitation is huge. See, e.g., John F. Sheehan, "Acid Rain Still a Scourge in Adirondacks," *Wild Earth* 6 (Spring 1996): 34–36.

23. Anthony N. D'Elia, *The Adirondack Rebellion: A Political, Economic and Social Exposé of the Adirondack State Park* (Loon Lake, N. Y.: Onchiota Books, 1979), v, 16.

24. "APA Opponent Anthony D'Elia Dies," *Hamilton County News,* Oct. 23–29, 1990.

25. Liroff and Davis, *Protecting Open Space*, 53–54.

26. Temporary Study Commission on the Future of the Adirondacks, *The Future of the Adirondacks, Technical Reports: Transportation and the Economy*, 21–22. The labor force participation rate is that percentage of the population in the labor force, i.e., either employed or looking for work.

27. William F. Hammond, Jr., "21 Years Later, APA Is Still Controversial," *Schenectady Daily Gazette*, May 18, 1992.

28. "Employment and Payrolls in the Adirondack Park" (Albany: Nelson A. Rockefeller Institute of Government, Center for New York State and Local Government Studies, 1994), v.

29. New York State Board of Equalization and Assessment, "The Taxation of State-Owned Lands" (typescript, 1982, Adirondack Museum Library), Taxes, 1.

30. New York State Board of Equalization and Assessment, "The Taxation of State-Owned Lands," 6.

31. All statistics on education are from the Univ. of the State of New York, State Education Department, *New York, The State of Learning: A Report to the Governor and the Legislature on the Educational Status of the State's Schools* (Albany: State Education Department, 1995) and Univ. of the State of New York, State Education Department, *Condition of Education in the Adirondack Blue Line* (Albany: State Education Department, 1992).

32. Liroff and Davis, *Protecting Open Space*, 53–54.

33. James Howard Kunstler, "For Sale," *New York Times Magazine* (June 18, 1989): 22–25, 30–33. See also William K. Verner, et al., "Report of the Citizens' Advisory Task Force on Open Space to the Adirondack Park Agency" (typescript, Adirondack Museum Library, April 18, 1980).

34. See David Cederstrom and Mark Frost, "Inside Finch Pruyn," *Glens Falls Chronicle*, Feb. 25, 1988: "Finch, Pruyn owns 158,000 acres of land in the Adirondacks, making it the second biggest private landowner in New York State behind International Paper." But according to Barbara McMartin, *The Great Forest*, 174, by 1990, Finch, Pruyn's holdings in the Adirondacks had dropped slightly, to 154,476 acres. That same year International Paper owned 205,714 acres (making it the largest owner of private land in New York State), and Champion International (the successor of the St. Regis Paper Co.) owned 118,265 acres.

35. The Commission on the Adirondacks in the Twenty-First Century, *The Adirondack Park in the Twenty-First Century* (Albany: State of New York, 1990). See also Commission on the Adirondacks in the Twenty-First Century, *The Adirondack Park in the Twenty-First Century: Technical Reports* (Albany: State of New York, 1990).

36. William F. Hammond, Jr., "Adirondack Park Faces Uncertain Future," *Schenectady Daily Gazette*, May 19, 1992.

37. "Legislation is Already Drafted," *Hamilton County News*, May 15, 1990.

38. "Second Freedom Drive is Planned," *Hamilton County News*, May 22, 1990.

39. "Stafford Leads Freedom Drive," *Hamilton County News*, June 5, 1990.

40. "Gerdts Calls for Adirondack Unity," *Hamilton County News*, June 5, 1990.

41. "The Development Interests have Lined up Their Spokesmen: Who's Going to Speak for You?" *Lake Placid News*, Sept. 12, 1990. For evidence that local opinion was split

among a number of positions, see Timothy Holmes, *The Future of the Adirondacks: A Survey of Attitudes* (Blue Mountain Lake, N.Y.: The Adirondack Museum, 1990).

42. Lucia Mouat, "NY's Adirondack Park Celebrates 100 Years," *Christian Science Monitor,* May 21, 1992. Sam Howe Verhovek, "For 100 Years, 'Forever Wild' and Forever in Dispute," *New York Times,* May 19, 1992. Will Nixon, "Fear and Loathing in the Adirondacks," *E Magazine* 3 (Sept.–Oct. 1992): 28–35.

43. Leo Wasserman, "New Roads, New Directions," *AJES: Adirondack Journal of Environmental Studies* 2 (Spring 1995): 10.

44. John Collins, letter to *Lake Placid News,* April 12, 1995.

45. Nixon, "Fear and Loathing in the Adirondacks," 31.

46. "C. V. Whitney, Horseman and Benefactor, Dies at 93," *New York Times,* Dec. 14, 1992.

47. William F. Hammond, Jr., "Whitney Park's Future at Stake," *Schenectady Gazette,* March 1, 1992.

48. Michael Shnayerson, "Mary, Queen of Spots," *Vanity Fair* (August 1995): 102–10, 154–56.

49. Paul Ertelt, "Whitneys Seek to Subdivide Park Property," *Glens Falls Post-Star,* July 26, 1996.

50. See, e.g., Leslie Zganjar, "Conservationists, Industry Join to Protect Adirondacks," *Rochester Democrat and Chronicle,* August 21, 1990.

51. The Commission on the Adirondacks in the Twenty-First Century, *The Adirondack Park in the Twenty-First Century,* 3.

52. Quoted in Roger Trancik, *Hamlets of the Adirondacks* (np., 1983), 7.

53. Mathias Oppersdorff and Alice Wolf Gilborn, *Adirondack Faces* (Blue Mountain Lake, N.Y.: The Adirondack Museum; Syracuse: Syracuse Univ. Press, 1991), 6.

54. Trancik, *Hamlets of the Adirondacks,* 9–10.

55. Bill McKibben develops this idea in *Hope, Human and Wild* (Boston: Little, Brown and Co., 1995), 172–227.

Selected Bibliography

Aber, Ted, and Stella King. *The History of Hamilton County.* Lake Pleasant, N.Y.: Great Wilderness Books, 1965.

Aldrich, Michele Alexis La Clerque. "New York Natural History Survey." Ph.D. diss., Univ. of Texas, 1974.

Allen, Ross F., et al. "An Archaeological Survey of Bloomery Forges in the Adirondacks." *IA: The Journal of the Society for Industrial Archaeology* 16 (1990).

Anderson, Patricia. *The Course of Empire: The Erie Canal and the New York Landscape.* Rochester: Memorial Art Gallery of the University of Rochester, 1984.

Association for the Protection of the Adirondacks. Miscellaneous minutes, papers, and correspondence. Adirondack Museum Library. Microfilm.

Barnes, Homer Francis. *Charles Fenno Hoffman.* New York: Columbia University Press, 1930.

Belasco, Warren James. *Americans on the Road: From Autocamp to Motel, 1910–1945.* Cambridge, Mass.: MIT Press, 1979.

[Benedict, Farrand N.] "The Wilds of Northern New York." *Putnam's Monthly Magazine* 4 (July–Dec. 1854).

Benson, Arthur L. *Adirondack Mountain Adventure.* North Hudson, N.Y.: Frontier Town Productions, n.d.

Berkhofer, Robert F., Jr. *The White Man's Indian: Images of the American Indian from Columbus to the Present.* New York: Alfred A. Knopf, 1978.

Bernard, Robert. "Years of Fires." *Adirondack Life* 20 (March–April 1981).

Bethke, Robert D. *Adirondack Voices: Woodsmen and Woods Lore.* Urbana: University of Illinois Press, 1981.

Birmingham, Stephen. *The Right People: A Portrait of the American Social Establishment.* Boston: Little, Brown, 1958.

Bond, Hallie E. *Boats and Boating in the Adirondacks.* Blue Mountain Lake, N.Y.: The Adirondack Museum; Syracuse: Syracuse Univ. Press, 1995.

Braden, Donna R. *Leisure and Entertainment in America*. Dearborn, Mich.: Henry Ford Museum & Greenfield Village, 1988.

Braden, Donna R., and Judith E. Endelman. *Americans on Vacation*. Dearborn, Mich.: Henry Ford Museum & Greenfield Village, 1990.

Buerger, Robert B., and Thomas E. Pasquarello. "The Adirondack Park: Changing Perceptions of Residents Towards Park Land Use Issues." *Journal of Recreation and Leisure* 13 (Spring 1993).

Burdick, Neal. "Who Killed Orrando P. Dexter?" *Adirondack Life* 12 (May–June 1982).

Byrne, Martin John. "Life in the North Country 100 Years Ago." Adirondack Museum Library. Microfilm 4.26.

Cadbury, Warder. "The Improbable Charles C. Ingham." *Adirondac* 51 (August 1987).

Cameron, Kenneth M. "Adirondack Fancies." *Adirondack Life* 3 (Spring 1972).

Canton, Sadie, Melba Wrisley, Marilyn Cross, and Sonja Aubin. *Growing Up Strong: Four North Country Women Recall Their Lives*. Elizabethtown, N.Y.: Pinto Press, 1995.

Carson, Russell M. L. *Peaks and People of the Adirondacks*. Garden City, N.Y.: Doubleday, Page, 1927; reprint, Glens Falls, N. Y.: Adirondack Mountain Club, 1973, 1986.

Champlain, Samuel de. *Voyages of Samuel de Champlain, 1604–1618*. Edited by W. L. Grant. New York: C. Scribner's Sons, 1907.

Clark, H. M. Diary. Adirondack Museum Library. Microfilm 4.51.

Colt, S. S. *The Tourist's Guide through the Empire State, Embracing All the Cities, Towns and Watering Places*. Albany: privately printed, 1871.

Colvin, Verplanck. *Seventh Annual Report on the Progress of the Topographical Survey of the Adirondack Region of New York*. Albany: Weed, Parsons, 1880.

Commission on the Adirondacks in the Twenty-First Century. *The Adirondack Park in the Twenty-First Century*. Albany: State of New York, 1990.

Commission on the Adirondacks in the Twenty-First Century. *The Adirondack Park in the Twenty-First Century: Technical Reports*. 2 vols. Albany: State of New York, 1990.

Comstock, Edward, Jr., ed. *The Adirondack League Club, 1890–1990*. Old Forge, N.Y.: The Adirondack League Club, 1990.

Conklin, Henry. *Through Poverty's Vale: A Hardscrabble Boyhood in Upstate New York, 1832–1862*. Syracuse: Syracuse Univ. Press, 1974.

Cox, Thomas R., Robert S. Maxwell, Phillip Drennon Thomas, and Joseph J. Malone, *This Well-Wooded Land: Americans and their Forests from Colonial Times to the Present*. Lincoln: Univ. of Nebraska Press, 1985.

Cronon, William. "A Place for Stories: Nature, History, and Narrative." *Journal of American History* 78 (March 1992).

Crowley, William. *Seneca Ray Stoddard: Adirondack Illustrator.* Blue Mountain Lake, N.Y.: The Adirondack Museum, 1982.

Delaware and Hudson Railroad. *A Summer Paradise.* Albany: Delaware and Hudson Railroad Passenger Department, 1898.

D'Elia, Anthony N. *The Adirondack Rebellion: A Political, Economic and Social Exposé of the Adirondack State Park.* Loon Lake, N.Y.: Onchiota Books, 1979.

Dodge, David. Diary. Adirondack Museum Library. Microfilm 4. 53.

Donaldson, Alfred L. *A History of the Adirondacks.* 2 vols. New York: Century, 1921; reprint, Harrison, N. Y.: Harbor Hill Books, 1977.

Dulles, Foster Rhea. *A History of Recreation: America Learns to Play.* Englewood Cliffs, N.J.: Prentice Hall, 1965.

Durant, Kenneth, and Helen Durant. *The Adirondack Guide-Boat.* Camden, Maine: International Marine Publishing, 1980; reprint, Blue Mountain Lake, N.Y.: The Adirondack Museum, 1986.

Ekirch, Arthur A., Jr. *Man and Nature in America.* New York: Columbia Univ. Press, 1963.

Elliott, Jeff. "Adirondack Vigilantes Assault EF!ers—Police Refuse to Halt Mob Violence." *Earth First! Journal* 10 (Sept. 22, 1990).

Ely, W. W. "A Trip to the Wilderness." *Moore's Rural New Yorker* 11 (1860).

Emerson, Livonia Stanton. "Early Life at Long Lake, N.Y." Adirondack Museum Library. Typescript.

Emerson, Ralph Waldo. *The Complete Works of Ralph Waldo Emerson.* Centenary Edition. Boston: Houghton Mifflin, 1903–4.

Emmons, Ebenezer. "Fifth Annual Report of Ebenezer Emmons, M.D., of the Survey of the Second Geological District." Assembly Document 150, 1841.

———. "First Annual Report of the Second Geological District of New York." Assembly Document 161, 1837.

———. "Fourth Annual Report of the Survey of the Second Geological District." Assembly Document 50, 1840.

———. *Geology of New-York, Part II: Comprising the Second Geological District.* Albany: Carroll and Cook, 1842–44.

———. "Report of E. Emmons, Geologist of the 2d Geological District of the State of New York." Assembly Document 200, 1838.

———. "Third Annual Report of the Survey of the Second Geological District." Assembly Document 275, 1839.

"Employment and Payrolls in the Adirondack Park." Albany: Nelson A. Rockefeller Institute of Government, Center for New York State and Local Government Studies, 1994.

Everest, Allan S. *Rum Across the Border: The Prohibition Era in Northern New York.* Syracuse: Syracuse Univ. Press, 1978.

Foster, Jeanne Robert. *Adirondack Portraits: A Piece of Time.* Edited by Noel Riedinger-Johnson. Syracuse: Syracuse Univ. Press, 1986.

Fox, William F. *History of the Lumber Industry in the State of New York.* Harrison, N.Y.: Harbor Hill Books, 1976.

Gilborn, Craig. *Durant: The Fortunes and Woodland Camps of a Family in the Adirondacks.* Utica: North Country Books, 1981; reprint, Blue Mountain Lake, N.Y.: The Adirondack Museum, 1986.

Gipson, Lawrence Henry. *Lewis Evans.* Philadelphia: Historical Society of Pennsylvania, 1939.

Glover, James M. *A Wilderness Original: The Life of Bob Marshall.* Seattle: The Mountaineers, 1986.

Goodspeed, Charles Eliot. *Angling in America.* Boston: Houghton Mifflin, 1939.

Graham, Frank, Jr. *The Adirondack Park: A Political History.* New York: Alfred A. Knopf, 1978.

Grover, Kathryn. "The Automobile Tourist in the Adirondacks." Unpublished report submitted to Adirondack Museum, Feb. 11, 1996.

Hallock, Charles. *The Fishing Tourist: Angler's Guide and Reference Book.* New York: Harper & Brothers, 1873.

———. *The Sportsman's Gazetteer and General Guide.* New York: Forest and Stream Publishing Co., 1877.

Halper, Louise. "'A Rich Man's Paradise': Constitutional Preservation of New York State's Adirondack Forest, a Centenary Consideration." *Ecology Law Quarterly* 19 (1992).

Hamilton, Lawrence, Barbara Askew, and Amy Odell. *Forest History: New York State Forest Resources Assessment, Report No. 1.* Albany: New York State Department of Environmental Conservation, 1980.

Hammond, Samuel H. *Hills, Lakes and Forest Streams.* New York: J. C. Derby, 1854.

———. *Wild Northern Scenes; or, Sporting Adventures with the Rifle and the Rod.* New York: Derby and Jackson, 1857.

Hammond, Samuel H., and L. N. Mansfield. *Country Margins and Ramblings of a Journalist.* New York: Baker and Scribner, 1849.

Headley, Joel Tyler. *The Adirondack; or, Life in the Woods.* New York: Baker and Scribner, 1849; reprint, Harrison, N.Y.: Harbor Hill Books, 1982.

Higby, Roy C. . . . *A Man from the Past.* Big Moose, N.Y.: Big Moose Press, 1974.

Hochschild, Harold K. *Adirondack Railroads, Real and Phantom.* Blue Mountain Lake, N. Y.: The Adirondack Museum, 1962.

———. *An Adirondack Resort in the Nineteenth Century.* Blue Mountain Lake, N. Y.: The Adirondack Museum, 1962.

———. *Doctor Durant and His Iron Horse.* Blue Mountain Lake, N. Y.: The Adirondack Museum, 1961.

———. *Life and Leisure in the Adirondack Backwoods.* Blue Mountain Lake, N. Y.: The Adirondack Museum, 1962.

———. *The MacIntyre Mine—From Failure to Fortune.* Blue Mountain Lake, N. Y.: The Adirondack Museum, 1962.

———. *Township 34.* New York: privately printed, 1952.

Hoffman, Charles Fenno. *Wild Scenes in the Forest and Prairie.* New York: W. H. Colyer, 1843.

Holmes, Timothy. *The Future of the Adirondacks: A Survey of Attitudes.* Blue Mountain Lake, N.Y.: The Adirondack Museum, 1990.

Howard, William G. *Forest Fires.* Albany: J. B. Lyon, 1914; State of New York Conservation Commission, Bulletin 10.

Hough, Franklin B. *A History of St. Lawrence and Franklin Counties, New York.* Albany: Little & Co., 1853.

Hoy, Ralph L. *An Adirondack Boyhood Remembered.* Santa Barbara, Calif.: Mendicus Press, 1978.

Hughes, J. Donald. "Ecology and Development as Narrative Themes of World History." *Environmental History Review* 19 (Spring 1995).

Huth, Hans. *Nature and the American: Three Centuries of Changing Attitudes.* Berkeley: University of California Press, 1957.

International Paper Corporation. "A Tradition in New York." Albany: n.d.

Jakle, John A. *The Tourist: Travel in Twentieth-Century America.* Lincoln: University of Nebraska Press, 1985.

Jamieson, Paul F. "Camping on State Lands Through the Years: The Adirondack Lean-to and the Forest Preserve." *The Conservationist* 19 (Feb.–March 1965).

———. " Emerson in the Adirondacks." *New York History* 39 (July 1958).

Johnson, William. *The Papers of Sir William Johnson.* 13 vols. Albany: Univ. of the State of New York, 1921–62.

Kaiser, Harvey H. *Great Camps of the Adirondacks.* Boston: David R. Godine, 1982.

Keith, Herbert. *Man of the Woods.* Blue Mountain Lake, N.Y.: The Adirondack Museum; Syracuse: Syracuse Univ. Press, 1972.

Kellogg, Juliet Baker. Diary. Ms. 61–83, Adirondack Museum Library.

Kranz, Marvin Wolf. "Pioneering in Conservation: A History of the Conservation Movement in New York State, 1865–1903." Ph.D. diss., Syracuse Univ., 1961.

Laing, Linda. "The Open Road: Wilderness, Politics and the Way to Crane Pond." *Adirondack Life* 27 (Annual Guide 1996).

Lanman, Charles. *Adventures of an Angler in Canada, Nova Scotia and the United States.* London: Richard Bentley, 1848.

Liroff, Richard A., and G. Gordon Davis. *Protecting Open Space: Land Use Control in the Adirondack Park.* Cambridge: Ballinger Publishing Co., 1981.

McKibben, Bill. "The People and the Park." *Sierra* 79 (March–April 1994).

McMartin, Barbara. *The Great Forest of the Adirondacks.* Utica, N.Y.: North Country Books, 1994.

————. *Hides, Hemlocks and Adirondack History.* Utica, N.Y.: North Country Books, 1992.

————. *To the Lake of the Skies: The Benedicts in the Adirondacks.* Canada Lake, N.Y.: Lake View Press, 1996.

Mandel, Patricia C. F. *Fair Wilderness: American Paintings in the Collection of the Adirondack Museum.* Blue Mountain Lake, N. Y.: The Adirondack Museum, 1990.

Martin, Roscoe C. *Water for New York: A Study in State Administration of Water Resources.* Syracuse: Syracuse Univ. Press, 1960.

Masten, Arthur H. *The Story of Adirondac.* New York: privately printed, 1923; reprint Blue Mountain Lake, N.Y.: The Adirondack Museum; Syracuse: Syracuse Univ. Press, 1968.

Moravek, John Richard. "The Iron Industry as a Geographic Force in the Adirondack-Champlain Region of New York State, 1800–1971." Ph.D. diss., Univ. of Tennessee, 1976.

Murray, William H. H. *Adventures in the Wilderness; or Camplife in the Adirondacks.* Blue Mountain Lake: The Adirondack Museum; Syracuse: Syracuse Univ. Press.

Nash, Roderick. *Wilderness and the American Mind.* 3rd ed. New Haven: Yale Univ. Press, 1982.

New York State Board of Equalization and Assessment. "The Taxation of State-Owned Lands." Adirondack Museum Library, Taxes. Typescript, 1982.

New York State Conservation Commission. *Annual Reports.* Albany: State of New York, 1911–1926.

New York State Forest, Fish and Game Commission. *Annual Reports.* Albany: State Printer, 1900–1910.

Nixon, Will. "Fear and Loathing in the Adirondacks," *E Magazine* 3 (Sept.–Oct. 1992).

Novak, Barbara. *Nature and Culture: American Landscape Painting, 1825–1875.* New York: Oxford Univ. Press, 1980.

Oelschlaeger, Max. *The Idea of Wilderness.* New Haven: Yale Univ. Press, 1991.

Oppersdorff, Mathias, and Alice Wolf Gilborn. *Adirondack Faces.* Blue Mountain Lake, N.Y.: The Adirondack Museum; Syracuse: Syracuse Univ. Press, 1991.

The Original People: Native Americans in the Champlain Valley. Plattsburgh, N.Y.: Clinton County Historical Museum, 1988.

Pilcher, Edith. *Up the Lake Road: The First Hundred Years of the Adirondack Mountain Reserve.* Keene Valley, N.Y.: Adirondack Mountain Reserve, 1987.

Pinkett, Harold T. *Gifford Pinchot: Private and Public Forester.* Urbana: Univ. of Illinois Press, 1970.

Pownall, Thomas. *Topographical Description of the Dominions of the United States of America.* Edited by Lois Mulkearn. Pittsburgh: Univ. of Pittsburgh Press, 1949.

Recknagel, A. B. *The Forests of New York State*. New York: Macmillan, 1923.

Redfield, William C. "Some Account of Two Visits to the Mountains in Essex County New York, in the Years 1836 and 1837; With a Sketch of the Northern Sources of the Hudson." *American Journal of Science and Arts* 33 (July–Dec. 1837).

Reed, William. *Life on the Border Sixty Years Ago*. Fall River, Mass., 1882; reprint, Saranac Lake, N.Y.: Saranac Lake Free Library, 1994.

Richards, T. Addison. "A Forest Story." *Harper's New Monthly Magazine* 19 (June–Nov. 1859).

Ritchie, William A. *The Archaeology of New York State*. Rev. ed. New York: Doubleday, 1980.

Robbins, William G. *Lumberjacks and Legislators: Political Economy of the U. S. Lumber Industry, 1890–1941*. College Station: Texas A&M Univ. Press, 1982.

Rosenquist, Valerie Beth. "The Iron Ore Eaters: A Portrait of the Mining Community of Moriah, New York." Ph.D. diss., Duke Univ., 1987.

Rothman, Sheila. *Living in the Shadow of Death: Tuberculosis and the Social Experience of Illness in American History*. New York: Basic Books, 1994.

Runte, Alfred. *National Parks: The American Experience*. Lincoln: Univ. of Nebraska Press, 1979.

Sacket's Harbor and Saratoga Railroad. [Broadside], 1853, Ms. 85-11, Adirondack Museum Library.

Samson, Nelson T. "Woods Labor in the Adirondacks." Ph.D. diss., State Univ. College of Forestry, Syracuse, 1952.

Schullery, Paul. *American Fly Fishing: A History*. New York: Nick Lyons Books, 1987.

Seaman, Frances B. "Life Was a Struggle for First Settlers at Long Lake." *Hamilton County News*, Oct. 4, 1994; Oct. 11, 1994; Oct. 25, 1994; Nov. 1, 1994.

Sears, John F. *Sacred Places: American Tourist Attractions in the Nineteenth Century*. New York: Oxford Univ. Press, 1989.

Sheehan, John F. "Acid Rain Still a Scourge in Adirondacks." *Wild Earth* 6 (Spring 1996).

Shnayerson, Michael. "Mary, Queen of Spots." *Vanity Fair* (August 1995).

Simms, Jeptha. *Trappers of New York*. Albany: J. Munsell, 1850.

Simmons, Louis J. *Mostly Spruce and Hemlock*. Tupper Lake, N.Y.: privately printed, 1976.

Smith, David C. "Wood Pulp Paper Comes to the Northeast, 1865–1900." *Forest History* 19 (April 1966).

Spears, Raymond S. "State Forest Fire Service." *The Angler and Hunter* 2 (March 1910).

Stanton, E. Lester. *Souvenirs of the Adirondack Mountains*. Batavia, Ill: privately printed, 1982.

Stanyon, Gladys, and Mildred S. Colvin. *Reflections: Wells on the Sacandaga.* N.p.: privately printed, 1975.

Stanyon, Minnie Patterson. *The Quiet Years.* N.p.: privately printed, 1965.

Steen, Harold K. *The U.S. Forest Service: A History.* Seattle: Univ. of Washington Press, 1976.

Stillman, William James. *The Autobiography of a Journalist.* 2 vols. Cambridge, Mass.: Houghton Mifflin, 1901.

————. "Sketchings." *The Crayon* 2 (July–Dec. 1855).

Stoddard, Seneca Ray. *The Adirondacks: Illustrated.* Albany: Weed, Parsons, 1874.

Street, Alfred B. *The Indian Pass.* New York: Hurd and Houghton, 1869.

————. *Woods and Waters; or, the Saranacs and Racket.* New York: M. Doolady, 1860.

Summerings Among the Thousand Islands. Syracuse: Boyd, 1882.

Temporary Study Commission on the Future of the Adirondacks. *The Future of the Adirondacks.* 2 vols. Blue Mountain Lake, N.Y.: The Adirondack Museum, 1971.

Terrie, Philip G. *Forever Wild: Environmental Aesthetics and the Adirondack Forest Preserve.* Philadelphia: Temple Univ. Press, 1985; reprint as *Forever Wild: A Cultural History of Wilderness in the Adirondacks,* Syracuse: Syracuse Univ. Press, 1994.

————. "Forever Wild Forever: The Forest Preserve Debate at the New York State Constitutional Convention of 1915." *New York History* 70 (July 1989).

————. *Wildlife and Wilderness: A History of Adirondack Mammals.* Fleischmanns, N.Y.: Purple Mountain Press, 1993.

Thompson, John H. , ed. *Geography of New York State.* Syracuse: Syracuse Univ. Press, 1966.

Thorpe, Thomas Bangs. "A Visit to John 'Brown's Tract.'" *Harper's New Monthly Magazine* 19 (June–Nov. 1859).

Todd, John. *Long Lake.* Pittsfield, Mass., 1845; reprint, Harrison, N.Y.: Harbor Hill Books, 1983.

Trancik, Roger. *Hamlets of the Adirondacks.* N.p., 1983.

Trigger, Bruce G. *The Children of Aataentsic: A History of the Huron People to 1660.* 2 vols. Montreal: McGill-Queens Univ. Press, 1976.

Tyler, Helen Escha. *Born Smart: The Story of Paul Smith.* Utica: North Country Books, 1988.

University of the State of New York, State Education Department, *Condition of Education in the Adirondack Blue Line.* Albany: State Education Department, 1992.

————. *New York, The State of Learning: A Report to the Governor and the Legislature on the Educational Status of the State's Schools.* Albany: State Education Department, 1995.

Van Valkenburgh, Norman J. *The Adirondack Forest Preserve: A Narrative of the Evolution of the Adirondack Forest Preserve of New York State.* Blue Mountain Lake, N.Y.: The Adirondack Museum, 1979.

———. "The Blue Line of the Adirondack Park, Part V—Expansion." *Adirondac* 59 (Jan–Feb. 1995).

Wallace, E. R. "A Reliable and Descriptive Guide to the Adirondacks." Appendix, H. Perry Smith, *The Modern Babes in the Wood Or Summerings in the Wilderness.* Hartford: Columbian Book Co., 1872.

Wasserman, Leo. "New Roads, New Directions." *AJES: Adirondack Journal of Environmental Studies* 2 (Spring 1995).

Waterman, Laura, and Guy Waterman. *Forest and Crag: A History of Hiking, Trail Blazing, and Adventure in the Northeast Mountains.* Boston: Appalachian Mountain Club, 1989.

Welsh, Peter C. *Jacks, Jobbers and Kings: Logging in the Adirondacks, 1850–1950.* Utica, N.Y.: North Country Books, 1995.

Williams, Michael. *Americans and their Forests: A Historical Geography.* Cambridge: Cambridge Univ. Press, 1989.

Woods, Lynn. "A History in Fragments: Following the Trail of Native Adirondack Cultures." *Adirondack Life* 25 (Nov.–Dec. 1994).

Index

Bartlett's Hotel, 87
Basselin, Theodore, 96
Bay Pond, 123
Benedict, Farrand, xvi, 16
Benedict, Lewis Elijah, 6, 11, 13, 16
Benedict, Sabael, 5, 6
Benson, 155
Berle, Peter A. A., 181
Bibby, William, 181
Big Blowup, 149
Big Boom (Glens Falls), 85
Big Moose, 152, 153, 154, 156
Big Wolf Lake, 143
Black River Regulating District, 150
blowdown, 149
Blue Mountain Lake, 66, 67, 69, 112, 125, 131
bobsled run, 146
Bog River, 47, 59
bounties, 43
Bowles, Samuel, 92
Brace, Charles Loring, 88, 92
Brandon, 23, 123, 124
Brandreth Park, 121
Brant Lake tract, 38
Bratt, Nicholas, 37
Burke, Edmund, 49
Burroughs, John, 65
Byrne, Martin, 28, 31, 32

campgrounds (state), 125, 127, 128, 135, 163
canoes, 135–36
Carr, Cal, 171
Champlain, Samuel de, xviii
Chateaugay Lakes, 21, 74, 110
Cheney, John, 38, 45
Chestertown, 76, 78, 80, 81
Civilian Conservation Corps, 155
Clark, Mrs. H. M., 82
Clark, Herbert, 140
class, 15, 116–18, 129, 172–73
climate, 5, 18, 26, 82

Clintonville, 34
Cold River, 59
Cole, Thomas, 44, 50
Collins, John, 178
Colt, S. S., 69–70
Colvin, Verplanck, 68, 89–92, 94–95, 104, 114
Commission on the Adirondacks in the Twenty-First Century, 176–78, 181
Commissioners of Parks (1872), 92–94
Conklin, Henry: forest clearing and, 28; hunting and fishing and, 40–41; logging and, 36–37, 38; poverty and, 24–25, 33; revival and, 32; sense of place of, 42; success and, 30–31
conservation, 83–84, 87–103, 165–78. *See also* Adirondack Forest Preserve; Adirondack Park; Adirondack Park Agency; Private Land Use and Development Plan
Conservation Commission, 127, 128, 134, 135, 149
Conservation Department, 140, 146, 147, 148
Conservationist, 149
Constitution (New York), 59; amendments to, 102, 140, 146, 150, 161–62; interpretations of, 147–48; of 1894, 102, 115; of 1915, 115; of 1938, 148. *See also* Article VII, Section 7; Article XIV, Section 1
consumption (tuberculosis), 64–65, 94
cottage industries, 33
Couxsachrage, 5
Cranberry Lake, 82
Crane Pond, 171
Cuomo, Mario, 176, 178

deer laws, 40-41, 131–32
DeKay, James, 11, 12
Delaware and Hudson Railroad, 74